BO'S WARRIORS

BO SCHEMBECHLER AND THE TRANSFORMATION OF MICHIGAN FOOTBALL

FRANK LIEBEF

TRIUMPH
B O O K S

Library of Congress Cataloging-in-Publication Data

Lieberman, Frank.
  Bo's warriors : Bo Schembechler and the transformation of Michigan football / Frank Lieberman.
     pages cm
  ISBN 978-1-62937-051-4 (paperback)
  1. Schembechler, Bo. 2. Football coaches—United States—Biography. 3. Michigan Wolverines (Football team)—History. 4. University of Michigan—Football—History. I. Title.
  GV939.S33L54 2014

                                                        796.332—dc23
  [B]

This book is available in quantity at special discounts for your group or organization. For further information, contact:
  Triumph Books LLC
  814 North Franklin Street
  Chicago, Illinois 60610
  (312) 337-0747
  www.triumphbooks.com

Printed in U.S.A.
ISBN: 978-1-62937-051-4
Design by Patricia Frey

Photos courtesy of Bentley Historical Library, University of Michigan

In memory of my parents

Contents

Foreword

Moving from a small Midwestern town to a huge university and premier institution of higher learning and athletics, how could I realize what was in store for me? While excited for the challenge, I was quite certain that someone entrusted with offering me a full-ride Grant-in-Aid scholarship had made an awful mistake. I did not feel that I belonged among the nationally recruited football players who would become my teammates. My thoughts on that were, *Well, that's not my problem. I will get a great education and set my path firmly in a positive direction for a career in...who knows what?*

All of that changed in December of my freshman year. Our head coach, Bump Elliott, was being "promoted" within the athletic department, and we were to meet our new head coach, Bo Schembechler. In that first meeting, among other things, we learned from Coach Schembechler that we were soft and undisciplined, with a national reputation as underachievers. "Well, boys," he said, "that is all going to change!"

In hindsight, that first Schembechler team at Michigan set the tone for a new and continued level of excellence for Michigan football. When youngsters decide to play for Michigan today, they know they will play in the greatest stadium in college football, in front of the most loyal fans and alumni, will prepare to play at the finest facilities, and will be taught by a great coaching staff.

I would not change anything from my four years in Ann Arbor. There were great victories as well as crushing defeats. As young men we were taught to live with both—not only as football players but as people, with an eye for what the world would hand us in the decades after we played. Our dedication to our alma mater is unshakable—as are the bonds of friendship we developed in competition and the driving force that molded us: Coach Schembechler and his inimitable staff.

Every day I am thankful for the men who will always be my teammates. I am thankful for my coaches, Gary Moeller and Jim Young, to whom I have not expressed my appreciation enough over the years. Most of all I am thankful for having a chance to play for Bo, who helped all of us learn how good we could be.

My life's journey has not been one anchored in the College of LS&A or Michigan Law School, although Michigan academics taught me how to think and organize. My career has been in professional sports—as a player, scout, and administrator, providing opportunities to hundreds of young men and women seeking the dream of working in sports. As my career winds down, it is altogether fitting to look back at those early days in Ann Arbor when I wondered, *What am I doing here?* Fortunately for me, there were those who believed in me. It's always a good time to pass it on.

—Mike Keller

Foreword

When I first heard about this book, I learned that the focus was going to be about mental toughness. One of my University of Michigan football teammates suggested that I would be a good source for Frank to talk to about the subject. I have no idea what medication my teammate was taking at the time that made him so delirious as to suggest to me, but the cat was out of the bag, and Dr. Frank and I began our journey.

We talked about my life. We talked about football. We talked about things totally unrelated to mental toughness. We talked about my college coach, Bo Schembechler. We talked about my friends on the team.

As time passed, and I spoke to some of the other guys who Frank had been interviewing, I realized that their experiences had been similar to mine. Not only that, but Frank was working these guys as hard as he was working me. Based on the conversations I had with my friends who helped Frank with the book, I knew this had to be more than a how-to manual on developing mental toughness. It was morphing into something else. It was becoming a story of young men developing into young adults.

I have often been asked to speak about my time as a University of Michigan football player and the lessons I learned from the game and my coach, Bo Schembechler. Yet I have never felt that I have done a great job of it. It was such a powerful time in my life, but it's difficult to impart to an audience the incredible impact it has on me to this day.

I believe *Bo's Warriors* can accomplish what I have failed to do in my speeches. What I think you have in your hands is a snapshot of history. It is a look back at this country in the late '60s and early '70s, as viewed through the eyes of us 18- to 21-year-old jocks. We were in the middle of a very unpopular war, racial tension was boiling, the drug culture was taking over college campuses, student unions were being occupied by militants…there was Woodstock, free love, free Angela Davis, burning draft cards, and burning bras. Meanwhile, with all this tumult bombarding us, we had to play football for a tyrant named Schembechler. How in the world did we survive? How in the world did we win a game? And how in the world did we learn lasting life lessons amidst the confusion?

That's the story you are about to read. When we saw the world crumbling around us, we had a pillar of strength to grab on to. When our life began to spin out of control, we had a safe haven. We had football. In football we knew where we stood. We had Schembechler. Sure, he was a conservative taskmaster. He did not like the counterculture, and the counterculture despised him. He did not suffer fools; it was his way or the highway.

But he demanded more from us. We delivered—sometimes grudgingly, but we delivered—and amidst the chaos came order, success, and growth. In that moment the group, through fate or providence, came together and something really positive happened. The blueprints were college football, but the architect was Bo.

—Jim Brandstatter

Acknowledgments

This book would not have been possible without the assistance of a number of special individuals. I begin with my wife, Linda. A few years ago, she was riding her horse Nails and I was running alongside them on the Olmstead Trail. She said to me that I was mentally tough. The idea planted a seed in me, and I began researching it. Then I incorporated my model into my Western States 100-Mile Endurance Run in 2002. After refining the concept of mental toughness, I published and gave presentations about my experience with it during my Western States Ultra.

It was then that I began to think about writing a book. It was a natural extension to write about the mental toughness of football players—especially those from the University of Michigan. A very special thanks goes to Mike Keller. With his quickness, he took the ball and ran with blazing speed. He then lateraled the ball to Jim Brandstatter. From there the ball was passed to Reggie McKenzie, Fritz Seyferth, Thom Darden, Gary Moeller, and Jim Betts, and then taken by Frank Gusich for a touchdown. Finally, Tom Curtis made an interception to save the win, and the project was completed. It was a team accomplishment and credit goes to this unique group of men. My gratitude goes to them.

Tom Bast of Triumph Books moved the Sierra Nevada Mountains to get this book published this year. And I can't forget Mitch Rogatz, Adam Motin, and the rest of the staff at Triumph for making this project a reality.

Introduction

It hit like a nuclear explosion when first-year athletic director Don Canham announced Glenn Edward "Bo" Schembechler as the new head football coach at the University of Michigan. Not only that, but Chalmers W. "Bump" Elliott was being transferred (booted) from head football coach to assistant athletic director. Could it really be true? How could this happen to the beloved Bump Elliott? It couldn't possibly set well with Bump, could it? His recruits and his Michigan friends couldn't possibly be happy with the news, could they?

And all this was going on during the 1960s. There was the pill, the Detroit and Watts race riots, the Vietnam War, political assassinations, the Black Panthers, "ban the bomb," and campus unrest throughout the United States. There was tumult everywhere. Yet that announcement in late December 1968 still resonates with Michigan fans today.

The well-respected Bump Elliott was, simply, a Michigan football legend. As a college athlete, Bump lettered in football, basketball, and baseball at rival Purdue University. He left Purdue, before graduating, to serve his country in 1944. Bump became a Marine lieutenant, seeing duty in China. After his service, instead of going back to Purdue to finish his studies, he enrolled at the University of Michigan and joined his brother Pete in the Michigan football backfield. Only this time, this handsome Marine became nationally known as one of the "Mad Magicians" in the Wolverines backfield. He was a spark plug that propelled the Wolverines to a Big 9 title in 1947, culminating in a 49–0 Rose Bowl victory on January 1, 1948, against the USC Trojans. On top of that, he was named All-American that season by the American Football Coaches Association.

Eleven years after that storied season, after initially coaching football at other colleges, Coach Elliott was named the Wolverines football head coach in 1959 by athletic director Fritz Crisler—his former head coach and another Michigan football legend. And in 1964, the Mad Magician coached his Wolverines squad to a Big Ten title and to a Rose Bowl victory over Oregon State University on January 1, 1965.

Elliott's overall head coaching record at the University of Michigan was 51–42–3 (.547 winning percentage). He also recruited such players as Jim Mandich, All-American end in 1969; Tom Curtis, All-American defensive back in 1969; Henry Hill, All-American guard in 1970; Dan Dierdorf, All-American tackle in 1970; Billy Taylor, All-American halfback in 1971; Reggie McKenzie, All-American guard in 1971; Thomas Darden, All-American defensive back in 1971; Mike Taylor, All-American linebacker in 1971; Mike Keller, All–Big Ten linebacker in 1971; Jim Brandstatter, All–Big Ten tackle in 1971; Frank Gusich, cocaptain and defensive back in 1971; Bruce Elliott, academic All-American and defensive back in 1971; defensive back Jim Betts, and numerous other notable names.

After the 1968 football season, Coach Elliott was removed by AD Don Canham, in spite of leading his Michigan Wolverines to an 8–2 record. In that final game of his last Michigan coaching assignment, 43-year-old Elliott's Wolverines were pitted against none other than Woody Hayes' Ohio State Buckeyes. The score was deadlocked at 14–14 in the second quarter and Michigan trailed 21–14 at the half; the outcome was very much in doubt. But the final score left no suspense, as the numbers were Ohio State 50, Michigan 14. To make that embarrassment worse and perhaps to rub Michigan's face in the mud, Coach Hayes went for a two-point conversion on Ohio State's last touchdown in the closing minutes of the game.

When sportswriters asked why after the game, Woody's reply was direct, clear, and to the point: "Because I couldn't go for three." That reply tells you everything you need to know about head coach Woody Hayes' competitive nature. "Woody just poured gasoline on that rivalry," an observer commented after the game. And the rivalry has burned strong ever since.

During Coach Elliott's reign, Michigan's football attendance was poor by what have now become Michigan standards. The average attendance was roughly 67,000, substandard given the size of their stadium. But did Bump deserve to be "bumped" by first-year AD Don Canham? You be the judge. And how long could Coach Elliott, who viewed his removal as a slap in the face, work under or in concert with Canham? As it turned out, not long. Bump served as assistant AD for a short time before leaving in 1970 to become athletic director at another Big Ten school and UM rival—the University of Iowa.

Not only did AD Canham not hesitate to remove All-American Bump Elliott as football coach, he made a second decision and hired a young, fiery, and spirited Bo Schembechler (an Ohioan, no less) to replace the revered coach. This quick decision, the story goes, was made after just a 15-minute conversation between Canham and Schembechler, at a restaurant, no less. Afterward, he would offer Bo the prestigious Michigan head coaching position. You might not be surprised that it took Bo even less time to accept the offer. (Just how much can you accomplish in just 15 minutes? In this instance, a lot!)

But what exactly was Canham seeking from this unknown young man? How did the AD envision Michigan football? Canham had already enjoyed an illustrious Michigan athletic and coaching history in his own right. He lettered in track at UM from 1939 to 1941. In 1940, he held the NCAA title in high jump and was named an All-American. From 1948 to 1968, he was the track-and-field coach for the Wolverines, leading them to 12 Big Ten Conference championships (11 in track-and-field and one in cross-country). His Michigan team also set world records in both the four-mile relay and the distance medley relay.

From 1968 to 1988, Canham rebuilt and solidified Michigan's dominance as a sports powerhouse as its athletic director. In fact, under his stewardship, Michigan's teams amassed 72 Big Ten championships. And behind his marketing leadership, the attendance for Michigan football reached unheard-of heights. Since 1975, the average attendance for home games has averaged more than 100,000. And from 1973 to 2004, Michigan led the nation in football attendance 30 times. Indeed, Michigan's stadium is known worldwide as "the Big House."

Canham used his business skills as a marketer, promoter, and fund-raiser wisely. In fact, he was the first ever to incorporate a direct-mail advertising program in soliciting attendees for football and other sports. This innovation, among other efforts, won him many awards as an athletic director. His counsel was sought by many others in higher education, and his model has been imitated in NCAA sports programs throughout the country. Put simply, Canham redefined the position of athletic director.

In selecting Schembechler, he felt confident that he could weather the storm he initiated. But just who was this 39-year-old man from Ohio named Bo? What did Don Canham see at the time that others did not? Was Canham really a genius, or was he just lucky?

Schembechler was born in Barberton, Ohio. Maybe being from a rural farming town suggests that Bo knew about the world of hard, physical work firsthand. He played high school football at the tackle position and achieved All-State honors in a state known for its very competitive prep football milieu. He attended college at Miami of Ohio, where he lettered as an offensive tackle in 1949 and in 1950. There he proved he could learn, follow directions, was teachable, loved the game of football, and was a significant contributor.

Schembechler was building the foundation for what was to come. If you're a football fan, you certainly know the name Sid Gilman. Mr. Gilman was considered a football man ahead of his time—in fact, some will say he was the architect of today's West Coast offense. Schembechler's other college coach was the one and only Woody Hayes. Bo was extremely fortunate to learn from the best of the best—and he didn't even have to travel very far from home to do it. I'll wager his impressionable young mind was being shaped and sharpened, especially in terms of offensive football philosophy, by the two coaches.

After college, Bo went into the service and learned more about discipline, giving and following direction, order, and working together for a common cause. He also coached as he was serving his country. All the while, he was developing even more insight into the social psychology of human behavior and group dynamics.

When his military service ended, he enrolled at Ohio State to get a master's in education. Being intelligent, he also reconnected with his mentor and became a graduate assistant under Coach Hayes. He spent five years with Hayes, learning from the master coach and paying his dues. While serving as line coach, he coached a young man named Gary Moeller, who was a captain on Woody's 1963 team (and a member of his superlative, undefeated 1961 squad); cocaptain Gary later became Coach Gary Moeller.

Schembechler coached at a number of other colleges (Presbyterian, Bowling Green, and Northwestern) before becoming the head coach at his alma mater, Miami of Ohio. At Northwestern, Coach Schembechler learned from and with another legend: former college teammate and Wildcats head coach Ara Parseghian. (Parseghian, of course, later reached fame and even legendary status as the head coach at Notre Dame.) At Miami, Schembechler compiled a 40–17–3 record from 1963 to 1968.

Clearly, Bo had been trained by the best minds in football. He had moved rapidly up the coaching ladder with determined motivation.

For those who do not know the whole story, Schembechler became the winningest head coach in Michigan football history, with a 194–48–5 record from 1969 to 1989. At the time of his retirement, he was also the winningest football head coach in the nation. He was also voted Big Ten Coach of the Year and National Coach of the Year by both the American Football Coaches Association and the Football Writers Association of America. Bo was now considered elite and became a football legend.

And what about Woody Hayes, who began as Bo's mentor and ultimately became his greatest rival? Hayes, too, started his coaching career at Miami of Ohio. Other notables who started their career at this university, known as the "Cradle of Coaches," included Paul Brown (Pro Football Hall of Fame, 1967), Ara Parseghian (national college football champion, Notre Dame, 1966 and

1973; College Football Hall of Fame, 1980), Weeb Ewbank (Pro Football Hall of Fame, 1978), Bill Mallory (Indiana Sports Hall of Fame, 1993), and Sid Gillman (Pro Football Hall of Fame, 1983, and one of ESPN's 20 greatest NFL coaches).

Hayes was the head coach at Ohio State University from 1951 to 1978. During that time, he won five national championships (1954, 1957, 1961, 1968, and 1970). His teams won 13 Big Ten conference titles and he compiled a 205–61–10 coaching record.

According to Buckeyes cocaptain Gary Moeller, "Woody hated the media. He told us players, 'If anyone comes up to you and tells you how good you are, blah blah blah, punch them in the nose—unless it's your parents.'" The one blemish on Woody's résumé was an incident with Clemson's Charlie Bauman. Bauman intercepted an Ohio State pass thrown by quarterback Art Schlichter to seal Clemson's win in the 1978 Gator Bowl. A physical altercation quickly followed when Woody assaulted the player and had to be physically pulled away by his own team. The legendary coach was quickly dismissed by Ohio State. He never coached again.

During the 10-year rivalry between Ohio State and Michigan from 1968 to 1977, either Schembechler's or Hayes' teams won (or shared) the Big Ten conference title; no other Big Ten school could wrest the title away from the powerhouses. Not only that, but both Michigan and Ohio State placed in national rankings every year during the same span. Indeed, the rivalry between Bo and Woody—and by extension Michigan and Ohio State—captured national attention. Their battles became legendary, their teams dominated, and their players became household names.

Schembechler may have put Michigan football permanently on the map, but the university's legacy was cemented long before that. The University of Michigan was founded in 1817, making it nearly 200 years old (and older than Ohio State!). Since its founding, the University of Michigan has been considered one of the top universities in the world. Today it is not only a multiethnic public institution of higher learning, but it also has reached unequaled achievement in research.

Intercollegiate competition began at Michigan in 1865. To put it into historical perspective, Abraham Lincoln was president and the country was entangled in a brutal civil war. In the ensuing years, Michigan athletics have become some of the best in the world. Michigan has won more NCAA Division I and more national titles in both hockey and in men's swimming and diving than any other Division I university. Prize swimmer Michael Fred Phelps ('09), has collected 22 Olympic medals, 18 of them gold. He is a world-record holder in the 100m butterfly, 200m butterfly, and 400m individual medley. He has earned more Olympic medals than anyone else, double that of his closest competitor. Yet Phelps is far from the only Olympian to have come from Michigan. From 1900 to 2014, Michigan athletes have attained 150 Olympic medals, including 73 gold medals.

The 1935 Big Ten championship in track-and-field was hosted by Michigan. Within 45 minutes of competition, Ohio State's Jesse Owens tied the 100-yard world record and set world records in the long jump, 220-yard sprint, and the low hurdles. In the Summer Olympics of 1936, held in Berlin, Jesse Owens won gold medals in the 100m and 200m dash, the long jump, and the 4×100 relay—and in the process drew the ire of German chancellor and Nazi propagandist Adolf Hitler.

If you are a basketball junkie, you know all about Cazzie Russell's exploits and his team's battle with John Wooden's UCLA Bruins in the 1965 NCAA Championship Game. In 1966, Russell was named the College Basketball Player of the Year and went on to become the No. 1 pick in the NBA Draft. Fittingly, Michigan's Crisler Arena was referred to as "the House that Cazzie Built."

Another Michigan All-American, Rudy Tomjanovich (whose jersey was retired by Michigan), went on to play and coach in the NBA. The five-time NBA All-Star coached the Houston Rockets to two consecutive NBA titles. He also was the head coach of the USA men's basketball team in the 2000 Summer Olympics that won the gold medal.

Michigan great Glen Rice (UM basketball's leading career and single-season scorer) led the Wolverines to a national title in 1989 and was named the tournament's most outstanding player. The fourth player selected in the

NBA Draft in 1989, he went on to win an NBA title in 2000 with the Los Angeles Lakers. His jersey number was recently retired by the University of Michigan.

In the 1990s "the Fab Five"—Chris Webber, Juwan Howard, Ray Jackson, Jalen Rose, and Jimmy King—led the Wolverines to two consecutive NCAA Championship Games. Webber, Rose, and Howard were named All-Americans and went on to tremendous NBA careers.

In 2012–13, Trey Burke (NCAA Player of the Year) and Tim Hardaway Jr. led Michigan to the NCAA Championship Game against Louisville. Both were drafted in the first round by the NBA.

When Wolverines football began in 1879, Rutherford B. Hayes was president of the United States. Born in Delaware, Ohio, he was a congressman and a two-term governor of Ohio. He assumed the presidency even though he lost the popular vote, by capturing 20 contested Electoral College votes. Several of the issues of the day related to the end of Reconstruction, the Great Railroad Strike, the gold standard debate, the Monroe Doctrine, and the building of the Panama Canal.

Meanwhile, Michigan was building something of its own: a fine football tradition. In 1925, '26, and '27, three-time All-American Bennie Oosterbaan led the Wolverines. Tom Harmon was an All-American halfback in 1939 and 1940 and a Heisman winner in 1940. Ron Kramer was an All-American end in 1955 and 1956. All three players' jersey numbers have been retired. And in a rare intersection of football and politics, our 38th president, Gerald Ford, played center and was an All-American at Michigan, too.

A few other more recent All-Americans, NFL football greats, and Super Bowl champions include Ty Law ('94), Desmond Howard ('91), and Charles Woodson ('97). Jim Harbaugh ('86) coached the San Francisco 49ers in the 2013 Super Bowl. Of course, Tom Brady ('00) has quarterbacked the New England Patriots to three Super Bowl championships (and counting).

More recent standouts include Jake Long ('07), who was a No. 1 overall draft pick and currently plays with the St. Louis Rams, and tackle Taylor Lewan, who was named an All-American in 2012 and 2013 and was a first-round pick of the Tennessee Titans in 2014.

Back to the Buckeyes and the Wolverines on the gridiron. Over the years, the two colleges have played 110 football games. Michigan has 58 wins with 6 ties to OSU's 46 wins. Michigan also owns 42 Big Ten championships, while Ohio State has 34. And in national championships, Michigan holds the edge 11–7. The Wolverines' overall record is 910 wins, 321 losses, and 36 ties for a .732 winning percentage; Ohio State University has 849 victories for a .716 winning percentage.

Individually, the Buckeyes have seven Heisman Trophy winners and the Wolverines three. The Buckeyes have a slight edge with 43 bowl appearances—one more than the Wolverines' 42. But in attendance, Michigan's Big House seats more than 111,000 compared to OSU's "Shoe," which seats more than 102,000. In 2010, Michigan set NCAA records with an average of 111,823 in attendance and a single-game record of 113,090. Quite simply, everything about this rivalry is huge.

On the lighter side, the Phi Gamma Delta (Fiji) chapters at Michigan and Ohio State came up with a creative way to give back during the rivalry, known as the greatest in North American collegiate sports. The Ohio State chapter has adopted the Stefanie Spielman Fund for Breast Cancer Research (named after All-American Chris Spielman's wife, who succumbed to the disease in 2009), while the Michigan chapter donates to the American Cancer Society. To raise funds, they run a relay each year. The visiting team's Fiji chapter carries an official game ball from their own stadium to the host team's stadium in time for the game's kickoff. The distance covered between the two stadiums is roughly 187 miles, and it takes the students more than 30 hours to make the journey. (Way to go, fellow Greeks. As an alumnus of Sigma Alpha Mu, I applaud your spirit and your giving back to society.)

And now here's the story of Bo Schembechler and Michigan football.

CHAPTER 1

Go Blue Go

This book is about a group of young men who played the game of football. The vehicle, in this case, is the game and its consequence. Some might view this book as a defense of football in light of the recent legitimate criticisms that have been made about the game. The impact (scientifically measurable) of football—and one game, in particular—is the focus here. The explosion has likely touched millions; in fact, what happened between gridiron rivals the University of Michigan and Ohio State University in 1969 still has tremors today.

On Saturday, November 22, the University of Michigan hosted the Ohio State University Buckeyes in Ann Arbor in front of 103,588 fans. Woody Hayes was coach of the nation's unbeaten (in 22 games) defending national champion top-ranked college football team. Some called them the greatest team of all time and compared them to the Minnesota Vikings, the NFL's gold standard at the time. Hayes believed this team was one of his best, if not his all-time best. If the Buckeyes were Goliath, then the Wolverines were David. Then again, you know what happened between David and Goliath.

Even though they were the home team, the Wolverines were 17-point underdogs going into the game. Michigan had suffered two early-season losses, but had since been on a roll and entered the game with a 7–2 record. They were led by a young first-year coach named Bo Schembechler. Coach Schembechler told his team that if they couldn't remember Schembechler, "just call me Bo." Previously, Coach Schembechler had been a head coach of Miami of Ohio, known as a hotbed of coaching talent. He brought with him young, talented, energetic, and intelligent football minds in assistants Gary Moeller, Jim Young, Chuck Stobart, Jerry Hanlon, and Rick Hunter, among others. These coaches also had experience as high school head coaches, which some believe contributed to their understanding of how to better communicate, teach, and motivate athletically gifted young men.

Bo was described by many as a psychological genius because of his ability to understand, teach, motivate, and underscore the importance of "team" to his players. He drilled the concept of teamwork over and over again, which resulted in the cohesion of his squads. It was about the team, the team, and the team. These young men became psychologically part of a group to which they belonged (what he called "bonded teammates"). As a result, for example, Mike Taylor, a defensive All-American specialist, got on Reggie McKenzie, an offensive All-American stalwart, for dogging it during practice drills. He said to Reggie, "Come on, they're watching you. Don't go through the motions."

Within their team practices and group drills, the teammates began to identify with each other, and developed unity; their goals became interdependent, and in the process they formed aspirations and expectations together. And as the teammates began to identify highly with the group and its goals, they gained camaraderie and satisfaction with the attainment of a goal. Even under certain circumstances, failure to meet a group goal also increased group bonding (as in that early-season loss to rival Michigan State). And when the teammates easily accepted a common goal (i.e., executing and minimizing mistakes of the I formation) and supported the actions required to reach it (practice, practice, practice; drill, drill, drill), teammates felt great and recognized contributions of their teammates (a solid block, a hard hit, or a key interception).

And team unity also positively influenced the personalities each player developed. As individuals, they became less self-centered, more giving. Simply, they cared about each other. And what Schembechler knew well was that membership in the group was paramount for security, achievement, competitiveness, and status. The team became "we"—forget about "I" or "me." So when Fritz Seyferth, a fullback, began sharing duties with a sophomore, he didn't complain or say "Poor me." Instead, he continued to work hard for the team.

Reggie McKenzie told a story about Preston Henry during one spring practice. On that day, Henry, a running back, had to practice offensive maneuvers for both the first- and second-string offense for some 130 plays or so. "After practice, everyone ran sprints. Even Preston Henry. We all felt sorry for him. Absolutely no one on the team would have been upset if Preston Henry was excused from running wind sprints."

With newfound cohesiveness, Michigan was able to mobilize its energies in their support of the group goals, which were to prepare physically (even if doing exhausting, unintelligible exercises like "slap and stomp") so that on-field performance (a win) became second to none. Solidarity was important and expressed by the final core players who didn't quit or leave the team. There was a sign on the wall that encouraged this ethos. It read, THOSE WHO STAY WILL BE CHAMPIONS. (One player who left the team named John Prusiecki added, jokingly, "Those who leave will be captains of industry, lawyers, and doctors.")

Roughly 75 to 80 players stayed with the team. They may have complained about some of the tactics employed by Bo, but they stayed. Along the way, one or two of them would be talked out of quitting the team—Reggie McKenzie, for one. McKenzie went through a spell thinking that Bo was unfairly on his back. He was reminded by his family, "McKenzie men do not quit." And from that point on, Reggie showed Bo his character. He told himself, "I'm not going to let Bo beat me."

These young men became strongly motivated to contribute to the team's welfare and advance its objectives instead of their own individual achievements. They bonded on the field and off. They roomed together, took the same classes, socialized, partied, got fixed up on dates by teammates, worked at the same places in the off-season, pledged the same fraternities, boycotted the same classes, and collectively they became inspired together. They were a part of something much larger than themselves (for one thing, University of Michigan's gridiron history). And with a campus undergoing serious racial unrest in the 1960s, their coach, according to Jim Brandstatter, told them, "we are one race—Michigan football. You guys are not about race. No one from the outside is going to get between us. Race is not an issue." Mike Keller remembered the coach putting it in more colorful terms: "Son of a bitch, you're not red, you're not white, you're not blue. You're Michigan." Bo also supported the Mellow Men's (comprised of seven African American football players) stand on boycotting the economics building during a campus demonstration.

The team's common needs for achievement, affiliation, competitiveness, recognition, and security were all being realized through team membership. Certainly, having the Ohio State game date written in red letters on the blackboard represented a clear group goal. No one had to verbalize the importance of that Buckeyes game; it was simply understood.

Bo also understood that his team needed to jell to win. He had learned from the best, coaches like Hayes himself. Bo also surrounded himself with smart football minds and valued his assistants' input. Serving in the U.S. military no doubt contributed to his understanding of the dynamics of groups, too. Indeed, many people compare the game of football to being in a foxhole with a buddy. Woody was a great field general and understood historical battles, and he taught his protégé Bo well.

Schembechler also understood psychology. He realized that external and situational factors play a part in group dynamics. He knew about focusing. He knew about expectations, about reward and reinforcement. He also was cognizant of the fact that reinforcement (feedback) didn't always have to be positive. He was smart enough to realize that negative or critical feedback also influences behavior. He could recognize who could take it and who couldn't. Some, like Brandstatter, remember comments from the coaches, such as, "You're the worst tackle in the history of intercollegiate sports" and "We wasted a scholarship on you." Bo called Gusich "a candy ass." (By the way, "candy-ass" cocaptain Gusich was described by his teammates as "the toughest dude on the team.") Bo also once said, according to Fritz Seyferth, that he had the 10 worst players in college football history on his squad.

The assistant coaches knew that Bo was going to break the men down so that he could rebuild them to excel at the highest level, and they provided some positive reinforcement in the face of the head coach's criticism. The players, in turn, responded by being obedient and eagerly following directions (of an authoritarian, no-nonsense disciplinarian, tough-love father figure: the head coach during that era). Bo may have been critical on the field, but his assistant coaches also knew that he was gentler with his young players one-on-one, behind closed doors. They also recognized that Bo (who himself had been warm and fuzzy as an assistant under Woody) somewhat imitated Woody when he became the man and ran his own program.

It was okay with Bo that the assistant coaches would be the good guys—gentle, personable, friendly, warm—who made football fun with their creative drills. Gary Moeller, for one, had his defensive men doing end-zone drills. They were laughing, having a good time, while Bo's offense was running their own not-so-fun drills. During one practice session, Fritz Seyferth was discouraged by Bo's criticism. Then assistant coach Jerry Hanlon came by to pat him on the back and say, "You are doing this right."

On one occasion, the offensive team was doing a punting drill. Bo said that he would give $10 to any defensive player who blocked the punt. As it happened, the punt got blocked and offensive tackle Jim Brandstatter shot downfield to make the tackle. Bo became irate and ran downfield after Brandstatter, thinking he had missed his block and created the blocked punt. When he finally caught up to the player, he began berating him. Quickly, Jerry Hanlon ran up and assured Bo that Jim had made his block. Do you think that the coach apologized for his mistake? Instead, he grumbled something to the effect of "He needed it."

Bo knew that the expectation of success creates incentive. Further, he knew that the expectation of failure can affect motivation as well, including the motivation to avoid failure. He knew that leadership, bonding, social pressure, and the desire to please could be nurtured in a group setting. He also knew, in launching that tirade, that the players would bond around Jim Brandstatter and that Jim himself could take the verbal abuse.

Coach Schembechler employed psychology in everything he did. He knew that purposive behavior / positive valence goals stoked competition. He knew that aversive stimulation or negative reinforcement worked, too. He also knew about intrinsic motivation (such as the desire to practice in order to become a better football player) and extrinsic motivation (such as a team win over OSU or MSU in red-letter games) as powerful motivators. Schembechler made it clear to his troops, "Do it my way or the highway, and do it right the first time." His communications were clear, not ambiguous.

He also was cognizant that success has a positive incentive value (it was important for the team, important for the coaches, important for the university, important for the tradition). It increased players' motivation and their behaviors associated with achieving the goal. Achievement and competitiveness were in the psychological DNA of the exceptional group of men that he was leading. He knew they would avoid failure at any cost.

Another significant and important part of Bo's psychological genius was related to conditioning. Bo Schembechler believed that being in top physical condition resulted not only in intellectual growth, but also in the development of mental toughness. The young warriors realized that if they could survive Bo's practices during the spring and fall, game day would be a breeze.

Perhaps Coach Schembechler's most significant contribution to success was his ability to get the most out of his young players by changing their thought process. He did that by challenging them, getting them to believe that the impossible was possible. His young men began to believe in him, in the team, and in themselves. The team mind-set changed, barriers and obstacles were overcome, and their on-field performance reached new heights. As these young men began to fulfill their football potential, their confidence soared. The sky was the limit.

Bo was, simply, a master social psychologist, a teacher/sage/mentor to the group of the highly athletic and competitive young men recruited by his predecessor, Bump Elliott. The 1968 team, which had an 8–2 record, had promised a high probability of success for that 1969 season. And with the crystallization of the team's goal, the cohesiveness of personalities, and their commitment to one another, the outcome of success left little doubt. Indeed, the foundation of Wolverines football success was set in stone for years to come.

Some argue that it was Bo who made the players successful. There are others who feel that the players, recruited by Bump, made Bo successful. After all, Bump Elliott was a football legend at the University of Michigan. The handsome former marine lieutenant was likely one of the most respected of Michigan's many living legends. He was a well-spoken, intelligent, meticulously dressed, and caring individual with great interpersonal skills. He knew football from a player's perspective—as a student from the University of Michigan—and was at ease with himself and his national recognition. If there was ever a spokesman for the University of Michigan, it was the unpretentious Elliott. Not only that, but his players loved him.

Thomas Darden remembered the coach coming to his Sandusky, Ohio, home for a recruitment visit. The soft-spoken Elliott had such a great presence that Darden's mother fell in love with him right away. Elliott referred to Thomas' parents as Mr. and Mrs. Darden. They told Thomas, "He's not like the other coaches." Thom felt Bump was "a kind man, someone you can trust. If he said something to you, you knew that he was telling the truth. I liked Bump and he made me feel that I was part of the Michigan experience. I also wanted to play for him, but he was fired."

Darden continued, "Bump was responsible for my six teammates and I leasing our house in my junior year. That house became the 'Den of the Mellow Men.' Mike Oldham and Glenn Doughty brought Bump the house listing. He took care of it from there. When I moved to Iowa, I looked Bump up, and continue to have contact with him."

Mike Keller said that Bump took a personal interest in him and his academics. "Bump knew that in order to play I had to be eligible," Keller said. Bump was easy to be around, like an uncle. Keller was also friends with Bruce, Pete Elliott's son (and Bump's nephew), and as a senior became friends with Bruce's brother Dave. Mike said that it was Bump who first approached him and asked him to run for the Board of Intercollegiate Athletics at the University of Michigan. He did, and won.

Frank Gusich remembered that Bump made a strong impression with both him and his mother. Elliott was "a real gentleman, a real classy guy. And it didn't hurt that Michigan had a good academic reputation."

Fritz Seyferth described Bump as a gentleman, respectful of every individual, dapper, well-spoken, perfect, like an Ivy Leaguer. He didn't think that Bump would have run Schembechler's slap-and-stomp drill because it disrespected the individual.

These Michigan Wolverines who spanned two iconic coaching tenures contributed greatly to and personify the Michigan tradition. Together they represent a cross-section of young men from different backgrounds who bonded and became relentless in achieving their common goal. They came together, and in 1969 they achieved together.

It is my pleasure to introduce you to some of the outstanding men of that 1969 Michigan football team: Jim Betts, Jim Brandstatter, Tom Curtis, Thom Darden, Frank Gusich, Mike Keller, Reggie McKenzie, Fritz Seyferth, and coach Gary Moeller, who learned about mental toughness firsthand from their legendary coach Bo Schembechler. These are their stories.

CHAPTER 2

The Duke:
Jim Brandstatter

Who can explain the 18-year-old's decision, in 1968, to attend and play football for his family's and community's hated rival? Not only that, consider that this teenager's father, Art Brandstatter, had been an All-American fullback at Michigan State—not to mention a sitting faculty member and director of the school of criminal justice. (The well-respected, well-traveled brigadier general and educator was appointed by none other than John Hannah, president of Michigan State University.) One other thing: this teenager's older brother Art Jr. had been a 6'3", 220-pound starting defensive end and offensive tight end for the Spartans in 1959, 1960, and 1961. And young Jim Brandstatter did *what?*

As the youngest of the athletic Brandstatter boys, he periodically heard "You have big shoes to fill" and "You are the last of the Brandstatters." Besides older brother Art Jr., who was All-State in both football and basketball (East Lansing High School and Lansing Halls of Fame), there was the All-Tournament basketball player John; middle linebacker, big-game (wild boar, caribou) bow hunter and fisherman, Bill; and Mike, a star on the state champion football team. That this family loved their sports cannot be denied, and both parents were supportive of their sons' various endeavors.

The highly competitive, athletic Brandstatter family was, not surprisingly, well known by administrators, coaches, and community leaders in East Lansing. It was not unusual at all to see Mrs. Mary Brandstatter driving her boys to the various practices or sitting in the stands with her husband at their kids' many games. It was like a full-time job, taking five sons to their various sports activities. Mary was well known, respected, and admired by all her boys' coaches. Once Art Jr.'s high school football coach, Vince Carrilot, asked Mrs. Brandstatter who her favorite coach was. It could've been Gus Ganakas, Art Jr.'s high school basketball coach (who later became Michigan State's head basketball coach). Instead, she surprised him by saying "Bo Schembechler." Perhaps it was a harbinger of things to come.

Aside from a strong academic modeling and emphasis on sports, young Jim was introduced to many cultures through the representatives from various countries (England, India, and Vietnam, to name a few) who attended his father's criminal justice program at Michigan State. Art Sr., being friendly, good-natured, and caring, invited his adult students to his home for dinner to meet his family to teach them about their own backgrounds. This created a dilemma for his wife, Mary. What could she prepare for dinner that would appease such diverse palates and did not disrespect the religion or mores of the individuals in question? Being intelligent and creative, she chose leg of lamb. To this day, Jim loves having leg of lamb because he associates it with the wonderful memories of those special, exciting, and intellectual international dinners.

Jim has fond memories of growing up in East Lansing. He remembers his father's mother, Grandmother Marie, who lived in Ecorse, Michigan, not far from Detroit. He has memories of his father participating in tug-of-war events with the Canadian Police Department and visiting Grandmother's for a good dinner afterward. On his mother's side were Grandfather and Grandmother Miles and Geraldine Walsh. They had a lake cottage in northern Michigan near Saginaw Bay and Lake Huron.

One childhood memory stands out vividly for Jim. It was either the late 1950s or early '60s, and the Brandstatter family was driving north in their Chevy station wagon to his grandparents' cottage. This was before Interstate 75 was built, so they were on a little road called US 13. On road trips, Jim's mother would have the boys playing such games as counting cows, spelling words from license plates, and of course reading all the Burma-Shave signs standing upright beside the road (THE WOLF / IS SHAVED / SO NEAT AND TRIM / RED RIDING HOOD / IS CHASING HIM / BURMA-SHAVE). On this particular occasion, there was a car behind them. It became clear to Jim that his father didn't want the other driver to pass; instead, he had increased his speed to maybe 60 to 65 mph. Mary was not happy and repeatedly asked her husband to slow down.

The boys liked that fast driving—but Mary held her own. The message was loud and clear. When his father was away traveling, mother ran the household. Jim said, "All she had to do was to give me that look of hers or say to me 'I'll tell your father.' And that was enough so that I didn't mess with her very much. I didn't get away with very much, and I'll bet she knew what I was doing." Indeed, with five sons, Mary had plenty of experience in dealing with her boys' mischief.

To Jim, the Great Lakes area was a paradise. Very early in life, he became a water person. He loved boating, fishing, and swimming. So it may not come as a surprise that Jim has a Lake Huron cottage of his own today.

In order to get a strong basic educational background, young Jim attended St. Ignatius Elementary School, which was headed by principal Sister Rose Gilbert. His favorite subjects back then were spelling and math. The nuns were strict, and when he misbehaved in Mrs. Wintermute's class, she grabbed him by the back of the shirt or twisted his ear. Jim would have attended a parochial high school, but there were none in East Lansing at the time. As a result, Jim attended the public high school, East Lansing High, located two blocks from his home.

As a sophomore, Leo Smedley was Jim's assistant high school football coach and wrestling coach. Jim remembered Coach Smedley pushing him like a marine drill sergeant—in fact, Jim often suspected he probably was a marine recruit. The coach would tell him, "You're going to find out just how good you are" whenever they faced a formidable opponent.

As a sophomore, Jim was 6'2" and weighed 225 pounds. He started out on the junior varsity football team but was quickly promoted to the varsity, on which he first lettered his sophomore year. Promoted to captain his junior year, he established himself as a team leader. On offense he played either center or tackle, and on defense he lined up in a three-point stance outside the opposing offensive tackle.

Jim also lettered in baseball, and received honors. He was an All-City first baseman in his junior year and an All-City catcher in his senior year. Jim even lettered in basketball; he was a center/forward on his high school team and a cocaptain in the last game of the postseason tourney.

Yet participating in sports did not keep Jim busy enough. He sang in the choir for four years and was elected homecoming king as a senior. A solid student academically, he thought of attending college and majoring in architectural design.

Jim was recruited to play football by Bump Elliott, the head football coach at the University of Michigan. He was well aware of the gridiron rivalry between UM and Michigan State. It was a difficult decision. Should he follow in the giant footsteps of his All-American father and brother Art Jr.? Or was that bar just too high, maybe unattainable?

Jim remembered that his brother Art Jr. and his football teammates expressed dissatisfaction during Art's playing days. Likely, these grumblings highly influenced Jim's decision not to attend and play ball for Michigan State. Luckily, his parents did not place pressure on him to attend MSU.

In fact, Michigan seemed to be a good fit for the young man. After all, Ann Arbor was still close to home. Two other factors sealed the deal: (1) he liked coach Bump Elliott and (2) he felt comfortable visiting Ann Arbor, saying, "It felt like home." At the time, he was aware that there was no guarantee that it was the right decision for him. Would he graduate with a degree in architectural design from the University of Michigan? Could he become a starter for the Wolverines? Should he even play football in college? And if he did, what kind of human being would he become?

In 1968, Jim joined the University of Michigan freshman football team, which was coached by Bill Dodd. The freshman team played only two games (Bowling Green and the University of Toledo) during the season. One of the things that stands out in Jim's mind were the difficult physical football practices along with the wind sprints that would take place afterward. One of the progressive sprints had the players running 10 yards at a time, then stopping, turning around, and running back to the goal line. They would continue this progression, increasing by 10-yard increments, until they ran the entire 100 yards of the football field. After this progression, they would decrease the sprints by 10 yards at a time until they reached their original starting place. One battery-mate was freshman player Reggie McKenzie. They would quietly complain and whine about wanting to kill the coach.

Aside from his dislike for his coach, he made new friends on the team while adjusting to college life. He bonded with buddies McKenzie, Mike Keller, Frank Gusich, Fritz Seyferth, and many others who became a sort of family. Early on, the groundwork for a band of brothers had been formed.

As a sophomore, Bo Schembechler was his new coach. Jim remembered Coach Schembechler saying, "Luck is when preparation meets opportunity." With proper preparation, behavior becomes instinctual, and muscle memory is developed. Muscle memory allows the player to react without thinking about what he is supposed to do. Schembechler also prepared his players to be mentally tough. For Jim, mental toughness "is never giving in. It's between your ears. It's attitude. It's not quitting." As an impressionable 18-year-old, Jim learned a lot from Coach Schembechler and his staff. He learned the value of practice and preparation, how to form good habits, and how to develop a winning attitude, regardless of the obstacles.

When he first arrived on the Michigan gridiron, he was filled with self-doubt. He wondered, *Can I compete? Do I have the ability to be a legitimate competitor, to contribute so I can play with these guys?* This insecurity quickly became a motivator, though, and Jim worked hard to develop his skills. To play for Bo, he simply had to test himself over and over. He learned not to take time off for any reason, not on any play during a game or practice. If he did, Bo would have gotten on him harshly.

Jim realized that failure was certainly possible because there was always somebody on the field who was better than him. He devoted himself to the fundamentals. On every play the coach had a job, so to speak, for him to do, which meant he had to focus. Under Bo's scheme, the tackle called out the line's blocking assignments, which fell to Jim. He had to anticipate what the defensive line was going to do on a particular play. At times, defensive linemen jumped before the snap, and then Jim had to call out another blocking assignment to compensate for the defensive shift. So he had to know his assignments and practice that job or block over and over. That meant using his arms, body, and legs properly and in concert. Of course, he knew that his opponent was likely doing the same thing. But he worked to make his play instinctive and become tough physically. Of course, the psychological came into play, too; Jim never wanted to let down his teammates.

Jim remembered, "We did drills and more drills, and had plenty of physical contact with pads. Our practice intensity was high—it was almost like game intensity—and our conditioning drills were very physical." Coach Schembechler didn't want his players to weigh in at more than 250 pounds. Jim exceeded that, so he had to run what was called "a penalty mile." At 6'3" and 260 pounds, he remembers that distance running being tough on him.

In order to improve his agility, foot speed, and balance, he did an exercise called "karaoke." This drill entailed standing with his feet shoulder-width apart, then crisscrossing his feet—first the right foot in front, then the left foot behind—and grapevining across the width of the field. Once completed, he went back, crisscrossing the field in the other direction. He worked on this drill numerous times before, during, and after practice. Jim also performed strengthening drills, such as getting into a three-point stance, firing off the ball, and landing on his two hands with arms extended. Then he would move down the field on all fours for about 10 yards. Another brutal strengthening drill was pushing a blocking sled with both arms extended.

Continually working on mental and physical preparation, he practiced over and over. And when he needed mental toughness to meet his goals, his self-talk went something like this: *Don't miss your assignment. Be your best. Be at your toughest. I can play with this guy. We are on an even field. Remember your technique and fundamentals. Stay with it, and don't get down.*

Some of Jim's goals included making the team, making the travel team, playing at critical game moments, and making significant contributions to the team. I explained to Jim that those goals were not totally under his control, at least according to my definition. I suggested that one goal could have been making and calling out the correct blocking assignment to his teammates. He replied that making the call was difficult because no one ever made it 100 percent of the time because the defensive opponents contributed to making errors. This suggests that there is no such thing as a mistake-free game. Yet that knowledge fuels the competitor to work hard to eliminate mistakes. And when mistakes do come, that doesn't mean quitting; it means that working hard and practicing are necessary.

Some of the harsh criticisms Jim heard from Coach Schembechler included "We wasted a scholarship on you." Assistant coach Terry Hanlon once told him, "You're the worst tackle in the history of intercollegiate football." Jim said that it was simply the way it was back then, and he realized at the time that he was being pushed. It challenged him to get better, and he did. He certainly wanted to be noticed by his coaches in a positive way. And he didn't want to be criticized, especially in front of the other players. Yet Jim added, "Bo knew I could take it, and I could."

Social unrest also visited the Michigan campus during those years. There were demonstrations about marijuana, gay rights, social injustice, and many other issues. Growing up in East Lansing, there were no African Americans in Jim's high school, though he did compete athletically against African Americans from other high schools. Perhaps because he was exposed to different races and religions at home, through his parents, he had a different outlook. He considered athletics to be the great equalizer. He said it's how you perform, period. There were no lines of color, no divisions.

Schembechler, too, talked to the team about being one race: Michigan football. He told the players that no one from the outside was going to get between them. Race was not an issue. Jim said that Bo had no color lines. "He treated us all like dogs," he quipped.

During his sophomore season, Jim served as a backup at both the right and left tackle position. In front of him was All-American tackle Dan Dierdorf. It wasn't until his junior year that Jim realized he was making a significant contribution. Because he played both the right and left tackle position, he knew the blocking assignments on both the strong side of the field as well as close to the sideline.

The Wolverines were playing the University of Arizona in a matchup that season. In this game, starting tackle Jack Harpring was injured, so Jim came on the field. The game was close, and the outcome still in doubt. Jim was in the huddle, and a screen pass was called. For Jim, this meant that he had to perform a "pretend" block on the defensive man in front of him, and then quickly get out in front of running back Billy Taylor, the pass target. The Wildcats cornerback came up to make the play to tackle Taylor, but Jim was in a good position and knocked that Wildcats player to the side and out of the way. Taylor scored, the crowd roared, and Michigan won the game. It was then, Jim confessed, that he realized perhaps for the first time that he could get the job done with the game on the line, he could play at this level, the coaches had confidence and trust in him, he could make a significant contribution, and he belonged on this team. "What a moment for me. It was such a positive experience, and it certainly built my confidence. I now knew that *I can do this*," he said.

I asked Jim to tell me about fond memories on the playing field. As a senior, he was a starter at offensive tackle. And the Wolverines were set to play against the very team he had rooted for all of his life growing up. (Remember, the Michigan State Spartans are in the DNA of the Brandstatter family.) Yet the youngest Brandstatter was playing and starting for the archrival Wolverines in Jim's hometown of East Lansing.

The expression "blood is thicker than water" is apt, but Jim can't be sure who his family members were rooting for that day. For his part, he was nervous and wanted to play his best game in front of his family and hometown. And that was no secret for either his teammates or the coaches.

Facing the young Brandstatter was All-American MSU tackle Ron Curl. And since Michigan had a power running offense, Jim had his hands full. Curl might've received the Kodak Player of the Game Award, but Jim thought that he played his best game and won the majority of the battles with the All-American. The coaches also thought Jim played well; he was graded somewhere around 80 percent by the coaches. The Wolverines won the game, and Jim delighted in his individual and team victory. His teammates, understanding the game's importance to Brandstatter, slapped him on the back after the game.

Indeed, it was clear that the Michigan State game was very important for Jim. Of course he was nervous going into it. But he knew that if he played well and if his teammates played well, the team would be successful. And of course he was right. Schembechler often stated that team success and individual success go hand in hand, that when the team becomes successful, the rewards for individuals follow. Indeed, that concept is true of all team sports, not just football. Just compare the Heisman winners in college football to the MVPs in basketball and baseball. Individual winners come from winning teams; that's just how it works.

I asked Jim to talk about that 1969 battle with Ohio State. Jim, a freshman in 1968, remembered the disappointment that the team felt after their devastating and humiliating 50–14 loss. He told me, "I knew the players were heartbroken.... I knew that team captain Jim Mandich wanted revenge." He also knew, written on the blackboard in the team meeting room, were two red-letter games: MSU and OSU. Their coach wanted those wins as much as they did.

Competitive Bo Schembechler had one overarching goal: to win the Big Ten championship outright. Since OSU had been dominating at that time, they became the coach's primary target. Bo was smart. He identified the two most competitive opponents. If his team was successful against them, Michigan would be the Big Ten champion. And with the Big Ten championship, a Rose Bowl would be another reward. In fact, Bo said upon arriving at Michigan, "I don't want to just win games. I'm not rebuilding. I'm here to win a championship."

Even though Jim was a backup tackle to Dierdorf on that 1969 team, he remembered the Iowa victory blowout the week before the OSU matchup. He also remembered the practices during the week before that final game of the season. These practices were clean, hard, crisp, and sharp. He said that it seemed that the drills were done differently, that they were more intense. The hitting seemed harder during the week. He also remembered assistant coach Jerry Hanlon saying, "Bo, maybe we should back off because we don't want these kids to peak on Thursday, we want them to peak on Saturday." Bo replied, "Let them go." The Michigan team was prepared, and Jim thought that they were going to win the game.

Here's an example of the clever coaching strategy Bo employed during that week. The second team (including Jim) wore white jerseys, and each player wore a red No. 50 on both his helmet and his jersey. The second-team offense practiced against the first-team defense and the second-team defense practiced against the first-team offense. That 50 signified the number of points scored by OSU the year before. The motivation worked. "Everyone seemed to be working their butts off. Everyone knew that he had to put out extra to be at your best for this game. And whatever you do, don't let your teammates down," Jim said.

On Saturday, game day, upon leaving the locker room and proceeding into the tunnel, Jim reached up and touched the sign above the door that reads Go BLUE Go. Indeed, everyone touched that sign on his way to the field for any game, yet it seemed to be much more vigorous that day.

"I was walking on air as I proceeded down the tunnel," Jim remembered. "I knew we were going to win, and likely my team did also. It was a unique experience walking through that tunnel, focusing on the field ahead. My senses seemed to heighten…. I just wanted to get on the playing field. I wanted to get on with it.

"In some ways it was almost like a group of cattle crowded in a confined space. My teammates were excited. The adrenaline was flowing. I don't remember talking to anyone. I was part of the moment. I remembered having butterflies in the locker room, but not once I got into the tunnel. I was chomping at the bit. Some guys were vomiting, but I didn't. Yes, I was nauseous in the locker room.

"In some ways it's like driving a car and not seeing what is going on around you. You go from point A to point B but don't remember the details. It was like a perfect storm for that moment, as it was so cool. This really intense experience in 1969 trumped everything. This was the best, and it has never been duplicated."

Even though he was not a first-string starter, he was still an important part of the team and made his contribution during practice and by being a good teammate. For Jim, it was about the team, the team, the team. As he said, "I felt special."

The last game in his senior year was again against Ohio State. In the fourth quarter, with about five minutes to go, Michigan was trailing 7–3. In order to win the game, Michigan had to drive the length of the field and score a touch-down; a field goal would not have been enough. In fact, chances were good it would be the last time that the Michigan offense would have the ball. The Wolverines had to score, simply put. Jim was confident and thought his fellow teammates were, too. *We are going to get this done, no panic. I want to be here*, he thought. Michigan was focused, and moved the ball downfield. The drive had a lot hinging on it. For one, it would keep Michigan unbeaten for the season— not to mention give them a win against their archrival. Jim didn't remember a lot of screaming in the huddle, but he thought, *I have to be my best during every snap, and I'm not going to let anyone down.* There was intensity to get the job done, and they succeeded. Touchdown, Billy Taylor. Michigan wins 10–7.

But football wasn't the only thing on Brandstatter's mind in college. He also went there for a top-quality education. When Jim enrolled at Michigan, he declared architectural design as a major. Since as a sophomore there was a heavy focus on football, he decided to take a less demanding class that didn't have a lab component. He chose a speech class as an elective. Who knew, maybe he might learn a bit about public speaking. Mike Keller, one of his teammates, took the class as well.

In one session, Jim gave a three-minute informative speech that was intended to sell, convince, and persuade the students. Young Jim played base-ball, and he also chewed tobacco. So intelligent Jim gave a speech about the benefits of chewing tobacco. Brilliant Jim tried to convince his fellow college students, sitting there chewing their pens and pencils, that chewing tobacco was okay. As he concluded his speech, the class clapped vigorously; the teacher gave him an A, saying, "You exuded confidence. You're a natural." Luckily Jim received some kudos during that difficult sophomore year, since he wasn't getting many on the practice field.

With his success, Jim took another speech class, this one focusing on TV and radio. He was learning and becoming more creative. Not only that, he even learned to direct a radio drama, which meant getting people to work together as a team.

But what about architectural design? He was really enjoying his speech, radio, and TV classes, so he talked to his advisor about changing majors. He thought about business and then realized he wanted to go in the direction of radio and TV broadcasting. Not only that, but he found a way to get around taking a foreign language course. Intelligent and creative Jim found out that he could receive a degree in general studies, and with it eschew foreign language study and pursue his interest in broadcasting.

Jim liked his radio classes. During class he wrote scripts, created a radio play, and picked out classmates to be the actors, engineers, sound effects crew, and production crew. He could be a coach with his team, or he could be a team member with a coach. Every student took a different role in each production, so he learned about producing, acting, and engineering, all while making presentations to the class. Moreover, the students graded each other's work. Jim got constant, to-the-point feedback. He found that quick reinforcement was important for his learning. On top of that, Jim's classmates told him that he was in everyone's top three as a director, which thrilled him.

He also learned a lot from his TV classes. Jim learned about various camera shots and techniques. It was during these classes, learning the roles of the various people who went into making a greater effort, that Jim learned to appreciate and respect all the different workers who made for an efficient production. Again, it was all about the team, the team, the team.

As a senior, he took an independent study class with Dr. Bill Coburn. By then it was crystal clear that Jim was on a mission. He was focused and knew what he wanted to do for the rest of his life. Clever Jim worked out a project with Dr. Coburn in which he would compare and contrast different styles of sports broadcasting. He knew that in radio there would be play-by-play narration, while in TV there would not be. Ray Scott, the CBS-TV broadcaster, would simply say, "Starr to Dowler. Touchdown." This meant that Bart Starr threw a touchdown pass to Boyd Dowler. Whereas Ernie Harwell, the Detroit

Tigers' broadcaster, might say something like, "It's going, it's going, it's going, and it's long gone." This meant that somebody smacked a home run. He also examined the styles of controversial Howard Cosell, as well as Curt Gowdy and Al Ackerman, all broadcasting legends.

Not surprisingly, Brandstatter's career path kept him firmly in the world of sports.

After making All–Big Ten honors in his senior year, he signed a free-agent contract with the New England Patriots but did not make the final squad. With professional football off the table, Jim turned to broadcasting. He got a position in WEYI-TV, a local Michigan station that covered Saginaw, Bay City, and Flint. The TV newcomer was suddenly a sports director, and at times he even handled the news and weather. Hardworking and enterprising Jim put in at least eight hours a day gathering and soliciting the news from city hall, PTAs, and other local government establishments in the surrounding communities. Laughingly, he remembered that his take-home pay was about $75 per week. In fact, once he couldn't afford to pay for a new fuel pump for his car, so like all good sons, he called home to get the money from his parents. His parents were understanding and paid for his fuel pump.

Jim remembered vividly when President Richard Nixon resigned. That day, Jim was handling the main news, weather, and sports all by himself. He cleverly picked out a couple of lines of Nixon's resignation speech, as well as a couple lines by Gerald Ford, the vice president and Republican congressman from Michigan, for his viewers. Although he did admit that he spent and focused most of the special program on the thing that he did best, which was sports. Those were the days back when he worked the night shift, which started at about 3:00 PM. The station's skeleton crew was just four people, and he loved being there. He learned from the ground up, and to this day he's proud of the fact that he paid his dues.

Soon ambitious Jim moved to a larger station with a greater viewing audience in the Jackson-Lansing market. While at WILX, Jim was able to cover Michigan State University sports, as well as local high school sports. This was perfect, since it was just where he grew up. He was already integrated into the community. And if he needed money, his parents were close by.

He did replay of Michigan games for television. He also did play-by-play for high school sports and interviewed the coaches before the games. All the while, he was laying the groundwork for what was to come. He was learning by doing. He was practicing and making his art form better, tenets learned from Coach Schembechler on the practice field. He was putting in the hard work for the later payoff.

Not only was he doing play-by-play and anchoring the 6:00 and 11:00 sports news, but he no longer had to call home for money. He even had his own apartment. What more could he want? It was around this time that he met his future wife, Ohio State (*Ohio State!*) graduate Robbie Timmons, at the station.

Jim was gaining more experience by covering the Detroit Tigers, Detroit Pistons, Detroit Lions, and Detroit Red Wings for his newscasts. He was holding press conferences as well as filming segments. He had more and more control over his professional life, and he loved it.

Once again, he received another opportunity—and this time it was a big one. He moved to Channel 4 in Detroit to be its sports producer. Still a young man, he was then in a big media market, making a good salary and working with veteran journalists. The news of the day determined who would get more of the airtime. Would it be the news, weather, or sports?

Jim quickly learned that he didn't want to be limited to just the 6:00 or the 11:00 sports news. After doing a short video segment on pitcher Steve Carlton, Jim knew he wanted to do play-by-play. So what did he do? He got involved in Michigan football, doing play-by-play on a TV setup. It was ostensibly a precursor to cable TV. He recorded commentary for replay of the Michigan football games that were aired on Saturday night at 11:00 PM through a special box that would fit on top of any television. With this new arrangement, Brandstatter made a couple hundred dollars per game, pretty good part-time money.

By then a television and radio star, in 1980 he added a half-hour talk show called *Michigan Replay*, with Coach Schembechler. The show was taped and televised after each week's game. Jim interviewed Bo about the game, played some highlights, and then there'd be a scouting report for the next matchup. This show was for the University of Michigan diehards. Even though the two had known each other for years, Jim acknowledged that at times Bo would get testy with him and say things like, "I thought that you knew more about the game of football, Jim. I still have the right to hire and fire."

In 1979, Jim landed a radio color commentator position for the Michigan Wolverines and added Detroit Lions broadcasts in 1987, positions he still holds decades later. He is doing what he loves and being paid for it. Over the years, he has interviewed Michigan head coaches Gary Moeller, Lloyd Carr, Rich Rodriguez, and Brady Hoke on both radio and TV for Michigan faithful. Today his TV show is called *Inside Michigan Football*. He also does a live radio show on Wednesday evenings during the football season in Ann Arbor, with current Michigan coach Hoke. For Michigan football broadcasts, starting in 2014, Brandstatter replaces Frank Beckmann as play-by-play announcer. Former teammate Dan Dierdorf and sideline reporter Doug Karsch fill out the staff. For Detroit Lions football, he's joined by Dan Miller and sideline reporter Tony Ortiz.

During Jim's illustrious career, he has twice been president of the Detroit Sports Broadcasters Association, and in 2004 and 2008 was the Sportscaster of the Year in Michigan. Jim has also written two bestselling books: *Tales from Michigan Stadium*, in two volumes. He was also inducted into the Michigan Sports Hall of Fame.

Reflecting on a career in sports broadcasting, Jim shared with this author a couple memorable moments.

Call Controversy

A few years ago, wide receiver Calvin Johnson made a touchdown catch. Nothing special about that. But on this play, he rolled over into the end zone, and as he was getting to his feet, he put the ball on the ground and left it there. One referee called it a touchdown, but the call was officially reviewed. After review, the referee ruled it an incomplete pass. On the air, Jim said to his fans, "Your team got hosed by the NFL and its rules." Reflecting on it years later, he stands his ground. "I used this word with passion because I meant it. And the word 'hose' is another word for another four-letter word."

A Bowl Misstep

Michigan met South Carolina in 2013 in the Outback Bowl. A great defensive South Carolina player, Jadeveon Clowney tackled the Michigan ball carrier in the backfield for a loss, knocking his helmet off his head. The media made a big deal of this play and even called it one of the best of 2013. In all the praise of Clowney, what they didn't say was that Michigan screwed up. The game film showed the offensive tackle blocking inside and the tight end going downfield. In other words, it was a missed assignment. No one, and I mean no one, from Michigan blocked this man. The result was a tremendous hit in the backfield. Jim reminds us that the eye in the sky or game film never lies. Clowney was probably their best defensive player, and he wasn't accounted for, resulting in this spectacular moment. Simply put, it was Michigan's mistake; Clowney simply capitalized.

Jim is clearly physically imposing, but also gentle. Known by his friends as Duke, he is kind, trustworthy, and caring. He befriends and even remembers the names of every one of his fellow freshman Wolverines. Not only is he well liked, but he is also intelligent and wise.

So how did he get his nickname, anyway? It does not take much prompting to get Brandstatter to do his impression of the one and only John Wayne; just ask him. (By the way, it's good.) The Duke continues to shine, and over the years he has made many contributions to his teammates, his craft, and his community. If you don't believe me, just ask his band of brothers about their fellow warrior.

CHAPTER 3

The Record Holder: Tom Curtis

Many of us have experienced disappointments in our life span. A disappointment can range from business, such as being passed over for that special promotion, to personal, such as failing to make a relationship work. Even though the disappointment may not be totally under our control, it still affects us. And of course, there are degrees of disappointment. For that matter, the disappointment can occur at any point in childhood, adolescence, or adulthood. It's also clear that one's disappointment is idiosyncratic; it takes place in the eye of the beholder. Others may or may not understand our disappointment, or even consider it irrational or foolish. In essence, it's very difficult to reconcile a personal disappointment. Don't forget there are very few, if any, do-overs.

Erik Erikson theorizes, in his Eight Ages of Man, that for an individual to become an emotionally mature adult his psychological task is to resolve, adapt, and come to grips with all the triumphs or disappointments of a lifetime in order to develop what he calls "ego integrity." This suggests that the individual who can accept his own life cycle issues and emotionally integrate the various conflicts while going through his various life stages will reach a sense of ego integrity rather than a sense of despair.

Consider this when reading the story of University of Michigan All-American and two-time Super Bowl champion Tom Newton Curtis. Curtis was born in Cleveland but reared in the small town of Aurora, Ohio, roughly 23 miles from Ohio's largest city. Tom, the youngest, was born to Dr. Henry Stoddard Curtis Jr., a psychologist, and Elizabeth Newton, a teacher. Both his parents were highly educated, holding master's degrees—dad from Michigan and mom from Northwestern University.

After Tom left to attend the University of Michigan, his parents returned to Cleveland, as his father took a job consulting with the Veterans Administration as well as a faculty position at Oberlin College. After Tom's mother died at age 87, Tom acknowledged that it was at first weird for him when his father remarried—but his dad didn't want to live alone. So he married Gail, a second cousin, and built a solar home for them in Delaware, Ohio.

Tom's older brother, Bob, attained a PhD from Indiana State and today is a superintendent of schools (he even taught former Buckeyes football coach Jim Tressel along the way). He has two older sisters. Ginger lives in Ocala, Florida, and Margaret, a nurse (and the angel in the family), works with hospice patients in Columbus, Ohio.

Tom's grandfather Henry Stoddard Curtis Sr., also a psychologist, lived in Ann Arbor. He wrote about parks and recreation in the U.S. and was a staunch supporter of President Teddy Roosevelt, who established national parks across the country. (Check out *Recreation for an Open Country*, written by Tom's grandfather.)

During summers as a young boy, he, like other athletic youngsters, played American Legion baseball. Tom claimed that baseball was his first love. Even though this impressionable young elementary school–aged child played catcher and shortstop, his two favorite Cleveland Indians players were Rocky Colavito and Minnie Minoso. Rocky, a right fielder, had 11 consecutive 20-home-run seasons (1956–66) and led the American League in home runs, RBIs, and slugging average during his career. At the time of his retirement, he ranked only behind Jimmie Foxx and Harmon Killebrew in home runs hit by right-handers. In 1965, Rocky played every game and became the first outfielder in American League history to complete a season with a perfect 1.000 fielding percentage. Quite deservedly, he earned a reputation for being a major power hitter, an excellent fielder, and strong-armed despite being flat-footed.

Minnie Minoso, on the other hand, played outfield for the Cleveland Indians (1949, 1951, 1958–1959) as well as for a number of other clubs over *five* decades of baseball. In 1951, he was even selected to the American League All-Star team for the first of seven times playing right field (and he actually played in eight All-Star Games). Minoso won three Gold Glove Awards and was an American League leader in hits, doubles, triples, sacrifice flies, stolen bases, on-base percentage, and total bases.

Tom was attracted to these two outstanding ballplayers in part because each of them overcame a physical trait to succeed (Rocky was flat-footed and Minnie was a man of color at the dawn of Major League Baseball's integration). Additionally, they were both excellent fielders, they both hit the ball with power and consistency, and they both had versatility (they could play more than one position and did). They were both exceptional and exciting athletes in their sport.

Since the age of six, Tom viewed himself as both a good athlete and leader in sports. He believed that he was a better athlete than his peers and acknowledged that in sports his personality changed. According to him, he became more aggressive ("like a dictator"); he screamed at people and bossed them around. He even did that with the older kids—no one was spared. He remembered an older boy named Randy Flora, who was 14 at the time, spiking him as he slid into second base during a pickup game. Tom was only eight or so, but he was angry about the incident and never warmed up to Randy. The fact that he still remembers it to this day should tell you something about the guy's grit.

Tom also played basketball with the older kids in his neighborhood—he was that good. In the ninth grade, he started on his high school's junior varsity team. After the first half of his very first game, the coach took the 5'10" freshman out of the lineup. Tom thought he was the best player on the floor and couldn't understand why the coach removed him from the game. Then his coach explained to him that if he played in the second half, he'd be ineligible to play for the varsity squad.

That was all the motivation he needed. Tom scored 10 points in that next game and remained a starter for the varsity for the rest of the year. As a junior in high school, he grew to 6'1" and scored at least 20 points per game in both his junior and senior years. He even played with a broken foot. He was also a gym rat and was fortunate enough to have friends who had an outdoor basketball court. In fact, he could not wait to finish his school day so he could play the game from day into night. He was agile, with great hands, but not fast. Most important, he loved the game.

Aside from baseball and basketball, Tom was an outstanding athlete in football and track-and-field. Tom participated in field events including the discus, shot put, and high jump. In his senior year, he competed in the state meet in the high jump, though he did not place.

His buddy and main competitor was a young man named Jim Mandich, who was from a neighboring town roughly five miles away called Solon. (Fittingly, Solon spelled backward is "no los(s).") Tom and Jim met during a track competition when they were about 15. Their friendship solidified off the field as they met at parties and other after-school events. The bigger, taller Mandich set school records in the shot put and discus throw and easily beat Tom in head-to-head field competition.

Tom's father was thrilled with his athletic son and took the young Tom to visit many colleges in Ohio during his sophomore and junior years. In his junior year, he and his father visited Miami of Ohio, where they met then-coach Bo Schembechler. Tom admitted that he was irritated that Bo had not heard about him—after all, he was the star quarterback on his high school team. Tom didn't like being an unknown. Returning to school as a senior, the star quarterback made sure that Bo knew about him, sending the coach media clippings of his exploits.

Curtis, the all-around athlete, was recruited by Tony Adamle and received a baseball and football scholarship offer from Northwestern. Further, both Ohio State and Coach Leo Strang of Kent State offered Tom a basketball and football scholarship. Bump Elliott, Wally Weber, and Bob Nussbaumer recruited Tom for Michigan. The boy thought that his mother, Elizabeth, loved Bump since he brought her a box of candy. Interestingly, Tom's father didn't talk with the coach during the visit; instead, it was just Bump, Tom, and Elizabeth in the family kitchen.

Visiting campus, Wally Weber met Tom at the Big House and took him up to the press box in the historic stadium. And from that viewpoint, overlooking the vast stadium, Tom knew he wanted to test himself against the best. Bob Nussbaumer was a member of the Cleveland Browns who also worked in their front office. He put in a few good words to Bump after seeing Tom play. Tom's high school football team was undefeated but didn't get much media attention because they were a small school. Despite that shortcoming, Tom made second-team All-State quarterback while playing in the lowest high school level in the state of Ohio. (Brian Healy, quarterback from Sandusky, Ohio, was the Ohio Player of the Year. Brian was recruited and enrolled at Michigan as well.)

When Tom asked his friend Jim where he planned to attend college, to his surprise, Jim said Michigan. Jim's high school football team was 22–0, on a serious roll. Tom thought that the outstanding Mandich would be heavily recruited and would likely choose Ohio State. When Tom learned he was going to Michigan, that pleased him; he had just committed to Michigan himself and would have a good friend there.

As a Bump Elliott–recruited freshman, Tom doubted his ability to play quarterback at the next level. The other quarterbacks on the practice field were Healy, Dick Vidmer, and Dennis Brown, among others. The 18-year-old Tom wondered, *Am I good enough?* Then, the three recruited quarterbacks started throwing the ball around. Tom began to evaluate them in comparison to himself. From there, his self-appraisal changed from *Am I good enough?* to *I can throw just as well as them.*

Michigan's freshman football team scheduled two games that season. The first was against the University of Wisconsin freshman team, and their second game was against the University of Toledo freshmen. During practices, Tom was the starting quarterback and Brian Healy was second-string.

They traveled to Wisconsin to play their freshman opponent. At the hotel prior to that game, freshman coach Bill Dowd visited Tom. The coach knocked on Tom's door, Tom opened it, and he was told by the coach that he was starting Brian Healy, not him, in the game. Tom admitted that he never got over the shock (disappointment) of that day. He remembered that knock on the door as if it was yesterday.

Healy started the first half and Michigan was soon down 21–0. Tom started the second half and threw a touchdown pass to Billy Harris; he also ran for 50 to 60 yards, he remembered. Two weeks later, against Toledo freshmen, Tom had the starting spot (no surprises this time from the coach); he started at defensive back as well. He threw for two touchdowns in the first half and also returned a punt for a touchdown.

Tom spent his sophomore season in the defensive backfield. At the time, there were at least two senior quarterbacks on the team. During spring practice, it was customary for the senior quarterbacks to be listed higher on the depth chart and get more opportunities as far as playing time. Finally, Tom was given his chance at quarterback during practice. He got his hands positioned underneath the center, barked the signals out loud, received the ball… and screwed up by being in the wrong position. He did something wrong but didn't fully remember exactly what it was; what he remembered clearly was that one of the offensive position coaches got in his face and chased him back to the defensive side of the field.

That spring practice was Tom's last opportunity to play quarterback for the University of Michigan; he was not allowed to take a snap from center again. Tom thought that his arm strength was okay, he had good instincts, and he was smart enough to play the position. In fact, he thought that he was destined to be a quarterback. He especially blamed Bump Elliott for taking away his dream. Not fulfilling what he felt to be his destiny was a major disappointment and continues to bother him even today.

Returning to a University of Michigan football game recently, he attended a players' reunion. There Tom saw Bump Elliott, age 86 at the time. He desperately wanted to ask Bump why he didn't give him a chance to play quarterback. It was Tom's opportunity, maybe his last, to finally get it off his chest. But he didn't, and the disappointment lingers.

There were three other recruited scholarship quarterbacks on that team, including Barry Pierson, Mark Warner, and Brian Healy. Mark was 6'2", while Barry and Brian were just six feet tall. Tom thought he had the strongest arm, but clearly, the other three were faster than him. And back then Michigan was primarily a running team. As it turned out, all four scholarship quarterbacks never played a down as Wolverines quarterback. Barry was a cornerback who started for two years. Mark was a defensive back and punter. Instead, the starting quarterbacks that year were Dick Vidmer, with Denny Brown in relief. And both of them were shorter than Tom! As a senior, starter Don Moorhead was 6'3", but none of them had a John Elway–type arm. Tom said, "He probably played too well as a safety, and they knew they had a sure thing with me playing safety. And of course when Bo got there he wasn't going to make me quarterback. If I was a coach in a similar situation, I would've given the player, like myself, a chance at quarterback—especially in my sophomore year. Once Bo got there, [when I was] a senior, it was just too late."

To make his point, Tom pointed out that the Miami Dolphins' Ryan Tannehill was primarily a wide receiver in college and then became a professional quarterback. Tannehill is now the first-string quarterback for the Miami Dolphins. His point was simply that some players have the talent to play at more than one position.

As a sophomore on defense, Tom was second on the depth chart behind Jerry Hartman, the right safety. The night before the first game, Curtis' position coach told him that he was going to be the starting left safety. At first, the insecure Tom was bothered by the good news / bad news that he was starting at left safety. Without having practiced the position, how could he be successful? He believed he needed practice learning the nuances of a specific position in order to play well. But he kept his insecurity to himself and didn't dare tell his position coach about his thoughts. And as it turned out, despite not practicing at left safety, Tom intercepted a pass in his first outing.

His performance earned him a starting position at left safety for the following game, against Navy. Even though he had a week of practice under his belt, he dropped a pass that could've been an interception. The pass hit him squarely in his hands. The sure-handed defender made a tragic mistake, and position coach Don James demoted him to second-string.

First-stringer Barry Pierson started the game against Michigan State. Of course it wasn't Barry's fault that Michigan State creamed the Wolverines that Saturday. Second-stringer Tom got to play in the game, too. He didn't make any interceptions against the Spartans, but he played well for the rest of the season. In fact, he made seven interceptions that year.

A productive athlete with terrific instincts, he excelled at intercepting the ball. He still holds Michigan's single-season record for interceptions (10). All told, he played in 31 games, the same as Michigan Heisman winner Charles Woodson. However, Tom holds the Michigan record for most career interceptions with 25 to Woodson's 18.

In one stunning game against Illinois, Tom intercepted three passes. The one and only Bennie Oosterbaan said on the team bus back to Ann Arbor, "Hey, Curtis, you just tied the Big Ten record for interceptions." It was a proud moment. And at the end of the 2013 college football season, according to NCAA statistics, Tom was tied for fourth place for Division I career interceptions.

With Bump Elliott was a coach, Tom admitted that the Wolverines didn't have much of an organized conditioning program in the off-season; it was more or less voluntary and without coach supervision. When he heard the news about Bump getting replaced, he was dumbfounded. At the time, he thought that Canham likely saw Bo's potential and recruited him, but he was still shocked to lose his coach.

Meanwhile, he still loved the game of basketball. Tom thought about playing Big Ten varsity basketball. Then as a senior, Tom asked Schembechler if he could go out for Wolverines basketball. Bo told him, "You can play basketball if you want, but you can't miss practice, because you're going to be a senior. Seniors have to lead." So Curtis instead decided to opt for intramurals. His IM teammate was Jim Mandich, and together they won the basketball championship as an independent team—they even beat teams that had a few of the Michigan varsity basketball players on them. "I was not big, nor was I fast, but I could drive to the basket," Tom said.

When Schembechler arrived on the scene, things changed drastically. Everyone had to be in shape—and he meant everyone. Tom remembered performing drills at the intramural building in more than 100-degree temperatures. He admitted the extreme workouts were not fun, but they helped immensely in getting him into condition.

Mental toughness, "being mentally prepared for the game," was the other big component. Tom said he knew the team wasn't ready for that MSU game in that 1969 season. "I had a bad feeling before the game. I can't quite describe it, nor can I remember my thinking before the game. It might've been an empty feeling. I knew how I felt and how the team probably felt. I wanted to change it. I wanted to change how I felt, but I just couldn't turn it around in my mind. It was a pivotal game for us, and was our second loss of the season," he said. He added that he knew he wasn't ready, and as a result, he played terribly—maybe the worst he ever played. He missed a number of tackles and failed to make any interceptions.

Tom redeemed himself in the next game, against Minnesota. In that game, he knocked down passes and his overall play was exceptional. In fact, he received Player of the Game honors. Then the Wolverines massacred the Hawkeyes 51–6. Tom wasn't totally excited about that blowout, though, because he realized that the following week's game against Ohio State was much more important. Michigan just *had* to beat Ohio State.

That next week of practice was very different and very demanding. Tom knew that his team had to beat Ohio State, pure and simple. He was focused and well prepared for that game. He knew that he had to execute and make plays. Tom and his team indeed executed, made plays, and thoroughly dominated the game—final score: Michigan 24, Ohio State 12.

The year before, Tom had really looked forward to playing that Ohio State game because it was in Columbus at the Shoe. His family attended all his games, but it was Tom's only opportunity to play in Ohio before all his friends, associates, and the people of his hometown of Aurora—perhaps especially one neighbor, the town crier John von Vrasik. Von Vrasik, for some reason, questioned Tom's ability to play at the University of Michigan. In fact, he went around the small town saying, "He'll never play a down at Michigan." John never said this to Tom's face, but he talked plenty behind Tom's back. It motivated Tom, but it also hit against a vulnerable spot since Tom's goal was to make the traveling squad—a goal that was concrete and measurable but yet not totally under his control.

Tom can't remember ever being so excited about playing a football game. Unfortunately, the week before the big game, Tom sprained his ankle against Wisconsin after intercepting a pass. As a result, he was limited in practice the week before the Ohio State game. He not only had difficulty running, he also had difficulty walking. His ankle was spongy. But the tough and athletic Tom took a needle in his ankle before the game for the team—probably not a good decision. But he was stuck, because he wanted so much to play in the Horseshoe.

In that memorable game, he couldn't plant on his bad ankle; he just couldn't tackle. He was at perhaps 70 percent, and maybe that 70 percent was better than his would-be replacement, but mentally he just wasn't there. He said he was in a daze. Buckeyes fullback John Brockington kept getting by him, slipping through his grasp. Curtis had so much to look forward to in that game, but he learned a valuable lesson: when a player is significantly hurt, he loses confidence as well.

However, in 1969, he knew his team was ready. He was mentally and physically prepared, and indeed he played one of his better games. He intercepted two passes, career numbers 24 and 25, and made a tackle on Jim Otis on a crucial fourth-down play. He said he was simply playing safety, the deepest guy in the field, and he gambled. He realized he should not have been there, but he wanted to make the play. And when you gamble, you *better* make that play. Luckily Curtis had Otis for the stop. On another spectacular play, Barry Pierson had a punt return of some 60 yards, aided in large part by the athletic and solid play of Tom, who made a key block during the return. After the game, Tom received credit for the play from one of his coaches.

With the game well in hand, Tom stood on the sideline counting down the waning seconds. He looked over to his right, and to his surprise he saw his high school football friend Geoff Jewett, drunk and standing next to him on the sideline. Geoff said to him, "I am here to celebrate your victory." The victory was monumental for Tom, but also for his high school friends. They had come from rural Ohio to see this game. After the game, SAE fraternity brother Jim Mandich and some other friends arrived and they all celebrated together. And on that day, most of Tom's hometown Ohio friends became Michigan fans.

Interestingly enough, growing up in Ohio, Tom did not realize the significance of the rivalry between Ohio State and Michigan. And his father even had a master's degree from Michigan. But as a college freshman, Tom quickly became aware of the rivalry's significance and intensity.

After concluding his Michigan career, Tom Newton Curtis was drafted in the 14th round (111th in 1970) by the Baltimore Colts; his buddy, fraternity brother, and roommate Jim Mandich was drafted in the second round by the Miami Dolphins. Tom had expected to be drafted in the third or fourth round—another disappointment. He thought that part of the reason he wasn't drafted earlier was that he refused to run the 40-yard dash at the Hula Bowl. He admitted that he didn't run the 40 because he was drinking and partying in Hawaii the entire time; he was a fine runner (his best time was 4.75). Some scouts later confirmed to him that his refusal indeed hurt him. Also drafted from UM were Barry Pierson, taken in the fifth round by St. Louis, and Brian Healy, who was drafted in the 17th round by Minnesota. All three had been quarterbacks recruited and then given football scholarships at Michigan. And all three ended up playing something other than quarterback.

Coincidentally, in their first professional preseason game, in their rookie year, the Baltimore Colts and Miami Dolphins played against each other. Baltimore rookie Tom Curtis was lined up on the kickoff team while Miami rookie Mandich was lined up opposite him, on the receiving team. The Colts kicked off and Tom looked up to see "Mad Dog" Mandich yelling, screaming at the top of his lungs while bearing down on Tom and attempting to knock his dear friend into the stands. Running at full speed, the hysterical Jim was slurring his words, with spittle coming from his mouth in his typical rage. Well, the smart Curtis played matador and did an "olé," getting out of Mad Dog's way and missing the collision.

As a rookie with the Colts, Tom played behind Rick Volk, himself a former Michigan Wolverine, and the old veteran Jerry Logan, who had been with this team for a long time. In those days, the NFL teams had a roster of 40, and Baltimore kept three safeties with the team. (Nowadays teams have larger rosters and they can carry more defensive backs.) When Rick Volk got hurt, Tom entered a game against the New York Jets. In that game, "Broadway Joe" Namath threw the record for most passes in any NFL game at that time: 62. Tom had an opportunity for interception, but he just dropped the ball—to this day he can't explain how that happened. Despite Namath's staggering numbers, the Colts managed to beat the Jets in the game.

The next week Tom had an opportunity to play against former Cal star Joe Kapp of the Boston Patriots. This time, the sure-handed Curtis did hold on to the ball, getting an interception off Kapp. After Jerry Logan came back from his injury, Tom didn't see much more action at safety for the remainder of his rookie year.

Volk was a talented player, and he monitored and mentored Tom. Logan and Tom, on the other hand, seemed to butt heads—likely because Tom wanted his job and Jerry knew it. By his estimation, Tom thought that Rick Volk was good but that he played better than Jerry Logan. Either way, he was playing with a veteran team, along with a number of younger players like Bubba Smith, Ted Hendricks, and others.

Curtis claimed that he was never hurt playing as a defensive back, but he was plenty injured on special teams. Today the NFL is attempting to deal with that part of the game, and he agrees that, without a doubt, it's the most dangerous part of the game for those vulnerable players.

It was midway through the season when the inevitable happened. The Colts were playing Buffalo. Tom attempted to make an open-field tackle on the infamous but brilliant O.J. Simpson when he injured his left knee. He didn't know exactly what was hurt, or even how it happened, but we all know how shifty Juice was.

Tom thought he was good enough to play, even though he was injured, because of his rehabilitation regime. He rehabbed during the rest of the season. Often, when playing and practicing, his knee locked up a few times when it got hyperextended. He was told by the team doctors and trainers that he required surgery; Tom felt he knew better and rationalized that he could still play.

Because of his injured status, he was put on what was then called the "move list." And when his team made the Super Bowl, he was upset that they didn't activate him for the game. He was part of the team, just not the playing part. Despite being out of action, Tom got paid and received the Super Bowl Ring (and $25,000) for being part of the team. It was yet another disappointment, and a decision made by management that Tom again had to go along with.

Curtis would've liked to have played more for the Colts and regrets that they did not give him more opportunities. Tom had 10 fair catches in his limited career, and stated that his highlight was a 21-yard punt return at the Packers on *Monday Night Football.*

After that Super Bowl in January 1971, Tom returned to Ann Arbor once more. He was visiting friends, and while playing basketball at the intramural building his knee locked up again. He decided to have that knee operation after all and returned to Baltimore. While in the hospital, he saw his Colts teammate Tom Mitchell; coincidentally, both were having operations on the same day.

After his surgery, wounded warrior Tom left and flew to Miami to recuperate with his buddy Jim Mandich. Tom was on crutches, but after a week or so he could walk on his own. Then he established his own rehabilitation program. He realized then that he was a fringe player, and he designed his own rehab workout that included running, sprints, isometrics, and weightlifting for strengthening. He got into great shape, and he made the Colts team again in 1971.

It just so happened that the football gods once again brought the two Michigan All-Americans together as opponents, once more when the Colts played the Dolphins, in the 1971 AFC Championship Game. The night before their big game, the injured Tom and tight end Jim got together and watched Michigan play Stanford in the Rose Bowl. (Unfortunately, Big Blue lost the game.) The next day, Miami and Baltimore squared off for the AFC championship. The game was not close, and it was Jim's Dolphins who prevailed, 21–0. With that win, Miami was headed to the Super Bowl, held in New Orleans that year. Tom traveled to the Big Easy and hung out with his friend.

Jim even had Tom ride on the team bus as they traveled to the Superdome to meet the Cowboys. Tom is certain no player would be allowed to travel on another team's bus today.

In 1972, the new Baltimore Colts head coach Don McCafferty drafted Jack Mildren, a quarterback from Oklahoma. Jack didn't play very well as quarterback and was placed on defense as a safety. In Tom's opinion, Jack couldn't play safety very well either ("He couldn't carry my jock"). However, the business of football being what it is, the Colts kept their high draft pick and traded Tom to the L.A. Rams. Not having much practice time in which to learn the Rams defensive scheme, Tom was ultimately cut by the Los Angeles Rams. Then–Dolphins head coach (and Tom's former coach) Don Shula picked up Tom on waivers.

As a result of ligament damage in the right knee, Tom went on injured reserve in 1972, the year the Dolphins went undefeated. But Tom received his second Super Bowl ring nonetheless. After rehabilitating his knee, Tom attempted to come back for the 1973 season. Unfortunately, his knee did not respond well to his rehabilitation program. Then he reinjured his knee on the second day of training camp. He got it taped but reinjured it again. Coach Shula told him, "I have to let you go." Tom replied, "Look, I'll agree to dress for the college All-Star Game, and after I get my check I'll retire."

Tom remembered standing for the national anthem in his shoulder pads, jersey, and pants at that game. He expressed that the experience was weird and unreal for him. It was his final appearance on the big stage, and he didn't even get to play.

After the game, Tom noticed that Shula was following him through the tunnel. He asked him, "Tom, you *are* going to retire tomorrow, right?" Tom replied, "Right." Tom regrets going along with that plan since he could've had a pension. It was a sad end to his professional career.

In September 1974, Tom and his wife, Debbie, married. They have three children: Tammi, the oldest, followed by boys Brad and Matthew. In 2001, Tammi married former Michigan football coach Lloyd Carr's son, Jason (a Michigan football player). Tom described Tammi as an outstanding athlete who was very competitive; apparently the apple did not fall too far from the tree.

Despite never taking a single journalism class, Tom has been in the publishing business since the 1970s. He started with a weekly digest called *Browns Beat*. Then for 40 years he ran the *Dolphin Digest*. He also published the *Steelers Digest* (working for the Rooneys was very rewarding, he said), *Eagles Insider*, *Draft Digest*, and *Football News*. Since 1981, he also has published a weekly newspaper called the *River City Gazette*. The publication covers five small Florida communities and is connected to the *Miami Herald*.

These days one can find Tom on the golf course, at a city council meeting, at the Rotary Club, playing poker on Tuesdays, and looking for local news to publish. If you want to know what's going on regarding women's shelters, charity fund-raising, Christmas parties, social activities, and business meetings, just consult with him; he knows. Although no longer intercepting passes, fielding punts, or driving to the basket, this competitor continues playing golf, bad knees and all.

Despite the disappointments in his football career, Tom always played his hardest. Yet those disappointments came not from his own efforts, but from the decisions of others. And looking back, Tom was indeed successful in becoming a player—and more important, a man—to be proud of.

CHAPTER 4

The Coach: Gary Moeller

H ow does an Ohio State Buckeyes cocaptain, one who shared a national championship (with a team as formidable as 1961's Alabama, no less), become a Michigan man?

As a collegian, Gary Moeller was coached by none other than Woody Hayes, the Ohio State legend. A two-way player, he played middle linebacker on defense and guard on offense, and lettered for three years. He was born January 26, 1941, in Lima, Ohio, a small town on the I-75 corridor. Lima, as the crow flies, is roughly halfway between Toledo and Dayton.

Gary came from an Ohio-rooted family. His father, Lloyd, modeled tough physical work, perseverance, and being in the here and now. Lloyd was not sports-minded, in part because he had to leave school in the eighth grade to help support his family by working on the farm. Gary's mother, Lucille, also lived on a farm, but was fortunate enough to graduate from high school.

Although Gary's older brother, Roger, never played high school sports, that didn't mean he didn't play at all. Back then, kids played sports and did not sit at home playing video games and watching television. Since Gary was a big, strong, athletic kid, the older kids Roger's age allowed him to play with them. Even then, Gary was competitive and could hold his own. Sports were a great way of managing his time productively, something that still holds true today.

When not participating in sports in high school, Gary worked at his father's dairy, where his father managed the evaporator machine for many years, turning milk into powdered milk. They also made ice cream at the dairy—not a bad fringe benefit for young Gary. Lucille was primarily a home-maker, but she occasionally worked at the factory, too. In fact, during World War II, she made tanks for the war effort at the local ironworks.

While attending high school, Gary played football, baseball, and basket-ball. His head basketball and baseball coach was also the assistant football coach—and he was tough. He'd place players on the wooden bench if they released the basketball underhanded when going up for the shot; he wanted them to release the ball off their fingertips. About 6'1" and 210 pounds, Gary was a forward on the basketball team.

The first in his family to attend college, Gary considered going to Bowling Green, Indiana, and Purdue to pursue football. But he didn't know much about those schools, so he chose Ohio State, which offered him a scholar-ship—and boasted the legendary Coach Hayes. Additionally, Columbus was only about 90 miles from home, so his parents could and did attend most of the home games.

It was on the football field at Ohio State that Gary first met Bo Schembechler, who was his line coach. He remembered that his teammates gravitated to Schembechler. They liked his personality, and everyone knew that he would assist them when needed. He a was nice, fair guy, and not at all like crotchety head coach Hayes. Schembechler certainly left an impression with Gary. So began what turned out to be a lifelong friendship for both men.

Moeller received a degree in education from OSU. He figured he would become a high school coach and teach. Why not, since he liked, was good at, and understood the game extremely well? (He did have a pro tryout with the San Francisco 49ers but didn't make the cut: "I wasn't fast enough, quite big enough; it would've been fun.")

He became head coach of the Bellefontaine High School football team. Soon, they won conference honors. Before long, he received a call from

Schembechler, who had become the head coach at Miami of Ohio, asking him if he'd consider becoming Miami's freshman football coach. He gladly replied yes and took the reins in 1967.

After the end of the 1968 football season, Schembechler was hired as the head coach at the University of Michigan. Moeller accompanied the coach and was promoted to be the Wolverines' outside linebackers coach for the 1969 season. He remained the position coach for three years, spent one year as the secondary coach, then became the defensive coordinator when Jim Young went on to become the head coach at the University of Arizona. Gary served in that capacity from 1973 to 1976. It was there that he truly shined; his Wolverines even led the nation in scoring defense in 1974 and 1976. It is clear that Gary knew the game of football and football strategy—just ask those Big Ten offensive coordinators.

A big reason why Gary became a Wolverine had to do with his love for Coach Schembechler. What Bo Schembechler was to football, Gary Moeller was to Bo Schembechler. In other words, the sport builds bonding experiences and can become symbiotic, with family roots thicker than water.

Reflecting on that special 1969 team, Moeller said it was one of the most athletically talented that he ever saw in his many coaching years. In fact, he said, they might have been the best Michigan ever fielded. "We put this group of young men through a lot of exercise drills, and many were weeded out or eliminated. The ones that stayed were a good group of mentally and physically tough young guys," he said.

Back when Gary had been a player for Ohio State, football conditioning was different. The players did a lot of running up and down stadium steps and conducted a lot of practicing and conditioning exercises on their own; it was simply not well organized. At Michigan in 1969, the coaches modeled their programs on difficult combat, wrestling, and conditioning exercises.

In particular, there was one drill called "slap and stomp" that got people's attention. It's "one that they'll never forget," said Moeller. In the intense physical drill, players would pair up and step on their opponent's toes while slapping them on their back. Of course, this was done in brutal temperatures and in close quarters (a boxing ring). Unsurprisingly, the competitive athletes got angry with one another, to say the least, and tempers flared. The coaches ordered this drill to get these athletes into shape, but some players thought that Bo was half-crazy. Yet Bo realized it was the perfect vehicle to get his players in really good physical and mental condition. He would say, "This is my way, and those who follow will become champions." Bo made sure that he had only the toughest on his team, and that's exactly what he accomplished with his "crazy" drills.

At Miami of Ohio and later at Michigan, Bo did lots of seemingly crazy things. He would have guys jump on players' backs and have them carry their teammate up and down the stadium steps. He had them working on agility. In essence, he attempted to break them. He wanted to prove to them that their minds were ready and capable of accomplishing more than they ever thought they could. And, according to Gary, it was always the mind telling the body what to do. This was a perfect illustration of mental toughness: learning that you can do more than what you ever thought you could do. The lesson never wavered: "You can always do more."

At Michigan, the coaches also incorporated on-the-field drills that penalized a player if he made a mistake. Gary and the other coaches had them run as fast as they could to tackle or block another player. The standing player or victim was positioned near a mat placed on the ground. If the coach didn't want the player to make the tackle or block, he quickly blew his whistle and had the player slide on the mat instead.

During football practices, the offense ran two plays a minute, the first and second teams running plays against the scouting team. The first team would start on one half of the field and the players ran maybe 15 plays to one side of the field. Then the offense would turn around and come back with running plays on the other side of the field. If one player made a mistake, the entire team had to run the play again. The game of football is not free from mistakes, but Bo wanted perfection, expected it. He also knew that his players would bond, especially in the face of criticism. He knew the other teammates would become supportive of the targeted player. And that's exactly what happened.

With Bo it was all about repetition. It was something he had picked up from Hayes. Both Woody and Bo were offensive-minded coaches. Yet Bo was more likable and team-oriented. He wanted players to support each other and to turn a mistake into a positive. His team's coming together was of the utmost importance to him. Of course, the coach didn't want to see mistakes, but if a mistake was to be made, he wanted them to make it in practice, not during the game.

Effectively, Bo put his players into simulated combat. They had to work hard and work together, just like soldiers in the military. Sure, these guys probably had good team relationships before Bo and Moeller came to Michigan, Gary acknowledged, but Bo wanted to make things even better.

Everything was disciplined. It was extremely important that the players arrived at the team meeting room on time; lateness was unacceptable. In the room, there was order to the seating arrangement; everyone knew his place. In the front row were the seniors. In the second row were the juniors, then the sophomores. The freshmen were in the last row. That was the pecking order. The freshmen were told to keep their mouths shut and listen since they didn't know anything anyway. Bo wanted the seniors to lead the way. And if a senior didn't do it right, he would not be part of the team.

Bo wanted guys who bought into the program wholeheartedly, and that's just what he got in that 1969 team. In particular, the seniors helped bring the team together by modeling leadership through concrete examples. They were integral to the success of that team. (This was true not only of the 1969 team but of all the teams that followed.)

As far as recruiting was concerned, Bo's coaching staff had advantages in going to Ohio to recruit because many on the Michigan staff had coached high school football in the state. These coaches included Chuck Stobart, Jerry Hanlon, Larry Smith, and Rick Hunter, in addition to Moeller. Bo wanted to focus on the state because there were a lot of good players there. He also knew the Ohio State–Michigan battles were always televised, and the rivalry was well known. Even if Ohio State took a lot of the state's most talented players, they couldn't get them all. Further, there was no predicting what the recruit would decide, or even how OSU recruited.

Bo acknowledged that Fielding H. Yost was the No. 1 Wolverine of all time. This Michigan legend was an All-American, coach, and athletic director. As a coach, Yost's teams won 165 games, lost 29, and tied 10. In fact, in 1901, Michigan outscored its opponents 550–0. Bo knew Wolverines history. And he wanted to bring it all back and put Michigan back in the spotlight. And that's exactly what he set out to do.

Moeller remembered the coaches' room back then, which was maybe a 20' x 20' room. In the room were 13 or 14 chairs that were placed in the middle of the room. There was a chain that worked the light switch. There were nails to hang your clothes on. "Bo would say, 'This is where Yost put in the nail, and this is my nail now. This is where I hang my clothes.' Things are very different today," Moeller said.

During that 1969 season, Bo gave his coaching staff five directives:

1. Coach hard.
2. Don't bitch or complain about the previous coaching staff.
3. Meet the previous coaches and do your best to win them over.
4. Work hard on conditioning players.
5. Evaluate certain player positions such as quarterback, since you don't know how or even if they are going to fit into our system.

At Miami of Ohio, Bo had run a scheme that was quite close to the Ohio State system—the running plays and the defensive alignments were particularly similar. He employed the same tactics at Michigan, which effectively meant that his Wolverines team practiced (especially in the spring) running the same plays that they would see Ohio State run against them in game action.

During the 1969 season, Michigan's second loss was to rival Michigan State (Missouri, ranked No. 9, was the first loss), to put them at three wins and two losses. "Things became so heated at that point. That was tenuous, to say the least. Our next game was at Minnesota, and we left our best running back at home because he did not practice during the week. The rule was that if a player didn't practice during the week, he didn't play. By leaving the best running back player at home, Bo sent a clear message to the team: no one was getting preferential treatment. The players practiced as a team and played as a team. There were no exceptions. The team was not set up like a pyramid.

Everyone knew who the better players were, and yet Bo was like a mom, as he loved them and treated them all equally," Moeller said.

Even though Michigan had resoundingly beat Iowa 51–6 in Iowa city the week preceding the Ohio State game, the nation's sportswriters were overwhelmingly predicting Ohio State would win the game, some going as far as to call the Buckeyes the greatest team in the last 100 years of college football. OSU had won 22 straight games with a team stacked with All-Americans, including "Assassin" Jack Tatum. To say they were the favorite would be a gross understatement.

Yet to Gary, it was an exciting matchup. After all, everyone knew that he had been a star player on the Buckeyes. Even the Michigan groundskeeper quipped, "Hey, are they going to let you come to that game?" To him, the matchup was like two brothers squaring against each other. Both wanted to win. Sure, you loved your brother, but you still wanted to beat him, and he wanted to beat you. It was good, clean competition, and winning was paramount. "With the victory, just think of all the respect you received. This was the ultimate sibling rivalry competition. You wanted to do your best and win. Let the blood flow and see what happens. Let the best person be victorious. Go Blue," Moeller said.

There was extra bad blood going into the '69 matchup. The year before, Hayes had gone for a two-point conversion after the last touchdown, when the Buckeyes were way ahead. Moeller was sure that revenge was a motivating factor, but vengeance alone would not bring victory. "Our team had a great group of seniors, like Jim Mandich. They bitched at winter conditioning, but just the same they worked hard. Bump did a tremendous job of recruiting, and this was one of his better combinations of players. Not only did we have offensive threat Jim Mandich, we also had Tom Curtis, Barry Pierson, Brian Healy, and Thom Darden in our defensive backfield. We had good and exceptional players.

"Also in our favor was the fact that our team was building momentum. The confidence was growing. After we put together a string of victories, the players were getting better with their techniques, and their on-the-field production was very impressive."

Practice in the week leading up to the Ohio State game was competitive, and the team's attention to detail was superb. "There was plenty of snow on the ground [on] Monday morning for our first day of practice," Moeller remembered. "Even under snow conditions, our players were chomping at the bit, ready to go and kick ass. I'd never seen a week of practice with so much intensity. Friday came and we moved to an Ann Arbor hotel. And In the late night, our hotel in Ann Arbor lost its power. To top that, during pregame warm-ups on Saturday, Woody purposely had his Ohio State players working out at our end of the field. *What would Bo do?* I thought. Bo told the manager in a firm voice, 'Tell him where he belongs, which is the other end of the field.'

"I thought that we had a really good chance of beating Ohio State. However, on their first drive, they went right down the field and scored a touchdown. We were offside during the extra point, and then they went for a two-point conversion but failed....

"I must admit, my confidence was shaken. Then we got the ball, went down the field, scored, and kicked the extra point. We kicked off, they got the ball, went down the field, and they scored again.... Again, they went for a two-point conversion and failed once again. They kicked off to us, we drove the field, we scored, and made the extra point, making it 14 to 12. We were never behind again and wound up scoring 10 more points.... By halftime, the game was essentially over.

"We ran our basic stuff...that day, but I never experienced anything like this. I knew our guys would not give up and our kids would play well. I had great expectations, and also I'm sure the other coaches had positive expectations as well. That also likely contributed to our victory."

Moeller also added that he especially liked going against great teams. He also liked the challenge of calling the defenses against Woody. After all, he learned a lot from the great coach. For instance, he learned everything that he needed to know about the media with this one Woody quote: "If anyone says nice things to you or about you other than your mother or your father, punch them in the nose." Woody's disdain for the media was clear: *They're not your friends.* What's more, it was crucial that the players did not start believing the hype, because it was not realistic. It was just words.

Gary also learned that being able to run a few plays to perfection was key. Woody wasn't necessarily creative, but he was detail oriented. He was an offensive-minded coach and went over and over certain plays to reduce the mistakes. He taught his players and coaches at the chalkboard. The play had to be run perfectly, no excuses. For him, his motto was "Practice makes perfect."

He learned firsthand about Woody's competitiveness, fire, and passion. "You [didn't] want to be around Woody when he lost the football game," he said. He remembered Woody once going nuts on the sideline and dismantling the field distance markers in anger. It was when Thom Darden made that fantastic interception in 1971 to seal the game for Michigan. (He also remembered the infamous moment when Woody punched that Clemson player on the sideline after he intercepted a pass to seal Ohio State's fate.)

Hayes perfected ball control and won with "three yards and a cloud of dust." Ask Gary, and he believes that the NFL is going to incorporate more and more running in their pro game. Indeed, the lessons taught by Hayes live on.

From Schembechler, he learned a lot about handling players. Bo called it "motivation through discipline." On the practice field, Bo appeared to be hard on them. However, after practice, he would call players in to talk with him individually. Maybe it was to smooth things over, but he got them to respect him, and he did it in private. They didn't carry grudges; even if he got on a guy, he was able to let it go. But if a player was in some kind of difficulty, he wanted to see him right away. He was clearly a player's coach and he also stayed involved in personal and non-football issues, such as academics and family life.

Like Hayes, he liked to go over plays. He also called the offensive plays for the team. Before practice, Bo would meet with all the players, and the coaches came up and determined the plays that we wanted to run for the next day's practice. Bo would then run all of those plays over and over until the players got it right. Then the assistant coaches would be in charge and run some drills, such as a seven-on-seven (seven offensive players practicing against seven players on the defensive squad). There, the assistant coaches would definitely be in charge, and Bo would go around the field and watch each drill.

There were set plays for both the offense as well as the way the defense practiced. For example, the first-string offense would run their plays against the scouting team (the scouting team would stand in for the next opponent). Likewise, the first-string defense would practice against the scouting team (and the scouting team would demonstrate offensive plays from the upcoming opponent's repertoire). This system was efficiently designed so that the team would be familiar with how its next opponent operated both on offense and defense.

Even though Bo was aggressive with his players, he was a great communicator. He used negative feedback as a technique to break down the players so that he could build them up. "And in that process they would get better as a result. Everybody knew that was his philosophy, especially the assistant coaches. So we had to be supportive with the players. It was never verbalized openly that the assistant coaches would be the good cop and Bo the bad cop. Some assistant coaches became critical, too, but Bo was fair with his criticism. He had no trouble getting after Dan Dierdorf, one of the more outstanding players. It didn't matter who the player was. Bo was just fair to all. He wanted his players to get better and to believe in themselves and that anything was possible," Moeller explained.

Gary defined mental toughness as a tremendous focus or commitment on a set goal. "You have to get the guy's mind to believe that he can and is able to compete. The mind had to see and believe what the body could achieve. That's what drives the machine. Sometimes you have to get guys tough." It wasn't hard for him. There are a lot of former players who do not consider coaching after their playing careers are done, but for Gary it's easy and fun.

He loves the game and loves and studies the tactics both on offense and defense. He watches game film over and over. He is a student of the game. He is also an expert. Over the course of his career he has been a high school, college, and professional football coach.

Along the way, he worked with countless talented players. Remembering Michigan offensive guard Reggie McKenzie, he said that Reggie was "self-made." Though Reggie may not have been "a real fluid athlete," Moeller thought that he was an outstanding football player. He gave an example:

When Reggie was playing professional ball with the Buffalo Bills, he believes that Reggie was *the* significant man blocking for O.J. Simpson, when the running back broke the NFL rushing record. Reggie was an ideal team player and would do whatever the coach asked, and was inspirational and a good leader. Reggie, he said, took pride in doing well.

Chuck Knox was Reggie's coach in Buffalo. And when Coach Knox left Buffalo to become the head coach for the Seattle Seahawks, he took Reggie with him to be that leader. He told Reggie, "I want you to continue doing what you are supposed to be doing." This meant that Reggie would get on players and push them to get better, and it didn't matter if it was in practice or during the games. Reggie was a leader. Some might call him an enforcer. Coaches need good leaders, and Gary thought Reggie was that leader.

Reflecting on his coaching practices, Gary talked about coming up with game plans and helping the players by painting pictures with his words. He would tell Elvis Grbac, the Michigan (and later the San Francisco 49ers and Kansas City Chiefs) quarterback, "Throw the ball or hit the receiver on your third drop-back step." He believed the quarterback had to visualize the play in order to complete it successfully. Likewise, he would tell Michigan wide receiver Desmond Howard, "If you don't get your release from the line, you're not going to be open to catch the pass." Or he might tell the offensive guard or tackle to take a short jab step so that the second foot would be underneath him, so that he could get his hands underneath the breast plate of the defenseman for his block. Practice, practice, practice in order to get better. Visualize it in your mind and then do it. Those were Moeller's mantras.

"With some college quarterbacks, you don't want to overload them," Gary said. "You might tell them to look at the first option, and if he is not open to catch a pass, then pull the ball back or go to the second option. It's very difficult to get to the third option because you'd need a great offensive line to keep away from being tackled from those opposing players." Some players can handle the overload like man-on-man or the timing between the quarterback and the receiver. This might be evident when the quarterback throws to a certain spot and expects the receiver to be there looking for the ball.

Gary likes talking to the players on or off the field. Yet with the pros, it's a very different game. "In the NFL, you're matching wits with the very best coaches in the game. With the pros, they are adults—and you expect more from them because they are older, more intelligent, more experienced—so that you can overload them. You wind up giving them more and more because that separates them at that level. If they can't take the overload, they won't be around for long. But of course you want to have players that are extraordinary. You want to turn them loose, but not to the extent that the player always gambles. If the gamble is successful, it's a great play. If the gamble is unsuccessful, the opposing team just scored a touchdown. The coach still has to coach, and it's a fine line," he said.

Gems from Gary

Gary said, "At Michigan, Bo ran the option. He had a good blocking fullback and good running back to complement the quarterback in the I-formation backfield. In this formation, the quarterback could either fake the ball to the fullback, fake the ball to the running back, keep the ball himself, or even throw a play-action pass off this formation—thus the 'option.' However, at Michigan, we were primarily a power/option running offense.

"In the NFL today, there's more 'option' by having your tight end or fullback spreading out wide. Normally, the fullback and the tight end can create a mismatch with the inside linebacker. This allows the quarterback to determine if the defense is playing man-to-man or some zone coverage. Once again, it's about the option and creating mismatches."

In talking about NFL quarterbacks, Tim Tebow came up in conversation. Moeller felt that Tebow just couldn't get it done, that he just didn't seem to have that touch. And if he ran the option like he did in college, he would not last long in the pros because of all the hard hitting. (Of course, Moeller's remarks were right on; as of this writing, Tim Tebow is unsigned and perhaps out of the NFL for good.) Gary added that most NFL quarterbacks don't seem to know how to fall or create separation like the running backs. "You have to know how to fall properly. The smart guys, like [Russell] Wilson in Seattle—he knows how to get out of bounds," Moeller said.

Gary also had an opinion on why it's difficult to repeat as a champion: "It may be a matter of complacency" but it also has to do with "the other teams figuring out a way to beat you." Every champion has a target on its back from the outset of the season.

Reflecting on Michigan glories, Gary said that Jim Mandich once told him that the 1969 victory against Ohio State was the most satisfying of his career. (Remember, Mandich was a two-time Super Bowl winner and member of the undefeated Miami Dolphins.)

Speaking of Coach Schembechler and his commitment to the game of football, Moeller said, "Bo probably didn't have a best friend. And he wasn't too social outside of football. Woody said, 'You can't have a best friend. Football is your best friend.'"

When Schembechler had his first heart attack on January 1, 1970 (his father had died from a heart condition), Gary was shocked to hear the news. He said, "I don't know if the doctors allowed him to watch the Michigan-USC Rose Bowl game." The following season, Bo moved his bed in the living room as part of rehabilitation. Of course, he continued coaching once he recuperated.

One last piece of advice to aspiring coaches: Gary thinks being a high school coach is a good way to start a football coaching career.

Politics in Football

In 1961, when Ohio State was ranked No. 1 in the nation, the faculty at Ohio State voted against going to the Rose Bowl that year, stressing that academics should come before athletics. The move suggested that the president of OSU ran everything and was likely threatened by the athletic director and football program. It was Gary's first taste of the battle between the administration and athletic department, one he witnessed firsthand as a player.

Fast-forward to 1973. Michigan's quarterback, Dennis Franklin, broke his arm and the Ohio State–Michigan game ended in a 10–10 tie. Both teams had identical records: undefeated with one tie. The Big Ten secretly voted 6–4 that Ohio State should get the nod to go to the Rose Bowl, sending Michigan to the Orange Bowl. Unfortunately, the Wolverines lost to Oklahoma in the

Orange Bowl that year; in the Rose Bowl, UCLA beat Ohio State. At the termination of the season, Notre Dame was ranked one, Ohio State two, and Alabama three. "And we were, I think, six," Moeller recalled.

He said, "The Big Ten rule was that no Big Ten school could go to the Rose Bowl two years in a row. At that time, the Big Ten's policy was only one team would go to a bowl, and that was the Rose Bowl. Bo was mad about that insane policy and raised hell in 1974. Then, in 1975, the Big Ten schools were allowed to participate in any bowl. Thank you, Bo Schembechler."

Family Life

Gary and his wife, Ann, have a son, Andy. In 1986, Andy was cocaptain of the Wolverines, along with Jim Harbaugh. Andy played linebacker on that Michigan team, while Jim played quarterback. Andy was a starter for three years. Meanwhile, Gary was the defensive coordinator—and had a lot of fun coaching his son. He enjoyed the experience because he got to see him often and got to see him play in all of his games. For him, coaching Andy was easy because as a player he worked his butt off. Sure, at times Gary got on his son. He told him that he had to get this done. But Gary doesn't remember cussing very much. (He added that what's important is how you say what you say.) He thought that Andy had a great understanding of the game.

Coincidentally, Jack Harbaugh also was coach on that team and got to coach his own son. As most football faithful know, Jack's son Jim today coaches the San Francisco 49ers and his other son, John, coaches the Baltimore Ravens. Incidentally, Andy was a position coach for the Baltimore Ravens for six years before joining the Cleveland Browns in 2014. Gary's very proud of him.

The 1986 Michigan team (with Andy and Jim) played in the Rose Bowl, but lost to Arizona State that year. ASU's coach was John Cooper, who later became coach at Ohio State. "I remember Michigan faked a punt, and that terrific play was called back because of a referee's call of holding. That might have changed the outcome of the game," Moeller remembered.

Moeller took the reins as Michigan's head coach in 1990. His overall record was 44–13–4, and among Big Ten opponents, Gary's record was 30–8–2. (Coach Moeller was also the head coach at the University of Illinois from

1977 to 1979). He also coached in the pros with the Detroit Lions, Cincinnati Bengals, Jacksonville Jaguars, and Chicago Bears. But the professional football business is just as mercurial for coaches as it is for players; Gary reminded me that the NFL also stands for "not for long."

Even today you can find Gary watching film and going to games—especially those of his grandkids. He also assists, occasionally, a former defensive player of his: Jim Lyall. Lyall coaches at a small Catholic college in Michigan that boasts some intimidatingly large linemen.

During Michigan's 40-year reunion for its 1973 team, Moeller pointed out to Jim that he was not a starter. Starting is important. However, it's finishing that is the key. And you can expect to find Moeller at practices and games, still a student and mentor of the game he loves.

CHAPTER 5

The Enforcer: Reggie McKenzie

T he city of Highland Park, Michigan, is surrounded by the much
larger city of Detroit. The working-class community of Highland
Park was home to Mr. and Mrs. Henry McKenzie. Mr. McKenzie
migrated from Georgia. According to Reggie, it is safe to say that McKenzie
was Henry's slave name. Reggie's great-great-grandmother was named Clarissa
and was bought by a Caucasian slave owner by the name of McKenzie in
Savannah, Georgia.

Henry, the oldest of 13 siblings, was just 13 years old when he began to
gain firsthand knowledge about mental toughness and hard work. His own
father told him something to the effect of, "You have to help out now with the
family." Young Henry McKenzie knew what his father meant. Since his family
lived and worked on a rural Georgia farm, it was time for him to accompany
his father in the field full-time. That also meant that Henry's formal school
education was terminated for good.

Henry Jr. married Hazel, and they soon started a family of their own.
Both Henry and Hazel were no-nonsense parents; they did not overindulge
their children. Hazel, like her husband, was tough—and at times she was a
disciplinarian, using a belt, ironing cord, or even a club when needed. She was

also strict about her children's schooling; she made sure that Reggie did well in school and simply wouldn't allow it any other way. To drive her point home, 5'9" Hazel told Reggie, "Son, you're not going to embarrass me. I'll kill you first." Reggie believed his mother's words and at an early age learned to respect adults. He also confessed that he was afraid of his mom.

Hazel McKenzie gave birth to eight children. And of Reggie's seven siblings, he was the first to graduate from college. He also became an All-American and an All-Pro football player.

Early on, Reggie knew about hard work, taking responsibility, academic discipline, and toughness. As a young boy, he earned money by mowing a neighbor's grass or performing other odd jobs. There was no such thing as an allowance in the McKenzie household. Aside from other occasional jobs, young Reggie had two newspaper routes: he delivered the *Detroit Free Press* and the *Highland Parker* from the age of 12 through high school. Not being afraid of hard work, and at the tender age of 16, he misled an employer about his age amidst a labor strike in Detroit. The tall lad got the job and began limited employment with the John F. Ivory Moving Company.

In the eighth grade, Reggie underwent a dramatic growth spurt, and his shoe size went from 11 to 14. Then during his junior year in high school, he grew four inches, shooting up from just taller than 6'0" to 6'4½" and 200 pounds. During those good old years, Reggie had a voracious appetite and consumed great amounts of food but burned it all off through work, exercise, and sports.

As a ninth-grader, he went out for freshman football, and played defensive end and offensive tackle. In the 10th grade, Reggie moved up and played on the reserve football team at both positions. In his junior and senior years, he started on both sides for the varsity team.

Reggie, being bright, was quick to realize that he had to get stronger and faster in order to improve in the game. He loved playing football. Yet when he compared himself to his other teammates, he realized that he wasn't the fastest runner. So lacking fleetness of foot, the young but physically large McKenzie went out for the track-and-field team. In his junior year, he threw the shot put (according to him, "not very far"). In track, he ran both the 100- and 200-yard dash, as well as the mile. This track-and-field experience indeed served him well because he learned to run on his toes while at the same time pumping his arms. With his new running form, he ran faster—and with a coordinated stride to boot. He by no means became a track-and-field star, but he improved his speed and in the process accomplished one of his goals.

In order to get physically stronger, Reggie became good friends with his neighbor and fellow shot-putter Oliver Parker, who also played fullback on the football team. Oliver had a badass reputation in the neighborhood. The word was out: *Don't mess with Oliver.* To reinforce that notion, Oliver would echo the sentiment himself. And all of the neighborhood rowdies took Oliver seriously; no one messed with or started a fistfight with him.

Oliver was extremely strong in part because he knew how to lift free weights properly. So the two teammates worked out together, doing a variety of weightlifting exercises including bench presses, military presses, and curls. And at home, Reggie and his brothers did push-ups while watching television. They'd start on their fingertips (strong fingers came in handy for that) and then rest on their palms only during commercials. By the time Reggie graduated from high school, he had vastly developed more strength in his arms and upper body, as well as improved his running skills.

Another significant influence during his high school years was his interest in the Boy Scouts. Not one to stand still, he progressed through the ranks of the brotherhood. And after a camping trip that lasted for about 20 nights under the stars, he became eligible for the coveted Order of the Arrow. During the prestigious ritual, Reggie was initiated into the Order of the Arrow (which promotes camping and responsible outdoor adventure; develops leaders with a willingness in character, spirit, and the ability to advance the activities of their scouting units; and crystallizes the Scout habit of helpfulness to life, with the purpose of leadership and cheerful service to others). In doing so, the young McKenzie learned how to survive in the wilds in addition to developing crucial leadership skills.

Henry McKenzie Jr., Reggie's big brother, graduated from high school in 1956. Although Henry played basketball in high school, there were few college opportunities for him back then, according to Reggie. As a result of limited opportunities, Henry Jr. instead went into the air force, in which he served for 24 years. He was honorably discharged and currently resides in Washington State.

When Reggie was a high school senior and nearing graduation, his father sat at the kitchen table reading the *Detroit Free Press*. Without looking up, he asked Reggie, "What are you going to do? You're turning 18 and graduating from high school." Before Reggie could respond, his father said, "You have three options, son. One, get a job. Two, go to school. Or three, join the military. These are your choices." That was the end of the father-and-son discussion. Reggie was well aware of his options, even before being told by his father. His father was very consistent; he had laid out the same choices to Henry Jr., Milton, and older sisters JoAnn, Margaret, and Dell, while reading the same daily newspaper at the same kitchen table.

Reggie considered attending Michigan State University, and met with one of their football coaches, Ed Rutherford. (Coincidentally, Coach Rutherford was this author's high school football coach at Denby High School.) According to Reggie, he believed that Rutherford didn't think he could play for the Spartans. The coach later denied saying that, but Reggie still believes otherwise. Either way, their initial meeting did not go well, and Reggie instead enrolled at the University of Michigan.

While standing on the sideline next to fellow freshman teammate and recruit Jim Brandstatter, Reggie remembered talking about "killing" the University of Michigan freshman coach, Bill Dowd. Reggie remembered well all the difficult practices and running progressions that the mean-spirited coach put those poor freshman football players through. And since they only played two games, the sadistic practices made even less sense to the young man.

Reggie believes that mental toughness is related to consistency, and follows Coach Schembechler's directive, "Do it right the first time, every time, and all the time." At the start, Reggie seemed to be in Bo's doghouse for a while. On one occasion as a sophomore, Reggie was going through the motions ("half speed at best") during practice. Reggie was clearly "fucking up." Future All-American middle linebacker Mike Taylor, one of the Mellow

Men, admonished him: "Come on, Reggie, they are filming our practice." But Reggie was discouraged when Coach Schembechler got on his case and said things to him like, "I should kick your ass off the team" and "Son of a bitch, you can do better." Schembechler, like only he could, rode him mercilessly.

The taunts had an adverse effect on him. Indeed, Reggie was having difficulty cutting it because of the onslaught of verbal abuse from Bo. He was embarrassed. He just *knew* Schembechler didn't like him. He even started questioning his own football abilities. He was confused, unable to think clearly. Initially he considered quitting the team. He talked to his mother and sister JoAnn about leaving the program. It was his big sister JoAnn who shot back, in no uncertain terms, "McKenzie men don't quit."

Reggie knew that he didn't want Bo to get on him during practice. He knew firsthand about that stare and about the coach's wrath. Schembechler said things like, "Son of a bitch, cocksucker, this is how I want it done." And he resolved to do something about it.

When Reggie was either a junior or senior, the offense was for some reason short on tailbacks in spring practice. As such, Preston Henry had to serve as tailback on every play for both the first- and second-team offenses during that fateful practice. Reggie remembered Henry being as tough as they come. He was not only street tough, he was football tough and mentally tough as well. Most if not all the players identified with Henry and felt very sorry for him. It was a grueling day for the player, who ran upwards of 130 plays in the session. At the end of the practice, Coach Schembechler had everyone line up on the sideline to run wind sprints. Even the workhorse, Preston Henry. Preston said, "I'm not going to let him beat me." With that, he had the players' respect.

That idea "I'm not going to let Bo beat me" was incorporated into Reggie's way of thinking, too. He learned to look through a guy. And when the coach said, "Keep your head up, don't look at the ground," Reggie did just that. He learned about mental toughness and physical toughness. Indeed, he knew it firsthand. After many practices, the players, despite being physically tired, had to run a mile. To get through those grueling times, Reggie thought to himself, *I have to keep going, one step after the other. To be the best you have to pay the*

price. Pick up your feet, keep pushing your arms. Keep at it; you're going to need it.
At times, Reggie verbalized aloud his self-motivations. He bought into Coach
Schembechler's proviso that he had to be both mentally and physically tough
to play the vicious game of football.

And proving that toughness to his coach became a prime motivation for
him. "I'm going to show you that I can play, Bo," he'd say. And in games,
he'd say to himself, *I want to destroy you because I can.* So in practice, facing
linebackers such as Mike Taylor and Marty Huff each day, he went at full
speed. He realized that "those cats were as tough as they come, and none were
tougher." With his new attitude, Reggie began to believe that he would win
those fierce physical battles. He said to himself, *If I can beat them, I can beat
anyone.* Reggie became intensely focused on practicing as hard as he could,
and in the process he got better and better.

Of course, that didn't mean that he loved winter conditioning. He remembered running from the Yost Fieldhouse and back to the intramural building
in the brutal weather. He also had to run on the inside track at Yost. It was
while doing winter conditioning that he began to appreciate teammate
"Wolfman" Frank Gusich. Of all of his tough-as-nails teammates, he told me
he felt Gusich was the toughest.

In February 1969, during winter conditioning, the players were doing
a slap-and-stomp drill. The big defensive end Cecil Pryor was in a boxing
ring and his teammate opponent hit him, possibly in the face. The strong,
burly jokester Pryor got mad and hit the young upstart with his left hand.
In so doing, he knocked him clear out of the ring. Schembechler immediately jumped into the ring and said, "If you want to fight someone, fight me,
Cecil." Of course Cecil chose not to fight the coach. However, Bo made a
clear statement. He was tough, he was in charge, and he was the boss.

Then, on January 1, 1970, when Bo had a heart attack before the USC-
Michigan Rose Bowl game, the coach was admitted into the hospital and was
not allowed any visitors. The players knew that Bo appreciated guys who were
tough and played tough, so they resolved to prove it to their leader. Everyone
on the team was concerned about Bo before, during, and after the game. Of
course, they also had to deal with their USC opponent.

After the Rose Bowl game, instead of traveling home with the team, Cecil left for the hospital. He quickly realized that he couldn't just walk in to see Bo (who was in critical condition). So the young, clever Pryor followed a young doctor in a white coat around the hospital. And after a while, it just so happened that this unnamed doctor removed his white coat and hung it on a rack. Quickly and furtively, Cecil put on the white coat and proceeded directly to Bo's room. Cecil entered quietly, alone, and found Bo with his eyes closed. He then headed toward Bo's bed, and while standing over and looking down at the helpless coach, he saw Bo's eyes open. The first thing that came out of Bo's mouth was, "Don't be messing with any one of those tools." Cecil started laughing and said to his coach, "I just wanted to see how you're doing." Pryor jokes that perhaps Schembechler thought he was going to physically hurt him.

Reggie learned from the older players, the juniors and seniors, about focusing. He knew he had to focus, pay attention, and be engaged—even when taking a water break. The older players modeled focusing all the time. And indeed, Reggie learned to focus for more than two and half hours in practice, day after day and week after week.

In time, Reggie realized he wasn't the only one who Bo singled out. He remembered the blocked-punt episode that was blamed on Jim Brandstatter. And he remembered Schembechler saying to Jim, "I'm going to kick your ass, but I'm afraid I'll lose my foot." Brandstatter wasn't immune to his coach's barbs. After one such incident, he was crying, and it took coach Jerry Hanlon to calm him, saying, "Bo didn't mean it." Reggie realized Bo got on everyone, though some more than others. He knew that Bo psyched players out and that everyone, especially all the young kids, had to learn how to deal with Bo. The coach wanted play perfection, which meant player consistency. He also told everyone that they could get better. Eventually Reggie began to understand all the mental torture inflicted by Schembechler.

Reggie also learned another valuable lesson from Bo: "We win as a team, we lose as a team. No one individual can win the game." The coach knew that his Michigan Wolverines had to become one, and that they could be only as strong as their leaders. For Bo, it began with the group. It's all about the group. And the group becomes the team. Bo wanted the seniors to lead. That fact was made very clear. Reggie believed that one way to lead was through exemplary play on the field. He learned about doing it right the first time, every time, and all the time. That expression became ingrained in him. He learned not to take time off. He learned to take responsibility for his play.

Reggie clearly remembered that 1969 season-finale game against Ohio State. He remembered going from the street into the famous Michigan tunnel, going down, down, down until he reached the stadium floor and playing field. In the tunnel with all his teammates, Reggie remembered the wild one, captain "Mad Dog" Jim Mandich, a senior, standing at the tunnel entrance, facing his teammates. Jim had his fists in the air and was making violent shaking gestures. With tears coming down his face, he uttered unintelligible grunts and sounds. That memory stands out and speaks to Jim's leadership and passion for the game. Without any words, it was clear to everyone how important that game was to Jim. For Reggie, that memory is as vivid today as it was more than 40 years ago. For him, it exemplifies the senior leadership, character modeling, and what was needed in order to play the game. That game was fueled by emotion, plain and simple.

Reggie thanked his mother and father for some of his early life experiences. He remembered that at times, dinner consisted of Spam, grits, toast, and eggs—and not necessarily all that. Sometimes dinner might've been just grits. And at times the McKenzie family received assistance. Reggie's mother said to him that she was sorry that the family did not have more, but Reggie didn't expect anything more. He knew that if he wanted something, he had to work for it. He had to take responsibility and make money on his own. He was thankful attending church helped him to develop a will and faith. Indeed, he thanked God for the many significant life decisions that He helped him make.

Reggie also was thankful to his high school coach and college coaches Jerry Hanlon, Larry Smith, Gary Moeller, Jim Young, Chuck Stobart, and Dick Hunter. He believes that what we learn is related to what we are taught. He acknowledges that his coaches were teachers and knows that they cared about him. And being cared about was very important to him.

Initially, coach Gary Moeller viewed Reggie as somewhat of an unnatural and uncoordinated athlete on the field. However, by the time Reggie graduated, the coach perceived him as one powerful force. He admired Reggie's self-determination, his will to improve, and his desire to become one of the best offensive linemen. He was a real leader and taught by example. He was one of Bo's warriors.

During the late '60s, while Reggie was attending the University of Michigan, his freshman football class included eight recruited African American football players. At that time, they were the most ever recruited by Michigan in a single class. They were Thom Darden, Glenn Doughty, Mike Taylor, Billy Taylor, Butch Carpenter, Mike Oldham, and McKenzie. The group was called the Mellow Men, a moniker bestowed by one of the parents.

Reggie understood that he and his fellow Mellow Men had to excel in sports and graduate in order to set the tempo for those who followed. They would be the models and the pioneers of their time, and football would be their vehicle. The group was very close, and remains bonded to this day. Representing a small minority of the student body (only about 10 percent of Michigan's students were African American), they wanted to make sure their presence was felt.

After a couple years in the professional ranks, Reggie realized that he wanted to give back and make a viable contribution to the boys and girls in his hometown, in the Highland Park community. He acknowledged that he didn't develop and achieve on his own; he had a lot of assistance along the way. So after coming to that realization, Reggie wanted to do what he could simply because he could. Initially, he established a football clinic to train kids who were like him growing up. He wanted to teach them early on about the dos and the don'ts, something his mother would've called "home training." Indeed, Reggie believed that a lot of these kids didn't have the same type of home training that he benefitted from. With that, he became a much-needed parental role model for many of the kids. When they arrived, many of them refused to take responsibility for their actions, and were selfish and egotistical. Reggie is a "we" person, a team player, and he wanted to teach that particular and important attribute to the youngsters.

A more mature Reggie returned to Ann Arbor to find none other than Coach Schembechler. He told Bo about his idea of giving back and asked the coach for his help. Bo helped Reggie get started in his endeavor. He gave Reggie footballs, cones, and other equipment on the condition that Reggie returned them when he was finished. So it was with the University of Michigan's training tools that Reggie started his clinic in Highland Park in June 1974. Initially the camp ran in the morning on Tuesdays, Wednesdays, and Thursdays, with boys aged 8 to 13. In the afternoon, he hosted high school boys at camp.

The clinic was conducted at Highland Park's educational facilities, which he arranged through his sister Eleanor, who was secretary to the superintendent of schools. So it was with assistance from others that Reggie was able to get his charitable efforts off the ground. Again, it takes a team.

The year 1974 saw Reggie begin a very different and mature relationship with Schembechler. He had perspective on Bo's teachings. He knew that Bo had cared about him and his human development, that he had expected nothing but the best from and for Reggie. It took time, but it is safe to say that over the years Reggie developed respect and love for Bo Schembechler. Once he understood that, he began to appreciate Bo's integrity.

In time, the Reggie McKenzie Foundation's approach was expanded to teach academics as well as basketball, football, track-and-field, tennis, and golf to both boys and girls. He even solicited All-Pro basketball player Joe Dumars of the Detroit Pistons (and an excellent tennis player) to teach tennis to the kids.

Over the years, Reggie has utilized the assistance of his Mellow Men to run his camp. He also lowered the admission age of the children to five years. He broadened the educational scope by including the necessary academics, such as reading, reading comprehension, math, and life training (such as teaching the kids right from wrong). By 1978, the Reggie McKenzie Foundation was incorporated. And for the past 40 years, Reggie has, by his estimation, empowered 4,000 to 5,000 kids through his foundation. He believes that the education component is one very important key.

At one time, Reggie asked Bo why he didn't recruit inner-city kids to Michigan. The coach replied that inner-city kids needed to improve their reading and reading comprehension in order to make it at the University of Michigan, a rigorous academic institution. According to McKenzie, Bo even contacted the Detroit Public Schools in efforts to create a program with the school district and the University of Michigan working in concert. What a loss for the kids of Highland Park, and the University of Michigan, McKenzie said recently.

Besides his clinics, he has also hosted a number of fund-raising banquets over the years. The guests of his first such event included O.J. Simpson, Schembechler, L.C. Greenwood, and Ahmad Rashad, among other football names. The proceeds went to fund his charitable foundation.

At another banquet, Reggie got ex-teammate Jack Kemp, the former Buffalo Bills quarterback, involved. At the time, Kemp was running for U.S. President. Jack got his political muscle behind Reggie's program, and there were perhaps 1,500 people at this one particular banquet—the largest-ever attendance. At another banquet, he recruited the first black brigadier general from West Point. With precision, Fred Gordon got up, stood tall, turned about-face, and marched to the podium. He faced the audience, saluted, and said, "My name is Fred Gordon. I'm the brigadier general, and I represent your military." People in the audience went wild, jumping to their feet and clapping.

In 1984 or 1985, a representative from Ford Motors attended, and the automaker became a partner in McKenzie's education efforts. He also has hosted Wilma Rudolph and Robin Roberts, among other leading lights. Reggie acknowledged that he has had a lot of assistance along the way. And he's made a point to give back. He believes that education is the key. To him, the words "empowerment and hope" are great motivators—and they seem to go hand in hand.

Going Pro

The Michigan All-American (1971) was drafted by the Buffalo Bills. He started 140 consecutive games over a 10-year period with the Buffalo Bills and later played for the Seattle Seahawks. With the Bills (1972–82), Reggie and teammate Joe DeLamielleure were the offensive pulling guards for O.J. Simpson when the runner set the NFL rushing record. In that role, Reggie was known as leader of the team's "Electric Company." The Electric Company, of course, turned on the "Juice" (O.J.).

In discussing mental toughness, Reggie said that Boy Scouts, running in the streets, weightlifting, track, and wrestling were all part of the equation. He also mentioned the importance of goal setting. In Buffalo, he wanted to set the bar at the highest level. Reggie got the offensive line together in 1973 and suggested that their goal should be for Simpson to rush for at least 2,000 yards and set an NFL record. They did just that during the ensuing (14-game) season. Line coach Jim Ringo, formerly of the Green Bay Packers, taught the run game, what he called "force and fill." In essence, the line works in concert to force the play and fill the hole. It is done when the defensive player forces the play. And when that happens, someone has to take his place. That came with the right guard leading the play by blocking or kicking out the linebacker while Reggie went inside and pushed his man to create a hole. Or, on the other hand, if DeLamielleure pinned the linebacker, Reggie had the speed to bounce to the outside by blocking the backside of his opponent's body—9 times out of 10 the strong safety. (McKenzie acknowledges that the Buffalo Bills were running the Green Bay sweep that Jerry Kramer, Jim Ringo, and Fuzzy Thurston made famous under coach Vince Lombardi.) The Bills' Electric Company ran the force and fill so effectively that there was nothing opposing defenses could do to stop O.J.

At other times, blocking for Simpson would consist of driving the opposing player to either the inside or the outside. Reggie was very efficient at making those blocks, what he called "pinning your opponent to the outside." Indeed, he learned his trade well; he was selected as a first-team All-NFL player in 1973 and 1974.

Reggie learned a number of tricks of the trade from Coach Ringo. For instance, when the opposing defender attempted to head-slap Reggie, Reggie would stick his fist up under his opponent's chin, driving his head back. It was a tactic he employed over and over and over. As he put it to his foes, it was "part of the business. Don't take this personally. It's my job."

He was widely known as an enforcer and motivator; others might call it simply being a team leader. In Buffalo, Reggie had a teammate, a wide receiver from Auburn, who didn't like going to the post because he would get clobbered by the safety. His teammates called the receiver "alligator arms" because he would invariably drop the pass from the quarterback. In one of the games, Reggie looked him in the eye during the huddle and said, "You better catch that ball, because I'm blocking for you." The message was received loud and clear.

On another occasion, the Bills had a place-kicker who was also from Auburn. Team owner Ralph Wilson was not known as a big spender, and this kicker was holding out for more money. Ultimately, an agreement was reached and the player signed a contract and came back after missing a few games. It was the third or fourth game of the season, and the Bills were playing New England. The Bills got the ball and started their drive from their own 5-yard line. They went 90 yards, all the way to their opponent's 5-yard line, when the drive stalled. The kicker came out to kick a field goal but missed it. Going to the sideline, Reggie's teammate DeLamielleure said to the kicker, "Listen, motherfucker, you miss another field goal, and I'm going to kick your ass." This kicker then looked at Reggie pleadingly, only to have him say, "You're lucky Joe got to you first."

When Chuck Knox became head coach of the Seattle Seahawks in 1983, he asked McKenzie to come with him and provide the same veteran leadership to his new team that he had in Buffalo. In 1984, the Seattle Seahawks were playing the San Francisco 49ers at Candlestick Park in the last preseason game. It was the second quarter, Seattle had the ball with second down and long. In the 49ers defensive backfield was All-Pro Ronnie Lott, along with another safety. Back then, employing a cutting block was legal, and Reggie wanted to cut both of them at their knees. He figured that since one was behind the other, he could take both of them out in one shot. He had done the same thing many times before. He made a terrific block and took out Lott, as well as the second safety. In fact, it was such a good block that Seattle made a first down on the play. Unfortunately, Reggie did not get his right hand extended as he fell to the ground, and his opponents landed on his elbow. The impact tore up his right shoulder. Reggie ultimately lost his muscle in the joint and never was the same afterward.

A Seattle orthopedist used some kind of twine to sew up what was left of his ravaged muscle. At season's beginning, he was only at 50 to 60 percent strength, which meant he needed to rely on his good left arm and limit use of his right arm. He described the experience as playing with one and a half arms. Still, he played left guard through this injury for the first seven or eight games of the season. Even though he had a severe right shoulder injury—a torn rotator cuff—he believed he had no other choice. He simply had to adjust and play injured without revealing its severity.

So how did he manage to block using only one side of his body? Well, the creative, mentally and physically tough Reggie made it happen. For example, on a running play he favored and blocked his opponent with his injury-free left side. He did that by using his face to make contact in the opposing player's numbers, and then grabbed that player's jersey with his right arm and held on with his strong fingers. In essence, Reggie's blocking philosophy came down to either focusing on the middle of his opponent's body or busting him in the mouth. On passing plays it was more difficult because he had to use both of his hands. Not only did he have to use his hands efficiently, but he had to have both of his feet positioned and balanced correctly. Of course, he favored his left side, his strong side. This technique worked fairly well for the first seven or eight games of that season—until Joe Gibbs, coach of the Washington Redskins, figured out there something wrong with the wounded warrior. The defensive opponents then identified that "Achilles" had a weakness, and the injury ended his playing career.

Once Reggie took off his Seattle Seahawks uniform, he stayed with the organization, moving to the team's front office. Unfortunately, Reggie took a pay cut to work as a team executive. (Yes, even back then players earned considerably more revenue than front-office personnel.) Over 12 years, Reggie was the assistant director of sales and marketing and assistant director of pro personnel. During that span, Seattle had two different owners and three different head coaches.

Reggie not only loved the Seattle organization, he also loved the Pacific Northwest. It just so happened that the Seahawks office was located on Seattle's east side, a wealthy and predominantly white area compared to the central district, where many people of color lived. He knew that it was important to engage the entire city of Seattle, as well as to give back. At that time, there wasn't one Seahawks player who lived in the central district. Not only that, but the only time a Seattle player would go into the central district was to enter Seahawks Stadium on game day. Reggie wanted to change the dynamics; he wanted to bring the two communities together. So the clever and knowledgeable Reggie initiated "Seahawks Sunday" in the central district. With it, players, cheerleaders, and live entertainment gathered for a community-wide celebration on Sundays during the off-season. The plan was highly successful.

Through his success with Seahawks Sundays, McKenzie learned that the only way to make things happen is for an individual to "take the bull by the horns, so to speak." Reggie became the team's ambassador of goodwill. He knew that people need each other in many ways.

He talked about Bill Gates, Paul Allen, and Jon Shirley of Microsoft—the people of means. He knew that some wealthy individuals often came from a second, third, or fourth generation of wealth, and that being born into wealth can shape one's attitude. For some, it didn't matter whether they created the money or not. Reggie also talked about one individual, a team owner, who said, "I do not want to be poor. I don't know how to be poor." Reggie then went on to talk about the haves and the have-nots, something he saw firsthand growing up in Michigan.

Perhaps one way to understand his highly disciplined driving force, he said, could be traced back to his ancestral past, of being a member of a tribe while living freely in Africa. The life of his ancestors was abruptly interrupted and changed dramatically by the slave traders. Many African people were rounded up, captured, separated from their families, beaten, sold, and against their will put on large oceangoing ships. Only the strong survived, in the face of limited food, scarce water, and other unthinkable conditions. The survivors were then bought and sold, considered pieces of property by slave owners. Perhaps these trials were passed on and on to succeeding generations through his evolutionary development. And if so, perhaps deep within Reggie's psyche was stored anger, resentment, and hate—which he was able to channel into not only a will to survive, but an imperative to dominate, destroy, and overpower others—and most important, a drive to assist and empower others less fortunate.

For Reggie, he found an opportunity to satisfy those inner needs by playing football. He realized at a young age, in high school, that he needed to become more physically powerful to be competitive. And he also had to be academically eligible. So he did what he had to do to meet those challenges.

As a freshman, he commented about "killing" his white football coach. As a sophomore, his de-facto master was Bo Schembechler. On the practice field, Bo shamed him, giving him frequent tongue-lashings.

However, Bo also taught Reggie that he could become more than he ever dreamed of becoming. He taught Reggie to do his job the right way, all the time, every time. He also taught Reggie the importance of teamwork, working together as one for the benefit of the whole. Bo taught him that no one succeeds entirely on his own, that there are friends, teachers, mentors, and others who give assistance all along the way.

It took Reggie a while to get it, but things finally clicked for him. He knew that he had to be the one to dominate, to bring his opponents to their knees. He would perform that task by literally cutting at his opponents' knees, putting his fists underneath his opponents' chins, or knocking them on their backs. He told himself that what he was doing was not personal, it was his job. But it did contribute to his development as a person. He was able to act out his anger, resentment, and hatred in the brutal and savage game of football.

His line play indeed exhibited physical savagery. He perfected his style of play and did not think twice about taking out two defensive players with one of his bone-crushing blocks. He was rewarded for his efforts with yearly salary increases, All-American and All-Pro honors, and acclaim from his coaches and teammates as a team leader. Reggie had become the master, and he and only he was in control of his fate and destiny.

Reggie also met his needs for giving back to others through his charitable organization in Michigan and community work in Seattle. He talks the talk and walks the walk—make no mistake about it.

Today he runs Reggie McKenzie Industrial Materials Incorporated and is making his magic in the business world. You might also find him on the golf links, hassling Joe DeLamielleure and other Michigan State Spartans. And if he's not there, you'd be best to find him at some football game helping the coach or his family. After a distinguished career on the gridiron, he was inducted into the College Football Hall of Fame and the Michigan Sports Hall of Fame. And after all these years, Reggie is still a passionate team player.

CHAPTER 6

The Overachiever: Fritz Seyferth

A number of individuals have researched and written about the idea of mental toughness. And for those in this book, including Fritz Seyferth, mental toughness is a central issue. It refers to a person's unique persistence, stick-to-itiveness, drive, energy, grit—all those factors that help individuals to achieve goals despite the various internal or external barriers or obstacles placed before them. Seyferth perfectly illustrated mental toughness during his lifetime. This is his story—and more important, his evolution.

It begins with his parents. Fritz's father, Jack, entered college at Michigan State University but left before graduating to enlist in the Army Air Corps during World War II. Fighting for his country at that time was more important to him than attaining a degree. Jack later returned to college in Southern California and finished the degree requirements for a bachelor's degree at USC. Jack was an athletic young man who had played football and wrestled during his high school years. He was also a high achiever. Later, his family moved around a lot while he advanced his career in such companies as Scott Paper Company, Crown Zellerbach, and Standard Packaging. Fritz described his father as a strong German who was highly disciplined, even with little things such as keeping his workbench and tools lined up and in perfect order.

He volunteered to take care of the neighborhood baseball diamonds, drawing the lines perfectly and raking an immaculate baseball field. He was very detail-oriented. He also took care of the chemicals for their swimming pool, and the grass in the front and back of the house was always neatly cropped. Fritz suspects his father's military service probably had something to do with that orderliness.

On the other hand, Jack was high-energy, confident, dynamic—the life of the party. Fritz watched his father work his way up the corporate ladder. Jack was very skilled in sales and managing others; he was also a great communicator. Fritz learned from his father that there is a right way to do things: with integrity, trust, and respect.

Jack worked hard and played hard. He was always there to protect his family and considered them of the utmost importance. Even though he spent time away from the family home working, coaching the neighborhood kids, and helping out at the sandlot, he always seemed to be there for his family when needed. And he knew how to slow down, too. One of Jack's favorite home activities was "take 10," what he called an afternoon nap lying in the sun.

Jack was born and raised in Muskegon, Michigan, where he met his future wife, Corrie, during their high school years. Corrie was an amazing and wise individual. She was a nurse, a Sunday school teacher, and later a broker in a very profitable real estate firm she helped start in Darien, Connecticut. She had a full life, was successful, and was at the top of her professional career. She employed the power of positive thinking and incorporated positive reinforcement with Fritz and others around her. She was full of wisdom, imparting in Fritz such lessons as, "If you have problems with other people, it is likely because they have problems of their own" and "Always be the bigger person and conduct yourself with maturity." She even told him, "I think you could be President of the United States." She was certainly a very supportive and positive influence on her son.

She was always the first one to rise in the morning. Often Fritz found her in the kitchen, at her ironing board, hard at work. It seemed she was always smiling about something; you could not find a scowl on her face. Fritz inherited this trait from his mom, he has no doubt. An intelligent and wise woman, she grew up one of nine siblings, the children of Dutch immigrants. It always seemed that people enjoyed her company and always wanted to be around her. Indeed, in Muskegon she had quite a reputation for being friendly and well respected.

Corrie's mother was a homemaker and her father a butcher by trade. Growing up, everyone in the family worked in the butcher store. One evening, while in high school, Corrie had a date. The date went to her house to pick her up but was directed to the butcher shop because she was still working. When he arrived, he asked for her. Her father replied, "She's in the basement, cutting off the chickens' heads." Apparently the date was either horrified or in shock. He simply turned around and, disgusted, left without her. Luckily, beheading chickens didn't dissuade Jack; he knew what he had in Corrie.

Fritz's grandfather, the butcher, was a minister as well. And all 11 family members lived in a tiny house that had one and a half bathrooms and four bedrooms—added to which, they always had relatives staying with them at the crowded house. Amazingly, his grandfather somehow found room for church meetings at the family home every Sunday.

Corrie was a positive thinker who believed that one should be able to get through any crisis, regardless of the circumstance. Fritz thought she was tough, and calmer under pressure than Jack. She also loved nature. If she wasn't in the house, you would likely find her socializing with friends. She was very social, a great storyteller, joked, loved the outdoors, and was a joy to be around.

It is very clear that Fritz's strength of character is directly related to his upbringing. His father loved sports, was mentally tough, was goal- and family-oriented, encouraged Fritz to participate in sports, and was a terrific role model, exemplifying values of integrity and respect. Likewise, his mother believed in him from the beginning. She believed he could accomplish anything he put his mind to. To have someone's, especially a mother's, unconditional love, support, and trust is one powerful motivator. Make no mistake about it: behind every successful person is a strong, steady supporter. Not many of us do it alone.

Fritz could be called "the Gypsy." His family relocated seven different times (Michigan, Illinois, Massachusetts, New York, and California) during the first five years of his young life. His father, Jack, was then vice president with the Scott Paper Company. After Fritz completed the third grade in the Covina (California) public schools, they relocated once more. Fritz and his mother met with the new school's principal; they assumed that Fritz would be entering the fourth grade. However, to his mother's surprise, the new school officials wanted to place Fritz in the second grade because he was only reading at a first-grade level.

Despite being behind in academic progress, he was physically ahead of his peers; indeed, he was taller than all of the fourth-graders. It was a dilemma for the Seyferths: How would tall, smiling, outgoing Fritz be viewed in a second-grade classroom? What would Fritz think about himself, and what would the younger kids think about him? Clearly he was behind in his reading skills. Was he dyslexic? If the school had been allowed to implement their recommendation and hold him back, Fritz's story would likely be different.

Instead, Fritz took his subpar reading as a challenge to overcome. Yet his stress level was acute for a young boy, and he experienced frequent stomachaches as a result. Fortunately, he understood and liked math. As a result, he excelled and found some sense of security inside the classroom. So all was not lost for him during those difficult elementary school years.

Neither Fritz, his parents, nor the school gave up on the youngster's education. Since Jack, the family's breadwinner, was often away from home making his living, Corrie became the boy's confidant. She assisted him with his schoolwork and set the standard for effectively tutoring him in reading. She also enrolled him each summer in reading classes. As a result, Fritz learned important skills early on: practice, repetition, and successfully overcoming and addressing challenges. By the time the school year finished, Fritz knew the program and realized what was expected of him. And the routine of tutelage from his mother and yearly summer school continued over the next five years.

By the time Fritz reached high school, he was reading above grade level. From the earliest age, Fritz demonstrated that he was tough enough to overcome big challenges by paying attention to details and evincing persistence, practice, and hard work. There were no shortcuts; one simply had to put in the work. Through his efforts, Fritz also learned the value of success.

Socially, being tall helped him, too—especially during recess and in his physical education classes. Young Fritz kicked and hit the ball farther than any of his classmates and that, along with his friendly personality, ingratiated him to his peers. In fact, he became a leader; everyone wanted to be on his team. So despite being challenged by his reading disability, his physical ability provided him a sense of belonging. As a consequence, he was neither isolated nor picked on. It was another important early lesson. It felt good to be part of a group. And that sense of belonging steered him more pointedly toward athletics, where he discovered that he could forge meaningful friendships. Another bonus of athletics was that he learned more about the importance of competition. Through competition, his self-esteem increased as well.

Despite greatly improving his reading comprehension, Fritz was still challenged by the written word. He had great difficulty writing book reports and term papers. Corrie once again came to his rescue and creatively assisted him with his school assignments. She sat him down at the family's Formica kitchen table. Despite her other responsibilities, she gave her loving, undivided attention to him as she sat with him at that table. Initially, she would ask him to answer a question from his assignment. Then young Fritz would verbally give an answer. Corrie wrote down his response in intelligible English and presented it to her son. Then it was Fritz's task to rewrite what his mother wrote, putting it into his own words. They repeated the process over and over again until the assignment was completed. Corrie's patience was rewarded; because of her ingenious technique, Fritz's writing skills started to improve, too.

Big for an eighth-grader, and still growing, Fritz went out for the football team. It was yet another community and a new set of classmates—this time, the Seyferth family had settled in Darien, Connecticut. A new kid in school, he didn't want to sit by himself during lunchtime. He quickly made friends by associating with the jocks, who bestowed upon him the nickname "Smiley." It was yet another move, and another lesson. He learned about assimilation, being adaptable, and he was able to fit in quite nicely with another peer group.

He made it onto the second-string football team in ninth grade. Going into the 10th grade (which would be his first year of high school in Darien's school system), Fritz was thinking about playing football in high school. It was a bit more of a commitment than the junior high team. In order to play for the high school team, besides playing and practicing in the regular season, players were also expected to practice in the winter and spring with the varsity squad. He decided to go for it.

Competition and participation as learned through athletics were very important virtues to Fritz's father, Jack. He was extremely sports-minded and was proud that his boy was playing the contact sport of football. Despite his work absences, Jack had ingrained a love of sports in his son. For example, when Fritz was around eight years old, he would punt the ball to his father and his father would catch the punted ball and then punt back to him. Jack coached his son in both football and baseball over the years; he also displayed groundskeeper qualities by chalking the baseball playing field in the summers. Athletic Jack even played ice hockey with the college kids.

Meanwhile, Fritz was discouraged being on the second-string football squad. He thought at that time that he was not good enough to make the varsity team, which had won the state football championship the previous year. An emotional teenager, he chose to exercise his disappointment by not attending the winter football practices. Fritz wanted to contribute and have an impact on the game, but he was an unhappy and discouraged second-string tight end.

During that time, his father away from the family on a work assignment, asked Fritz how football practice was progressing. When he found out about Fritz's state of mind, he would have none of it, and said very clearly: "Son, you can fail in trying, but never fail to try. Get a haircut, go to your coach, apologize to him for missing practice, and see if you can still go out for the team." With his father's encouragement, Fritz didn't quit; he followed his father's instruction and went on to play on that high school team. At that time, the first-string tight end was a boy named Dan Murray. Three years later, as seniors, he and Murray were cocaptains of the team. It was a tough lesson, but Fritz took to heart that quitting was never an option.

By the end of high school, it had become apparent that Fritz had learned how to be mentally tough—both academically and athletically. The importance of his parents cannot be overstated. They were emotionally and physically there for him, and believed in him even when he did not. In fact, it took both of them, in their own ways, to provide, as parents can do, the right formula for their son. Many parents have difficulty with providing the necessary balance of tough love, demanding responsibility, displaying integrity, and being hands-on. Some parents exercise too much control and overprotection, which can stifle a child's development and/or growth; others are too permissive, overindulgent, and accepting, unwilling to set proper limits and boundaries. As any parent can tell you, raising a child is no easy task.

Fritz played three years of high school football in addition to three years of high school baseball; he also played one year of basketball and one year of hockey. While practicing football, Fritz repeatedly fell on his elbow while carrying the ball. The hard ground and rocks eventually caused a problem that only surgery could fix. The surgery to his elbow interfered with his ability to play basketball his senior year.

Because high school was a much more positive experience for Fritz academically than in previous years, he remembers the names of his influential teachers. His math teacher, who was also his baseball coach, was George Nelson. Mr. Nelson had a big impact on him. He also remembers his running backs coach, Navio Ottavi. Of his two head football coaches, he respected John Maher, who employed discipline like a tough marine. Vic Crump was his other head football coach, though his teams did not have the success of the legendary Maher.

While playing high school football, Fritz suffered his first neck injury. As a sophomore, he was blocking a dummy in a practice drill. During the exercise, the person holding the dummy thrust it at Fritz's head before he was ready. The impact jammed his long neck, which pinched a nerve. As a consequence of the injury, he was unable to raise his right arm for weeks. He could not even brush his teeth or comb his hair. Unfortunately, his injury caused him to miss the rest of the season.

At the time, Fritz dismissed the significance of this injury; he would get better. Still, he wanted to strengthen his neck, so he religiously, even compulsively, performed neck exercises such as bridges (an inverted exercise that works the back and neck muscles). His neck strengthening and conditioning program seemed to work. Once recuperated, Fritz never missed another practice. Additionally, Fritz's neck grew to 19¾" in diameter by the time he finished college. And for further protection to his neck, Fritz wore a neck roll to add more stability to his neck during practice.

Since experiencing that injury in the 10th grade, Fritz has had many stingers (pinched nerves) from physical football contact. Typically, the neck hurts like hell for about two minutes before the pain subsides. Today, Fritz has stenosis, bone spurs, and arthritis—but he's not complaining.

As a high school senior, Fritz was recruited by Yale, Penn, and Dartmouth in football. He had his sights on playing and receiving an education from an Ivy League college, but he did not get in, despite his improved academics. His father suggested he visit a few Big Ten campuses. They went on a road trip and visited Michigan State University and the University of Michigan. Jack's first choice for Fritz was West Point, and arrangements had been made for the boy to be admitted. Fritz was faced with an important decision about what to do about football and his education.

Even though Fritz knew hardly anything about the Michigan Wolverines football tradition or history, he immediately fell in love with the small-town campus atmosphere in Ann Arbor and the remarkable person in head coach Bump Elliott. After research, he found out that Michigan had the top-ranked industrial engineering program in the nation. Upon learning that, his decision was made. Jack, on the other hand, was already well aware of Michigan's illustrious academic and football tradition and was supportive of his son's decision. It didn't hurt that Fritz would be coming back to the state of Michigan, source of the family roots and home state of both his parents.

As a boy, he did not perceive himself as a natural, fluid, or skilled athlete, even though he excelled in baseball and football. He knew he had to work extremely hard and practice to get better. Soon Fritz set his sights on playing football and baseball at Michigan. He was on track to do so until Bo Schembechler arrived and gave anyone thinking of playing baseball a tough choice to make: football or baseball, but not both. It ended up being an easy decision, even if it was disappointing.

In 1968 Fritz went out, without a scholarship, for the freshman football team at the University of Michigan. (In other words, he was considered a walk-on.) A week into the season, freshman coach Bill Dodd had him listed as a sixth-string running back on the freshman squad. Ultimately, Fritz wound up starting in the defensive backfield. There happened to be several other defensive backs faster than him, but he had one thing going for him that they didn't have: he liked the physical contact of tackling. Then all of a sudden, the freshman team became short of fullbacks. The coach had him practice as a fullback with the second-team offense. It was a break for Fritz, and he took full advantage of his promotion, and of being on offense. Although it took a lot of hard work, practice, and training, he thrived under the new challenges and accordingly developed his skills.

About six weeks into the season, Fritz and his teammates expected that they would not have a typical Friday practice since the varsity was away for a road game. But Coach Dodd called the freshman team for practice. Fritz and his teammates weren't too happy, and to make matters worse, the brutal coach had the freshmen scrimmage for about two hours. And if that was not hard enough, he had them run wind sprints after practice. Considering this, it's easy to understand why these freshman players disliked their coach. Fritz remembered teammate Reggie McKenzie once saying, "He's crazy." These practices with Coach Dodd were painful to say the least. Even though he was tough on him then, Fritz smiles when he sees his old coach today.

Fritz wound up starting as a punter, fullback, and free safety as a walk-on on that freshman team. Amazingly, that squad boasted 14 members who were drafted into the NFL a few years later.

Fritz's roommate on campus was teammate Bruce Elliott. Bruce's father was assistant coach Pete Elliott, Bump's brother. Bruce's girlfriend fixed Fritz up on a blind date with Lynn, a Kappa Kappa Gamma pledge and soon-to-be sorority sister. Years later, Fritz and Lynn married. And Bruce continues to be Fritz's great friend, as well as his attorney.

At Michigan, Bruce Elliott was a defensive back and an academic All-American. He was tough and he knew the game. Though undersized, he was really fast—and a brutal tackler, he used to put his nose on the running backs' numbers. His father, Pete, was a head coach at Nebraska, Cal, Illinois, and Miami. He also was a 12-time letter winner at Michigan. It's easy to see that the Elliotts, with their strong tradition of athletics and academics at UM, are indeed the picture of the "Michigan man." They conduct themselves with integrity, and everybody looks up to them and their family.

After completing the freshman football season Fritz returned home to Darien, Connecticut, during a welcome winter break. A winter sports lover, he went on a skiing trip to Vermont at the end of December. While watching TV at the Brattleboro Bowling alley, Fritz heard a report that Bump Elliott, Michigan's head coach, was retiring and would be replaced by Bo Schembechler. *Who?* he and everyone else wondered. He had no idea at the time who this Schembechler was. There was cause for concern. For one thing, Fritz thought that he was in line to receive a scholarship for the following school year based on his freshman play. Suddenly with a new coach, he had to prove all over again that he was worthy of the scholarship. It didn't matter to Fritz that his father could afford to pay for his Michigan education; it was about principle. He had played well enough to earn a scholarship, in his estimation.

Sometime in early January 1969, Fritz met Coach Schembechler for the first time. At that initial team meeting, Fritz clearly understood as Bo made it loud and clear that he was the boss and would not put up with anyone's nonsense. It was going to be his way or the highway. Bo told him, "I will get more out of you than you know what's inside of you. You should be embarrassed by the way you have been performing." At first, Bo reminded Fritz of his no-nonsense father, yet he was still intimidated by the new coach.

Winter conditioning soon followed as freezing temperatures fell on Ann Arbor. And Coach Schembechler had his players doing the slap and stomp. The drill was timed for about one and a half minutes, but sometimes it seemed as if it continued for an eternity. No one wanted to back off from the contact. It was simply exhausting, but the winner would be the one who could continue this physical activity the longest. Sometimes elbows would fly and connect with a teammate's jaw, occasionally leading to fistfights. Fritz admits that at one point he might've gotten into a fight with Mike Keller. But supposedly the drill helped with developing agility, conditioning, and toughness.

While Fritz was performing all those slap-and-stomp drills during the winter, Jack and Corrie decided to take the rest of the family for a holiday to Puerto Rico. Jack, being a thoughtful father, invited his football-playing son to join them. That meant Fritz would have to ask Coach Schembechler if he could be excused from his Friday workout so he could accompany his family to soak up the sun. Brave Fritz admitted he was scared to ask for his permission. But after a while he got over his butterflies and mustered up his courage. He went into Coach Schembechler's office and told him about his father's invitation. To his surprise, Bo told him that missing practice was okay since he was going to be with his family. For Schembechler, family was paramount. Was that a contradiction, since the cost of football mandated that Schembechler be separated from his family for such great lengths of time? In any event, Fritz was thrilled. And at a very early stage in their relationship, Fritz saw a different, caring side of the rough, tough, larger-than-life coach.

Coach Bump Elliott had always made it clear that he respected each person for whom he was as an individual. With Bo, there was a clear contrast. For him, it was team, team, and team. It was all about team purpose and team goals, not about the person or egos. Yet Bo was a great communicator and a terrific listener. When he talked, the players paid attention. Bo clearly realized how to challenge a person's will, and he also knew how to build the person to become a component of one tight family. He taught his troops that everything should be for the best interests of the team.

He wanted to find out who could take it and who couldn't. He wanted the strongest, toughest young men to lead. And his belief that the individual can always do better stemmed from the fact that no one is ever perfect, so by definition there was always room for improvement. "Is that the best you can do?" he'd challenge them.

The 1969 Missouri game was humbling for this second-string fullback, Seyferth. Fritz was a backup to senior Garvie Craw. The University of Missouri team was both physically and mentally better than the Michigan team on that day. Michigan fumbled the opening kickoff, and that foreshadowed the events for the rest of the game. Michigan came far from playing their best football, and Bo was extremely upset. Missouri made Michigan look terrible—and Michigan made Missouri look brilliant. The final score: Missouri 40, Michigan 17—perhaps Bo's worst defeat as Michigan's coach. He told the team, "You guys are not ready mentally or physically to play football." It was something they had heard before. Yet young Fritz thought the team was getting better and wondered to himself how the team could improve, and fast.

Against Michigan State, in the fifth game of the season, Fritz didn't make the traveling squad. The coach had another player, a senior, travel with the squad instead. After that game, Bo told the team he left sophomore Fritz home even though he wanted to win more than any of the seniors. Meanwhile, Fritz was upset because his father and other relatives and family members planned to attend that game. (Remember, his father attended Michigan State. He even had a Sparty patch on his car windshield.) Unfortunately, the players didn't find out if they'd made the traveling squad until Thursday evening, and by then it was too late. Then again, whether or not Fritz played wouldn't have mattered because Fritz's father attended all the Michigan games, as well as many practices. He even attended the two spring games they had one year. Jack was a real fan of his son.

For the Minnesota game, the sixth game of the season, Bo installed the I or Oklahoma formation, with the option. The timing seemed to go well, the offense began to trust the I. And as the execution got better, it seemed that team confidence started to build, too. That week of practice went well.

Around that time, it seemed to Seyferth that Michigan had become more of a "we" and were on to something special. Fritz was still backing up fullback Craw, and Garvie was a senior and the starter. When running the option play, the fullback had to run fast in order to get out in front of the running back while running laterally to the sideline as lead blocker. This challenged Fritz to move, quickly and get out in front of the running back. It was something he had to work on—especially getting out of the stance so that he would be in front of and out of the way of that running back. The second running back was lined up as a flanker, whose purpose was to confuse the defense. (This was possible because there were so many running or passing options off that formation.) Michigan scored 35 points in that game, winning the Little Brown Jug (trophy of the Minnesota-Michigan contest that dates back to 1903), while Minnesota scored 9. The team was jelling on both sides of the ball.

The team was high with excitement and energy after defeating Iowa in the penultimate game of the season. Their final game was against hated rival Ohio State. Things were coming together, and everyone understood the tremendous obstacle that lay ahead. Fritz found it difficult to keep focused on the task at hand because there were a lot of distractions, like attending class. During the week, he realized that he had to prepare himself for all the hard hitting in practice. He was expected to hit harder and expected to be hit harder in return. Timing had to be crisp and sharp. The offense and defense had to be perfect for the big game.

Unsurprising for the end of November, there happened to be a snowstorm that week, and the coaches brought shovels to scoop the snow off the field. Those dedicated coaches were in the cold, shoveling snow, while the players sat inside, warm. Their gesture symbolized a lot to the team. It told the players that the coaches were behind them. By Friday, the team seemed completely confident.

Friday night, before Saturday's game, the Michigan team was staying at the Sheraton Hotel. Late that evening, there was a fire alarm. The players were awakened from their slumber and had to take their blankets with them to the lobby of the hotel to cover themselves. In all the commotion, they didn't get much sleep that night. Yet there's a fine line between being uptight and being ready. Perhaps the fire alarm worked to the Wolverines' advantage because it was a distraction. Everyone knew about the importance of that first meeting between Bo and Woody. The atmosphere was much more intense compared to other games because of the serious task at hand.

Going into the Michigan tunnel on the way to the playing field, Fritz said his feet didn't seem to touch the ground. There was lots of adrenaline flowing through the players' tunnel. Everything seemed as if it were scripted. Fritz's assignment was to block Jack Tatum on the kickoff, and he knew all about the All-American.

Then the game started, and Ohio State received the ball and easily went down the field to score a touchdown. On the ensuing kickoff, Michigan lined up to receive the kickoff. There, young Fritz saw his man. Just as Schembechler had anticipated, Woody Hayes inserted the Assassin into the lineup for special teams in addition to his other duties. It was Fritz's job to block Tatum and get him out of bounds in an attempt to open up a lane for Michigan's returner. Fritz looked across the field. This Tatum looked five years older and more muscle-bound than the rest. Fritz was taller, but Tatum clearly outweighed him. A whistle, a thud, and the ball was in the air. Fritz saw Tatum charging down the field in his direction. Then there was a loud collision as Fritz, in a perfect blocking position, used his strength and agility to make a perfect hit on Tatum, belting the All-American cleanly out of bounds.

Then the two teams traded a pair of touchdowns, which sent Fritz back to the line on special teams. Again Fritz looked down the field at the fierce, angry Tatum, who might've been embarrassed and wanted revenge. Indeed, he seemed to be running faster than before, bearing down on him quick. This time, the very clever Fritz changed his strategy and cut the All-American at his knees. It was a terrific block, and again he knocked Tatum to the sideline and out of bounds. Fritz undoubtedly did his job well in the first half of that game. The Wolverines went into the locker room leading 24–12.

Ohio State kicked off to Michigan to start the second half, and again came Tatum. If it was possible, he might have been coming even faster this time. Then, to Fritz's surprise, Tatum avoided a hit from Fritz and ran out of bounds of his own volition. Apparently, he was tired of being knocked around by the fullback. As it turned out, Ohio State did not score at all in the second half, and the Wolverines cruised to a resounding victory.

After that game, the Michigan teammates went to a party as one team. As Marvin Gaye's "I Heard It Through the Grapevine" blared, the players belted out their own lyrics: "Going to the Rose Bowl." They celebrated through the night.

The following season, 1970, Fritz played second-string fullback until the third game, against Texas A&M. Billy Taylor was first-string fullback and Glenn Doughty the running back. Michigan was losing at the half, and Schembechler inserted Fritz as starting fullback for the second half. Late in the half, Fritz contributed 45 yards on a 63-yard drive, paving the way for quarterback Don Moorhead to score. Michigan took the lead and won the game 14–10. Fritz showed that he was a better blocker than Billy Taylor, and Billy was moved over to running back. Glenn Doughty was moved to wing-back to make room for Fritz. Bo wanted his run-based offense to accrue at least 200 yards in every game and maybe pass for 150 more. With Fritz's play in the A&M game, the position was his for the duration.

Against Minnesota at Minnesota—the Gophers' homecoming game—Fritz was the spoiler, scoring four touchdowns. Back then Dan Dierdorf, the Wolverines' All-American tackle, barked out, "I own these guys. Just run off my tail." Fritz did just that and scored all those touchdowns running behind Dierdorf's bone-crushing blocks. Fritz didn't receive verbal praise from his coaches (even when he tied for the most touchdowns in a single game). Adulation like that was unheard of back then. In the Schembechler system, players had a job to do, and they were expected to do it. No one individual was more important than the team.

The last game of the season was set to be played in Columbus against Ohio State. Going into that last game, Michigan was undefeated. But playing in Ohio State's stadium was always very difficult. For one thing, the Buckeyes had the loudest fans—they were (and still are) out of their mind, to put it mildly. Overall, it was an intimidating atmosphere. But on that day, Michigan was dominating the game, and the rowdy crowd was mostly silent. The silence coming from the ordinarily antagonistic crowd was so powerful that Fritz still remembers that eerie feeling. Unfortunately, the tide turned and Michigan lost the game (20–9) on a couple mistakes.

Fritz hated to lose that game in particular. He took it hard, not even talking about it with his teammates. In fact, he did not talk about any game (there were not many during his career) that Michigan lost. Fritz was extremely bitter and could not wait to play the Buckeyes again the next year.

That one loss ate at him that whole next year. He wanted his revenge, the sooner the better.

The fifth game of the 1971 season was against Michigan State. That rivalry was also very intense, and that year the game was in East Lansing. Prior to the contest, the Spartans' All-American Ron Curl quipped that he would eat a towel if his team lost. Michigan won that game 24–13; none of the Wolverines can be sure if Curl actually ate that towel.

The Wolverines were terrific in 1971, going undefeated by playing smash-mouth football. It was just the way that Bo wanted all their games to be played. The '71 squad challenged records for rushing yardage, touchdowns, and extra points. They were a running juggernaut that season. Their reputation of "three yards and a cloud of dust" was etched in stone. Yet even though the Wolverines were winning, practices still remained brutal. And not every game was a blowout. They had one close call in a game against Purdue. Michigan's Dana Coin had to kick a field goal to clinch the win. Perhaps Michigan was distracted looking ahead at the last game of the season, against Ohio State, instead of focusing on the Boilermakers.

Even though the feelings of intensity from the 1969 Ohio State–Michigan game could not be repeated, the Wolverines were plenty fired up for their 1971 matchup with the Buckeyes. In the waning minutes of the game, the Buckeyes led 7–3. Michigan had the ball on the Ohio State 24-yard line with fourth-and-1 to go. In the huddle, Fritz's number was called; he would run the ball between center and left guard. The quarterback called the signals, the center snapped the ball, and the QB pivoted to his left, handing off the ball to Fritz. There was a lot of noise as bodies slammed into each other, but Fritz picked up a precious yard and a half. First down on the 22-yard line.

Years later, Fritz commented that it was one of Michigan's traditional or bread-and-butter plays, one that they practiced over and over again. It was his job to get the hard yards for that first down, plain and simple. He was focused. And he wasn't tired when he went back to his team's huddle, with the clock ticking and the next play set to be called. Michigan was still alive.

Another bread-and-butter, fundamental running play was called for the next down. This time, Fritz was supposed to run like hell, but coordinated and in control, toward the sideline and then sharply turn upfield, staying in front of the ball carrier, Billy Taylor, and blocking the wide man's path. Getting in front of Billy Taylor was not easy, but Fritz accomplished just that. The first person Fritz saw was Ohio State safety Tom Campana (who earlier in the game ran back a punt 85 yards for OSU's sole touchdown). Fritz was positioned between Billy and Tom and in position to make a block. Campana was coming fast and getting in position to make the tackle. Then Fritz was able to block Tom squarely on his outside thigh pad with such brute force that the collision brought them both to the gridiron turf at about the 15-yard line, creating daylight for Taylor. The announcer then gleefully shouted, "Touchdown, Billy Taylor!"

After receiving the kickoff the OSU offense came on the field and quickly lined up in the huddle; they still had a chance. A few plays later the quarterback, Don Lamka, went back to pass and All-American Darden somehow hurdled his muscled body over the outstretched hands and body of Ohio State's tight end Dick Wakefield to intercept the ball at the Michigan 32-yard line. Woody Hayes went nuts on the sideline, and his team fell 10–7.

Because of the importance of the game and the rivalry, the Armed Forces Radio Network broadcast the game to troops all over the world. And indeed, for Fritz, it was his most satisfying block—as someone said much later, "It was the block heard 'round the world." Yet at game's end Bo said, "The Ohio State game ball goes to Fritz," it came as a huge surprise. After all, a player is just supposed to do his job. Besides, no one had talked to him about that play at the time.

Leading up to his senior year at Michigan, he received letters and questionnaires, as did his teammates, from professional football teams requesting biographical information. Receiving letters from the pros was pretty cool to the youngsters, but Schembechler considered them a distraction to his Michigan players—and Bo didn't like distractions. When Seyferth completed his Michigan career in 1972, he didn't have high expectations about being drafted, despite the pros' letters. But during the last round of the draft, he received a call from head coach Alex Webster of the New York Giants. He said yes to the Giants immediately.

The 6'3½", 225-pound fullback was driving down the I-95 Turnpike, heading for the Giants preseason training camp, when out of the blue he experienced an anxiety attack. *I'm going to get killed. What am I getting myself into?* He had never before been so consciously insecure in his football abilities. Although he realized he was not the fastest, most coordinated, or most natural athlete on the planet, he also knew he wasn't a total slacker. Still, he worried.

Arriving at the Giants camp, Fritz met with his position coach, Jim Garrett. He worked his way up to second-team fullback but often ran with the first team during practice. He noticed that he was the tallest of all the starters in the huddle. And once he experienced contact, his anxiety and doubt faded away. Likewise, during film sessions, the coaches complimented him and he felt their respect. Ahead of him on the Giants depth chart was five-year veteran Charlie Evans, who was neither bigger nor faster. However, the seasoned veteran did not make mistakes.

During the summer Giants practices, his father would often drive up with friends from Darien to watch Fritz's workouts. He had Fritz shake hands, sign autographs, and take pictures with all of his cronies. Jack's father was proud, to put it mildly; he saw Fritz fulfilling his destiny. Deep down, Jack knew that he had a lot to do with his son's success. Not only that, but an exhibition game during that camp was played in the Yale Bowl. (New Haven, Connecticut, was near Darien.) The day after the game, Fritz hosted his fellow football buddies. These players were celebrities and were the toast of the town. And Fritz enjoyed showing his friends his neighborhood. Even then, professional football players were larger than life.

The news in the camp was that a big trade had taken place in the off-season between the Giants and the Minnesota Vikings. The Giants traded away star quarterback Fran Tarkenton for a number of players, including a fullback. Ultimately, the Giants kept the former Vikings player and cut rookie Fritz. Fritz felt horrible, humiliated at the time. It was difficult for Fritz to accept. How could he face his family and friends and tell them about his being cut from the Giants?

Giants executive Jim Trimble, in part to boost his spirits, mentioned to Fritz that he had also been drafted by the Calgary Stampeders of the Canadian

Football League. And on top of that, the year before the team had won the Grey Cup, the CFL's version of the Super Bowl. The team offered Fritz a five-day tryout to determine if he could make their roster.

Even though Fritz was given another opportunity to play professional football, he was shaken by his dismissal in New York. What would his family and friends think? And what would Bo and his former Michigan teammates think? It didn't matter that professional football is the top of the mountain and only a very small percentage of players ever attained that status. Fritz's personal bar for excellence was set that high.

What made matters worse was Fritz's evaluation of the player who got his spot. The fullback the Giants kept on their roster was behind Fritz in the depth chart. Perhaps politics played a part in the decision to release him. After all, when a team trades its star player, it expects to get quality in return. The powerful New York press criticized the Tarkenton trade; every move by the coach and management was scrutinized by the press vultures. The papers reported that the Giants received practically nothing of value in the deal. But whoever said that things are fair in life or sports? At that juncture Fritz was expendable, and it would have made team management look foolish if they had cut the player whom they received in the unpopular "blockbuster" trade. Fritz, being young and immature, let his ego get in the way. He failed to understand that professional sports was a business, and that the people in power prefer to stay in power and avoid looking foolish.

Still stinging, Fritz decided to go to Calgary for the tryout. He asked his father to drive him to Kennedy Airport. Fritz got up his nerve and told his father he had been cut. Jack reiterated that he was there for his son. "You gave it your best shot, and that's all you can do," he said. It was true; Fritz had no control over making the team. All he could do was to work hard, do his best during each practice, attend team meetings on time, and have a good attitude—but one can never control the subjective opinion of others. It was another important lesson.

Even though the Stampeders had won the Grey Cup, coach Jim Duncan was under pressure. At one team meeting, he said something to the effect of, "They are after my ass, and I will get every one of you before they get me."

That message didn't go over too well with young Fritz. Duncan was nothing like his revered Coach Bo. Unfortunately, Fritz's attitude was poor. He was still down in the dumps and had neither his head nor body in the game. After about three days, Coach Duncan singled out Fritz and told him, "I understand you may be hurt by being cut by the Giants, but if you don't get your head out of your ass, you are not going to make this team either." It took that jarring dose of reality for Fritz to snap out of it. He had left New York on a plane to Calgary in body only. A very different, uncharacteristic Fritz was playing on a football field in Canada.

Fritz got his head out of his ass, and in doing so he took the job of the previous year's CFL Rookie of the Year. Coach Duncan made good by keeping Fritz over the award-winning player. Of the 32 players on the team, 15 were "imports," or American players. In his first game in the CFL, Fritz certainly earned his stripes. He was named Player of the Game despite Calgary losing to rival Edmonton. In Canada, he was catching passes on a playing field that was wider than in the U.S., which favored the more mobile option quarterbacks, as well as speedy running backs. Even though his shoulder continued to pop out, he was able to play by wearing a harness, and eventually had surgery in the off-season. He admitted that he had shoulder issues throughout his undergraduate career, too.

To his amazement, his former Michigan teammate Billy Taylor was brought up to challenge his place. Billy didn't make the team, but management wanted Billy to live with Fritz. Fritz went along with the nonsense, and Billy Taylor practiced with the team illegally (the CFL does not permit more than 15 "imports" to practice with one team). What was he to do, tell his friend and former teammate, "No, you can't stay with me"? Then, during the second-to-last game of the season Fritz was kicked in the calf and injured. With that, Billy Taylor became legal and took Fritz's place on the field for the final game.

That season's Calgary Stampeders team didn't do well enough to make the playoffs that year. Still, playoffs or not, Fritz fell in love with Calgary. In the charming small town, professional football player Fritz was once again a celebrity, just like back home in Darien and Ann Arbor. He was different, but he was able to fit in to the rugged Canadian milieu. He made new friends and acquired new teammates. However, there was something missing. He was lacking the connections of the close, solid support group he had from his teammates in Ann Arbor. He admitted that the Canadian people treated him with respect, but it was clear to him that they didn't want to hear about how great America was. And who could blame them? At the end of the season, he returned to Ann Arbor to finish school and marry Lynn.

In his second season with the Stampeders, Michigan teammate Billy Taylor was again playing second string behind Fritz. This was a switch, because Billy Taylor had been the backfield star at the University of Michigan. While practicing, Fritz developed a serious hamstring injury and the team moved a Canadian player to fullback. Billy Taylor remained at second string. As Fritz's hamstring started to heal, to his surprise he was told, "You are now the tight end." Fritz was stunned but said, "Okay, you're the boss. Football is paid slavery." He was not happy, and certainly didn't want to move to the unfamiliar position.

The current starting tight end was a 13-year veteran and also the captain of the team, beloved in the community and respected by all. Fritz called Lynn the night before the final player cuts to say he would most likely be home soon. To his surprise (again), the Stampeders cut the captain. Suddenly Fritz was on TV being asked what it was like to unseat the captain and hero.

Having made the team as a tight end, he was once again unsure of himself. He started thinking too much, and he didn't know the blocking technique for the new position, at which he hadn't played since junior high school. How can you compare the junior high experience with the professional experience? There was no comparison, period. To make matters worse, Fritz seriously injured his tender and vulnerable shoulder while playing. With no injured reserve list in the CFL, Fritz was cut from the team. It was time to reassess his options.

Fritz immediately returned to Ann Arbor to get an expert opinion from the University of Michigan team doctor. He pleaded, "I still want to play professional football. What if I made another team?" The doctor, without hesitation, very clearly replied, "I would call that team doctor and tell him, 'Fritz cannot play because of the seriousness of head and neck injuries.'" As unceremoniously as that, Fritz's playing days were behind him. One option eliminated.

In 1973 Fritz had married Lynn and also completed the requirements for his engineering degree, graduating from the University of Michigan. They separated when Fritz headed back to Calgary for camp six weeks later, then Lynn joined Fritz in September after completing her own requirements for a physical therapy degree.

After being cut that fall by the Stampeders, they both returned to Michigan. Fritz initially went to work for the BFGoodrich company, performed corporate consulting, and entered an MBA program at the University of Akron as well. After a short time, the ex–football player left that company for a position with Arthur Young & Company, doing management consulting in NYC; he also went for his MBA at UConn.

It was during this corporate-work phase of his life that he experienced his first identity crisis, so to speak. It became crystal clear to Fritz that the major concern in the corporate world had to do with what you do to make money. Do corporate giants invest in people or do they invest in physical plants? The answer seemed obvious. Aside from these troubling corporate values, it soon became apparent to Fritz that he didn't respect the unblinking pursuit of the dollar. On top of that, Fritz had a son, Sean, and newborn daughter, Courtney, to consider. Up to that point, Fritz had been working long hours moving up the corporate ladder and attending night school toward his MBA. It all left very little time for his family or himself.

A couple of incidents put Fritz in touch with the unpleasant realities of his life. First, Fritz arrived home after being gone for a week and saw to his surprise that Lynn had posted a picture of him in his New York Giants uniform on their shiny refrigerator door. She then sarcastically said to her young husband, "I want our kids to know what their dad looks like." What could Fritz say?

Shortly after this incident, young Fritz, just 28, was having dinner with one of the partners of the company, who was 42. This partner had houses in Connecticut, Vermont, and Florida, and drove a spiffy Mercedes. He had everything—or did he? As they sat at dinner, Mr. Everything confessed, "I don't know my own 16-year-old boy. It is his birthday today." The conversation hit home. Roughly four months later, Fritz was driving two hours each way to commute to a corporate client, in addition to being away from home attending night school for that precious MBA. While visiting his client, Fritz received a call from a neighbor who said that Sean had been taken in an ambulance to the nearby hospital. Worse, in his race to the hospital, Fritz heard a report on the radio that the No. 1 cause of death for children under four years of age was the flu, which Sean had.

Over the next five days and four nights, Fritz spent his time in the hospital with his son. During this stressful time in the Seyferth household, he made the painful and difficult decision to leave New York and Arthur Young & Company. In the process of resigning, he had a meeting with the 63-year-old managing partner about his decision. The executive, who had it all himself, was sitting back with his feet on his credenza, overlooking the magnificent New York skyline. He said, "God, I envy you."

Fritz had begun his pursuit of an MBA at the University of Akron, then transferred his credits to Kent State. When his job brought him to New York, he left Kent State and enrolled at the University of Connecticut. Leaving for Michigan after departing Arthur Young, he transferred his credits to the University of Michigan. Eventually, his MBA degree was conferred by the University of Connecticut. How's that for goal-oriented behavior?

Initially, Fritz believed that he wanted to be in the corporate world because of his love for people and the dynamics of business. Why not follow in the footsteps of his father, a successful businessman? He wanted to be at the top of the pyramid in that arena, too. According to Fritz, he wasn't good in English, history, or languages, but he was good at math, physics, and geometry, so pursuing a degree in engineering had made sense. He fantasized about being plant manager, running the plant, and eventually becoming head of the company. However, he finally admitted to himself that he was chasing a hollow dream.

Meanwhile, Coach Schembechler and his dad, Jack, had become good friends. During one visit with Bo, Jack mentioned that Fritz would be changing jobs. And out of the blue (as in "go blue go"), Schembechler called Fritz in the fall of 1978 about taking a position as recruiting director for the University of Michigan. It was a great offer, but more self-doubts surfaced. Was the job a good fit for him? What would it be like working for Coach Schembechler? Bo promised him, "Make a commitment to help me for four years, and when you figure out what you want to do [with the rest of your life], we can go into business together."

Fritz took on the challenge of this new experience and worked tirelessly as recruiting director from 1979 to 1988—far beyond those first four years. And when Bo became Michigan's athletic director, Fritz was promoted to associate athletic director under his former coach. Fritz had come back to Ann Arbor, to Lynn's hometown, and was fully entrenched at the locus of his greatest football success.

Although Fritz was no longer wearing the traditional (back then) business uniform of suit and tie, he worked his butt off from August through February—92 hours per week, seven days a week—each year. After February, Fritz and the staff had a "reprieve" and worked only 60 hours per week. Of course, it had long been obvious that Fritz was no stranger to hard work.

He had a schedule that was similar to the coaches'. Meetings would start at roughly 8:00 in the morning and continue until the end of practice, which was about 6:30 in the evening. There would be a dinner break, and then everyone would go back to the office from 7:30 until about 11:00. He wasn't a coach, but he worked closely alongside them. In fact, Fritz was the only non-coach with Bo and his coaching staff. As a result of this time spent with Schembechler, Fritz really got to know the man much better. And for the first time in his life, he started to become more in touch with himself as well.

Fritz's work was more fulfilling than it had ever been. He found purpose and meaning, which nurtured his soul. He was back in a comfort zone with his mentor Bo, once again an eager protégé on a quest for learning. He had a clear purpose in his life and was fully committed to it. As it turned out, his being away from home for long hours happened to be okay with Lynn because she always knew where he was: he was in the same town! And on one Sunday afternoon when his son Nicholas broke his leg, Fritz was able to quickly meet her at the hospital.

During his tenure, Fritz created five new positions in the Michigan athletic department: recruiting coordinator, director of football operations, director of development, director of external relations, and executive associate director of athletics. He knew that in order to succeed, he had to compensate by working harder than anyone else. And he soon found out that he had a passion for working with Bo and making Michigan football and Michigan athletics the best ever. Once again, for him it was about team and working as a team.

In his position in the athletic department, he originated the first-ever widespread recruiting network for Michigan football. The network went from a small number of large cities including Detroit, Cleveland, and Chicago, to 34 cities. He figured out that Michigan alumni are not only all over this country, but are also placed in strategic industries in myriad positions of power. This far-flung network could reach out to and recruit the best players in the nation. The alumni would become the eyes, ears, and helping hands of the Michigan recruiting factory.

To give an example of the power of the network, let's say there is an outstanding recruit in Los Angeles. That recruit might receive letters from five captains of industry (all Michigan alumni) in the Los Angeles area telling him that the Maize and Blue people are there for him. That recruit might also receive five or more letters from Michigan alumni power figures throughout the state telling him the same thing. And then, to top it off, the recruit might receive a letter from President Gerald Ford. How is that for networking?

Fritz visited high school recruits, evaluated high school and junior college transcripts, and evaluated players' game film. It was a lot of work for him, but he loved it. It became clear that his energy was contagious, and it also had a ripple effect: it pumped energy into the alumni. Their enthusiasm in turn became contagious and was passed on to the potential recruits. This special program allowed the alumni to play a significant role in Michigan athletics themselves; they were part of the family. And on a personal level, the smiling Fritz honed his skills, became much more of a people person and, in the process, became the face of the Michigan athletics system through his innovations.

Although initially Fritz didn't want to be involved in fund-raising, his coach and mentor convinced him of its importance and eased his doubts about asking alumni for donations. Fritz hesitantly agreed. Fritz knew how to focus and how to complete a significant goal. So what did he do? He set up an efficient system that raised more than $54 million over seven years; they had never raised $1 million previously.

His biggest hesitation in fund-raising was his discomfort in going to people and asking them for money he could not give himself. He felt very uncomfortable about doing so. However, once he perceived that it was not about him but more about them (he remembered what his mother told him), a "no" response carried much less weight. He no longer felt the sting of rejection, which allowed him to more vigorously approach the alumni. It was not a personal rejection. Instead, they simply had other financial priorities, period.

Through fund-raising he also learned something really unexpected: that people actually become happier when they give. And giving back became central to Fritz's character and helped define who he is today. He began to view giving as a win-win situation for every party. It was a win for the university, a win for Bo, it was a win for the athletic program, a win for the athletes, a win for the alumni, and it was a win for him personally. It was one of the most important developments in his young life. It gave him inspiration, and through it he developed a passion to be part of something greater than himself.

Although the new face of Michigan recruiting became involved in many projects, one major project was the building of Schembechler Hall. The cost of this project was estimated at $12 million. Fritz, to no one's surprise, beat that fund-raising goal by a long shot, and actually raised $15.5 million in record time. Through Seyferth's tenure, the role of the alumni evolved from recruiting athletes to raising money for much-needed university programs. All the while, the Michigan alumni family grew and became a significant part of the athletic program for the university.

As recently as 2013, Fritz continued to play an important role for the university and its athletic program. A donor recently gave money for a bust of Bo to be installed in the Frankel Cardiovascular Center. Fritz played a role in bringing the project to fruition and said something to the donor about doing something similar for athletics. And in 2014 a larger-than-life statue (a first on the Michigan campus) of Schembechler was unveiled in front of Schembechler Hall. The only stipulation made by the sculptor was that the rendering was first approved by Fritz, as well as Bo's wife, Cathy. Both of them gave their ready approval to the Missouri artist. When asked what Bo might say about the statue, Fritz replied, "Bo might say, 'If it's to benefit mankind, it's okay. If it's to honor me, forget it!'"

During Fritz's career with the athletic department, he met and interacted with many interesting and amazing people. A number of his favorite stories include President Gerald Ford, whom he first met in 1980. Fritz was surprised by the president's humility and found him, in some ways, like everyone else. Bo wanted the president to head up one of the fund-raising campaigns. So Fritz traveled to Palm Springs for golf and a meeting with the president and former Michigan football player. On the golf course, Fritz asked Ford if he had kept up with Michigan athletics during his administration. Ford replied that he started every day in the White House with the sports section. After that, the conversation flowed easily. Fritz has a picture with his dad, brother Steve, and Ford. He laughs that in the picture, the only person wearing a name tag is President Ford.

On another occasion, Fritz was giving a fund-raising talk to a large audience, and spotted none other than Gerald Ford seated in the front row. After concluding his presentation, Fritz asked the members of the audience if there were questions. Fritz was taken aback when the President of the United States raised his hand. So shocked was he, he can't remember what the question was, or even if he answered it.

At one kickoff fund-raising dinner, Fritz sent the president a brief note regarding the topic for his evening talk. He conveyed that Michigan was progressing to the next level and asked the president if he would tie that concept in with his own life and accomplishments. In doing so, he also took the liberty to give the president some suggestions that he might consider. A few days later, Secret Service men came and picked up Fritz in an unwashed, old automobile. They arrived at the airport to pick up the president. Ford smiled, said hello, shook Fritz's hand, and got in the backseat of the dirty jalopy with him.

During their conversation, Fritz asked Ford if he had received and read his note. Ford replied that he hadn't. So Fritz, being on top of things, reiterated some of the suggested topics that the president might consider when giving his address later that evening.

At the dinner, Fritz was impressed by the wonderful speech that Ford gave, as well as his ability to tie in the things that Fritz had mentioned to him just that day. He was impressed by the politician's vision, his ability to relate to people, and especially his brainpower.

In 1988, Bo Schembechler became the Michigan athletic director in addition to his coaching duties. The Michigan president at the time, Jim Duderstadt, informed Bo that he had to hire Jack Weidenbach to be an assistant athletic director. Ostensibly, the president wanted control over the athletic department and put in his own man. Fritz, unhappy with this new turn of events, talked with both his wife and Bo. Since Coach Schembechler's health wasn't getting any better, and now the president had a say in and an ear to the athletic department's plans, Fritz was concerned about his career choice. After all, the new assistant AD was in his sixties, and while he had a passion for athletics had no athletic business experience whatsoever. Would Fritz get screwed in the long term? At the moment his job seemed secure, but his future could easily be compromised.

Under doctor's orders, Schembechler resigned as athletic director two years later because of his heart condition, in 1990. Michigan president Duderstadt quickly promoted Weidenbach to AD. Though not a surprise, it was a bitter pill for Fritz to swallow. Still, loyal Fritz stayed on and worked under Jack, whom he liked, until Jack left in 1993.

It finally looked as if it were going to be Fritz's turn to take the helm of Michigan athletics and join the group of illustrious ADs that preceded him— including greats from Fielding H. Yost, Herbert Orin, and Fritz Crisler to Donald Canham and Glenn E. "Bo" Schembechler. Fritz had the overwhelming support of the Michigan alumni, he was a protégé of Bo's, he installed the recruiting and fund-raising machine, and he was well-known in the university and the town of Ann Arbor. He, along with his family, expected to be rewarded for his experience, commitment, and devotion to, as well as knowledge about, Michigan athletics.

It seemed like a lifetime passed while Duderstadt made his decision. Finally, enough was enough, and Seyferth set a meeting with the president. The next day, Fritz met with President Duderstadt, who informed Fritz that he was going to appoint Joe Roberson as the new AD. In disbelief, Fritz shot back, "He's not the most qualified." Duderstadt replied, "This is not a popularity contest. The athletic director is an appointment [made] by the president."

Disappointed to say the least, Fritz left the office to go pick up his two boys—Sean, age 17, who was doing a marketing internship at UM at the time, and Nicholas, age 13. While in the parking lot, the radio was on, and the station announced over the air that Roberson was the new AD. The news brought tears to his sons' eyes, too. Fritz then had to conduct an interview with a volleyball prospect in from California instead of attending the press conference.

The unhappy Fritz stayed on in the Michigan athletic department for a few more years, and was again passed over by new president Lee Bollinger, who hired Tom Goss in 1997. Fritz knew he had to go, but he was torn about working for another university. After everything, he *was* a Michigan man.

Fritz interviewed for and was offered the AD job at Miami of Ohio and Tulane, and was a finalist for the AD jobs at Penn State and Boston College as well. After much soul-searching, he asked himself why he would leave the town that he had been a part of since 1968. He realized that his connections and family were all part of his community and asked himself if he wanted to relocate once again. In the end it came down to whether he wanted to continue to be part of the Michigan tradition and remain in Ann Arbor. The answer was yes. So in Ann Arbor the Seyferth family remains. Fritz went on to aid the directors of the UM cardiovascular center and helped raise $104 million for the project as a part-time employee.

The Great Outdoors

You might be surprised at how the 64-year-young Fritz spends his summer vacations. In the summer of 2013, Fritz embarked on a two-week wilderness trip led by Michigan's hockey coach, Red Berenson. According to Fritz,

Red has been leading trips into the Canadian wilderness for 50 years. Red was initially brought up to play hockey for the Montreal Canadiens of the National Hockey League after Michigan was eliminated from the NCAA championship his senior year. It just so happened that three years later the Canadiens won the Stanley Cup, coached by Toe Blake. With his championship earnings, Red bought a canoe. And these wilderness trips have been going on every year since. Berenson began coaching Michigan's hockey team in 1984.

The 2013 trip was Fritz's fifth trip. Red, in charge of gear, left Ann Arbor with five men. They drove 20 hours—with two Wenonah Spirit canoes, Red's single-man canoe, food, tents, two axes, two saws, and sealed containers full of food—to Winnipeg, Manitoba, to pick up a driver. Then the six of them drove to a float plane that would take the group deep into the wilderness, along the Bloodvein River. The single task was to return safely. This meant they had to paddle, cut trails, and portage their way back to civilization 10 to 12 days later. In the two-man canoes, each man carried roughly 125 pounds of gear—and the canoe itself weighed about 71 pounds. Sometimes it took four of them to carry a loaded canoe over a large log or other impediment. And when they had to portage, they generally took their gear out of the canoe because of all the weight. Thankfully, Red was the expert on everything from the way to cut trails to the type of gear that was needed.

During the two-week trips, Fritz has learned a lot about human nature. He realized quickly that even a world-class athlete might not be mentally tough. That old discipline, focus, and preparation in him kicked in. This was something he first learned from his father and then from Bo—not to do various tasks halfheartedly and to pay attention to detail.

Teamwork was also crucial on their trips, and indeed the sum of their parts was greater than the whole. Everyone had to be on the same page, to communicate. There was a tremendous amount of work to be done and no one there to give direction or tell you what to do. Each man had to take responsibility, to fulfill his role. Fritz likes being part of a group that can focus and accomplish the task at hand. For him, the work that needed to be accomplished to make the trips successful became obvious. Under Red's leadership, Fritz was reminded of his Michigan football experience with Schembechler; in fact, at times, Fritz has even called Red "Bo."

His initial wilderness trip with Red was by far his most dangerous. Fritz was somewhere in the wilds of the Yukon, heading north to the Arctic Circle, and the raging rivers were at a flood stage. The terrifying roar of the water scared him. He had never experienced or seen the awesome, raw power of nature like that before. Red told him, "I take people who have high character. It's about getting out of jams, it's not about 'me.' And it's not about complaining or whining." That brought it into focus for Fritz.

He loves these primitive trips—making fires, fixing things when they break, and figuring out what to do when faced with constant obstacles. Nature is an intimidating power. He begins to focus by "thinking, evaluating, assessing variables like the wind, speed of the water, direction of the water, weight of the boat, and where you need to place your paddle," he said.

During Fritz's first trip, one of the comrades' canoes somehow got wedged, raging waters pushing it against some very large river boulders. Joe O'Donnell, former captain of the UM football team (and an 11-year NFL player), was dangerously stuck. The canoe somehow got trapped on a huge boulder even though Red was seated and paddled from the position of the stern. Unfortunately, Joe was in the bow position and was not an experienced paddler. And so they got into trouble. Fritz said to himself, *You're not going to die if you don't panic. Go underwater and then come up for air and breathe. Then go back down and try to get out.* Luckily, they were wearing life preservers. The pair somehow managed to get free and exited the canoe.

Once ashore, they put their heads together and came up with a plan. The plan was to dislodge the canoe while keeping comrade Fritz safe. Fritz would walk back upstream, get into the cold water, and propel toward the disabled canoe. His fellow partners would hold him by a sturdy rope tied around his waist. If not harnessed, he would have become a torpedo speeding toward the dangerous boulders that lay in the river ahead of him. The team figured that he would go straight toward that large rock or boulder where the canoe was pinned. It would be his job to somehow secure or lasso the canoe with his rope and carabiner.

Because of the hazardous water conditions and cold temperature, Fritz was only able to secure a loop around the canoe's seat. Although not perfect, it was the best he could do. After securing the canoe, they pulled the cold, wet Fritz to shore. Then for the next 10 to 15 minutes, the six men, with all their strength, pulled, grunted, swore, and groaned until the canoe was dislodged.

Fritz has told the story many times. He will never forget the experience. It again reinforced the importance of teamwork. His "teammates" on that terrifying trip included Barry Salovaara, a former Red Wings teammate of Red's; O'Donnell; wilderness expert Ken Waggoner; Dr. Deke Mackesy; and Red.

On another trip, it was raining and cold on the day in question. Normally, the group would paddle from about 10:00 or 10:30 in the morning until about 4:00 in the afternoon. But on this particular day, they were unable to find a suitable campsite and had to keep going. It was so cold they could not hold a map to read because they all were shaking so badly. It started to get a little scary, until about 8:00 that eventful evening, when Matt Hunwick, then with the Colorado Avalanche, noticed a cabin on shore. The paddlers found it, unlocked it, and were able to get out of the uncomfortable weather conditions. They were fortunate. They eagerly and quickly started a fire, and within a short time the welcome cabin heated up quickly so that they were able to remove some of their wet layers. Experienced woodsmen know that vacant cabins are purposely left unlocked because it's impossible to keep out desperate people. The unwritten rule of the forest is "Leave it clean, replace the wood, and make sure it's better than when you found it." And they did.

Fritz believes that mankind is hardwired to face challenges and added that too many people today unfortunately are in jobs that are not challenging. Many times, because their bosses do not know how to challenge them, boredom sets in. "This is why we enjoy these canoe trips. It's primitive. I love the new challenges, and it's physical being in nature, meditative, and spiritual with reflection," he said.

He added that every participant is humble and that there's no pretending and no pretense. Masks and false social layers are peeled away; you quickly reveal who you are, and no one is able to hide their fear. It is that reality, being in the present, that is so special because it is so rare. Ordinarily, Fritz feels he

UM athletic director Don Canham (center) announces Bo Schembechler (left) as the Wolverines' new football head coach and Bump Elliott (right) as the new assistant AD.

Coach Schembechler conducts spring practice in 1969.

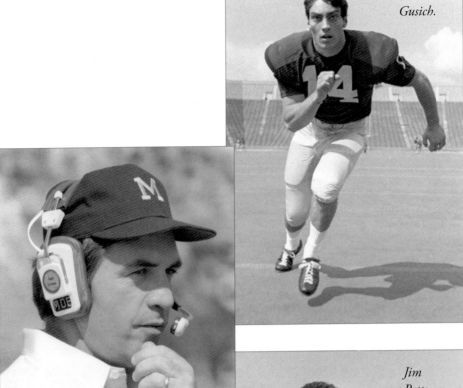

Frank Gusich.

Jim Betts.

Assistant coach Gary Moeller.

Thom Darden intercepts a pass against the Buckeyes.

Jim Brandstatter.

Fritz Seyferth (32) charges against a Vanderbilt in 1969 while Jim Betts (23) runs interference.

An aerial shot of Michigan
Stadium on November 22,
1969: game day.

Bo Schembechler
leads his team on
to the field.

Tom Curtis picks off a pass against Ohio State.

Cecil Pryor (55) and Mike Keller (90) nab Buckeyes QB Rex Kern.

Jim Mandich beats his man.

Wolverines (left to right) Dan Dierdorf, Don Moorhead, and Dick Caldarazzo celebrate against the Buckeyes during game action.

Coach Bo Schembechler is carried off the field by players after defeating former mentor Woody Hayes and his Buckeyes team.

Reggie McKenzie celebrates in the locker room after the game.

Wolverine fans storm the field and tear down the goal post after the unlikely victory.

Coach Bo Schembechler and Coach Woody Hayes in a calmer moment. The two would square off 10 times during their respective careers, in what came to be known as the 10-Year War.

In the ensuing years, Schembechler led the Michigan football team—Bo's warriors—to extraordinary heights.

must be in control most of the time, but on these trips he can let go. A cell phone is of no use. Fritz falls out of contact with the rest of the world, and the rest of the world goes on just fine without him for a while. The wilderness trips put Fritz in touch with his inner self.

On Bo

It was Bo's mission to develop the individual, to make him better by reframing his players' self-concept. Practice, practice, and more practice was the method used to instill the belief that the individual can always do more and perform better. Behind Bo's thinking was his belief that man is inherently lazy and that it was his job to change his charges for the better. He did this by constantly challenging them.

Bo would initially break you down and after that build you up in order to mold you as part of one tight and unified family. Fritz, along with his other teammates, learned that it was never about the individual; it was always about best interests of the team. Bo tested the players to see who could take it and who couldn't. Bo was judgmental on every play; he employed a lot of criticism and few compliments. But it worked for him because every one of his players knew he cared about them as individuals, whether or not he got after them in practice and during games.

Bo reminded the players and the alumni not to embarrass the university. He wanted everyone to play by the rules. In fact, if an individual didn't play by the rules, there were serious consequences. For example, there was a doctor who lived in New York who was part of the alumni network. This doctor hired a football player to mow his mother's lawn in Buffalo. According to the NCAA, an individual cannot be hired just because he's a football player. When the NCAA found out about the infraction, so did Bo. Bo was mad and had Fritz immediately call the doctor and tell him that he was fired, he no longer had season tickets, and he was expelled from his association with the athletic department. Bo always meant what he said and followed through.

On the field, he was also known as an SOB. However, during the season and throughout the year, Bo would have his secretary contact the players to summon them to the coach's office. At first, they thought they were in trouble.

But they quickly learned that he was interested in them and cared about their welfare. He had a great memory about the things that they told him. And through this further interaction, Bo eventually got his players to believe in him. They realized that he was not manipulating them but loving them in his own way.

Fritz said that Bo's strength was his weakness, too. Consider when Michigan played Stanford in the Rose Bowl. Fritz said that the undefeated Michigan team didn't respect Stanford as an opponent because they lost to San Jose State during the regular season. Meanwhile, Michigan had set records for rushing; for Bo that year it was run, run, and run. In the Rose Bowl, even though Stanford packed the line of scrimmage—putting more defensive men on the line than Michigan had blockers, which made it very difficult to run the ball—Bo still stubbornly called for the rush. If Bo had replaced the running quarterback with the quarterback who could throw the ball, Fritz said, the outcome of the game would likely have been different. But the efficient-throwing quarterback was in Bo's doghouse.

The moral of the story is not to allow your strength to get in your way. Or, to paraphrase Einstein, if you keep on doing the same thing over and over and expect a different outcome, that's insanity. Bo wasn't crazy, but he was certainly committed to his own singular way of thinking.

Family Life

Sadly, Fritz's father, Jack, passed away from leukemia at the age of 71 in 1997. Unfortunately, Fritz's mother, Corrie, didn't cope well with the loss of her spouse. Prior to Jack's death, while living in Muskegon, they had lived in Darien, Connecticut, where she was a real estate broker. She was doing extremely well businesswise, as well as socially. Then when real estate was at its peak, Jack was offered a job with the family business back in Muskegon. The Seyferths sold their Darien home and moved back to Muskegon. Businesswise, Jack did well in Muskegon. And socially, he even joined the country club, where he eventually became president. Meanwhile, Corrie sold real estate in Muskegon. Unfortunately, the real estate market in Muskegon did not compare favorably to affluent Darien, but still, they were both doing great. They built a large home on Lake Michigan and she spent time with her sisters and many friends, decorating, working in the woods and yard, and selling real estate.

Then Jack was diagnosed with leukemia. They had five good years before he passed. Toward the end they sold the large family home and the family business and were about to move into a condo when Jack passed suddenly. The once happy and strong Corrie was suddenly left without a deep, meaningful purpose. She was no longer helping take care of Jack and his business and didn't have her kids to look after. Corrie's gypsy spirit kicked in and she moved a few years later to Ann Arbor, to be with her two sons and grandchildren.

During his dad's illness, Fritz revealed to Schembechler that his father had been diagnosed with leukemia and given only five years to live. Bo was resolute, saying, "We are going to be there with him, and make sure he gets the best care available on earth." Bo was supportive of Fritz and always asked about Jack and how he was doing, as they had developed a mutual admiration through the years.

One way that Fritz has dealt with his father's loss is by incorporating the things that he learned from his father into everyday life. "I attempt to honor him each day by being proactive. I want to be more proactive. He set a high standard. He taught me not to associate with people who do not have a sense of purpose," he said.

Fritz has a younger brother and two younger sisters. Jane was born in 1951, a year after Fritz. During her career, Jane's main employer was the Georgia-Pacific Company. He describes her as strong, independent, and the best aunt his kids could have. Today she lives outside Atlanta, Georgia, taking great care of Corrie.

Fritz's younger brother, Steve, was born in 1954 and resides in Ann Arbor with his wife and four children. A gifted athlete, he played baseball at Michigan. He spent his career in the sports marketing industry and is a great advertising genius—very social and extremely bright. A career highlight: he was part of the marketing team led by Bill Schmidt at Gatorade that lured Michael Jordan away from Coke and created the iconic "Be like

Mike" campaign. Aside from being a great communicator, he also has a photographic memory. Three of Steve's children won the Michigan high school state championship in tennis and the other a state championship in baseball. The athletic brothers Fritz and Steve remain close, attending games and hanging out on a regular basis.

Fritz's youngest sister, Lisa, was born in 1956. Lisa graduated from Michigan State University, like her father, and was a stockbroker in both New York City and Chicago. She's married to a University of Michigan–educated lawyer and they have three children, all of whom happen to have graduated from Michigan themselves.

Lynn, Fritz's wife, was a Michigan high school champion in tennis. He admitted that Lynn loves sports, especially football, but there are more important things in her world—children, grandchildren, and parents to take care of. Fritz described her as brilliant, smart, respectful, and kind. Upon meeting her in college, Fritz was swept away by her beauty, brightness, and deep character. As a young college woman, she seemed mature, and could carry on intelligent conversations. Not only that, but Lynn employed common sense and used good judgment uncharacteristic for her age. She was focused and clear about her values. She declined drinking alcohol before they went out to parties, and that was fine with him. Together they have a beautiful family.

Handsome and gifted as both a student and as an athlete, their oldest son, Sean, has had success in all aspects of his life. Married to a wonderful gal, Vincenza, they reside in Chicago with their three children. In the ninth grade, Sean wanted to play on a traveling hockey team. But his parents didn't want him to dedicate his whole life to hockey, so he was told no. Fritz thought he would go out for football and be the high school quarterback, but he rebelled and went out for golf instead. Then, of all things, he was drafted the next year to play junior hockey. He could play in the league at the highest level without losing his college eligibility. His parents allowed him to try out for the team, which he made. Sean wanted to have his ear pierced like the majority of his hockey buddies. His parents said, "Show us some accomplishment at a high level." "How about if we win a national championship?" he suggested. The smart kid won the argument and, later, the team took the national championship. And with that, Sean had his ear pierced, just like his buddies.

Sean attended Notre Dame University, and after playing hockey there he was invited to try out for the Detroit Red Wings. After a short professional hockey career, Sean entered the financial world, where he found great success.

Courtney, the Seyferths' middle child, lives in Evanston, Illinois, with her husband, Ryan, a former hockey teammate of Sean's at Notre Dame. Although she was not as deeply entrenched in competitive athletics as her brother, she is a complete winner and would have likely been the best football coach ever, according to her proud father. While Sean was playing hockey, Courtney brought along her schoolbooks and studied. She captained her high school field hockey and lacrosse teams and went on to play field hockey for Miami of Ohio, where she was honored as the Female Athlete of the Year in her senior year after walking on to the field hockey team as a freshman. She has coached high school field hockey and currently coaches field hockey and lacrosse at the recreational level in Evanston. She and her husband have three children.

Nicholas is the youngest, and played ice hockey like his big brother. He attended Eastern Michigan University, earning a degree in business administration. Today a builder by trade, he lives in Traverse City, Michigan, about 240 miles from Ann Arbor, and has four children with his wife, Rebecca. According to Fritz, Nicholas thinks differently than most people and is able to figure out complex problems. He's actually an artist who uses wood and can easily figure out in his mind the angles necessary to complete the job. Like his father, he also thought of himself as having to work harder than others.

Today you'll likely find Fritz tailgating at Michigan games, snow skiing, taking long walks, or rowing on the Huron River. His family, friends, and teammates remain important people in his life. Outgoing, positive Fritz also has a new business position: coaching executives. Over the years he has learned many things from Bo Schembechler and has incorporated those ideas into working with his clients. In part, he helps them connect with their hearts in such a way that no hurdles can stop them from achieving their goals. He underscores that to be exceptional one has to live an integrated life that has clear priorities. He is still a firm believer in "the team," whether the family, community, business, or our nation as a whole. He also incorporates ideas from his readings, including *The Spirit of Leadership* and *The Four Levels of Happiness*. He knows that preparation, hard work, discipline, giving back, and leaving a legacy are all important, too. After a lifetime of experience, he has learned that there's more to life than chasing the almighty dollar, and like the great coach, he follows through on what he says.

If you are a CEO or COO and want to learn about reaching higher levels personally and professionally, improving your focus, goal setting, and interpersonal relationships, then Fritz is the man to see. This warrior has built on the lessons of his father, Bo Schembechler, and others, becoming a mentor in his own right. To know him is to respect him, admire him, and like him.

CHAPTER 7

The First Wolfman: Thom Darden

Thomas Vincent Darden first experienced notoriety as a skinny seven-year-old southpaw in the projects of Sandusky, Ohio. At that young age, Thomas was a left-handed pitcher in the Adam Baseball League. The story goes that this southpaw was the best hitter on his team as well. He was scheduled to pitch an important playoff game when a most unlikely event occurred. A pesky mosquito bit him on his pitching hand. That bite not only hurt, but in the process his hand swelled up so much that it was impossible for him to grip and throw the ball with any accuracy or velocity.

What was the manager of the team to do? Thom was his best pitcher. Well, the young, precocious Darden had a solution for his coach. "I'll pitch with my other hand, my right hand. My right hand is good," the little boy assured him. (Coincidentally, Bo Rather, future Michigan and NFL wide receiver was his main competitor and opposing pitcher back in those Little League days.)

After watching Thom warm up as a right-hander, the manager was spellbound and in disbelief. He quickly determined that Thom should start the game on the mound for the important game. And not only did the skinny left-hander pitch right-handed, but his team also won the game. This was news, and it traveled fast. A reporter from the *Elyria Chronicle*, about 30 miles away, quickly drove to Sandusky to interview the young boy. The skeptical reporter wanted to see firsthand this remarkable feat, so he had Thom throw the ball with his right hand. Wowed after the reporter had him throwing the baseball with his right hand, he had him then throw the baseball with his by-now-unswollen left hand. The reporter was completely satisfied, and after the interview he had pictures taken of this remarkable and sensational ballplayer. It was Thom's first sports interview, but far from his last. Indeed, his first newspaper story, with picture included, foreshadowed things to come for the outstanding athlete.

There is plenty in his background that accounts for his natural athleti-cism. According to Thom, his father, Thomas Edward, was an amazing athlete himself. He could've been an All-American in baseball, basketball, or football if given the opportunity. He excelled in and also coached fast-pitch softball (young Thom was the ball boy) and played a mean game of basketball up to the age of 65.

Thom learned from his athletic father that he was not allowed to wallow in a loss or whine about his performance, during or after a game. His wise and intelligent father taught him, "You' re not going to win every game every time. There is always another game, there is always another time. Just do your best." He had kept that excellent advice close to his heart his entire life, and passed it on to his own son. Even so, Thomas Edward never complimented his only child, because he instilled in him the idea that Thom could always have done better (something Bo Schembechler instilled in his players). "My father didn't want me to get a big head, and made sure that I didn't," Thom said.

At a young age, the slender Thom also learned valuable lessons from his father about hard work and not taking shortcuts. He taught his son about pitching and, more important, about controlling where the ball was sup-posed to go. Thomas Sr. worked at the aluminum-magnesium company in the area and used materials from the plant to fashion a home plate with which they would practice. Thom had to throw the ball repeatedly to his father, the catcher, and make sure that he "hit" both corners of the plate. He threw that hardball over and over, and eventually developed great control. He thanks his father for that commitment. Those invaluable lessons from his father gave

Thom a foundation for things to come, both at the University of Michigan and with the Cleveland Browns in the NFL.

Unfortunately, that aluminum-magnesium company closed (Thomas Edward had been involved in quality control—a good fit), and he went to work for General Motors in the 1990s. Even though Thomas senior had pleurisy, he never complained. The stoic Darden did not swear, smoke, or drink, and always treated people with dignity and respect. He became heavily involved in the scripture and became very active in the African Methodist Episcopalian Church. In fact, he became a minister in his late forties at the church near Mansfield, Ohio, and served there until he turned 75 when, because of church rules, he became a "pastor in supply." This meant that the bishops and elders figured out that he had a good church following and was still able to raise money, but they wanted younger blood at the pulpit, since they also realized they needed a continued supply of young men in the congregation. It doesn't sound like they know much about this focused and goal-oriented Darden, since they were worried that Thomas Sr. might be too old. Hopefully, said Thom, the church people will figure it out and get it right soon.

The young Darden also learned other valuable character lessons from his mother's side of the family. Her family, after Reconstruction, migrated from Mississippi to Ohio. Thom's grandfather, Esau Simmons, arrived in Sandusky looking for work. The story goes that he was the first African American in town to own his own house, in the 1920s. Thom's mother was one of 13 children, and Mr. Simmons did not want his kids to be without a home. So he walked into the neighborhood bank, found the appropriate man, and came straight to the point with the mortgage lender: "I have a job. Are you going to give me a loan?" The bank agreed, and the house was his to purchase. It still stands, and is today being upgraded.

Unsurprisingly, Thom is part of a large extended family and has many cousins. And 9 of his 12 aunts and uncles have stayed in Sandusky, making for a large family contingent in the small town. Every Thanksgiving 40 to 45 of the Simmonses return to that Sandusky home. And among them, being responsible, family-oriented, and talking straight are terrific common character traits to have been taught and incorporated.

Thom thought that his mother, Thelma Wilma Simmons Darden, should have been a boy. He said she thought like a man, and was very pragmatic. Although the family was neither rich nor poor, in order for young Thom to get his school "digs," Thelma took on a second job. She also played the piano at church and made sure that Thom was in the youth choir along with many of his relatives. He remembered that she had a mirror on her piano so she could watch the choir kids while playing that church piano. All she had to do was give you that special look, and you knew you were in trouble, and you'd better behave, he said. And no one wanted to deal with an angry Thelma. She also worked as a secretary for the Philco Company and then after it closed went to work for General Motors.

Sadly, Thom's mother passed away from diabetes. Today, Thomas Sr. and his second wife reside in Crestline, Ohio, and are in their eighties. Even though he had his thyroid removed a few years ago and suffered a stroke, today Thomas Sr. is doing okay. He can still fix or repair anything, and his mind is still sharp.

* * *

Competition called on young Thom as a seventh-grader. A great speedster, despite his lack of enthusiasm for running, he entered a junior college community track event. He ran fast and because of his finish entered the state track meet. Competing in a state track meet meant that the small-town Sandusky kid would go up against other boys his own age from the larger cities. He felt like an underdog. After all, he was no track-and-field guy; he was trained for the running event by his seventh-grade football coach, Tony Munafo. And even though the seventh-grader was the best runner in Sandusky, he said he got smoked in the finals, finishing in sixth place. Sure, he was fast, but the dose of reality in competing against other talented athletes planted some seeds of insecurity in the youngster.

In football, fast Thom was a left-handed quarterback. Yet he admitted that the first-string quarterback was better than him, and the smart coaches were wise to play him somewhere else, where they could utilize his talents. The versatile and talented quarterback wound up playing as a wide receiver, defensive back, and middle linebacker in high school.

Thom was a good student in the racially segregated Sandusky school system. In fact, he was placed in the college prep classes with mostly whites, while his neighborhood friends were in the non–college prep curriculum. At the time, he was a tall, skinny, acne-prone teenager. And when the gangly kid looked around the classroom, he quickly found out that he was the only one of color. Being shy and insecure, he had some difficulty making friends; he certainly didn't feel as if he had anyone that he could talk with about fitting in or about his anxious feelings. To make matters worse, he wore braces because two of his front teeth were misaligned, and as a result it affected his smile. As it stood, the scholastic-minded Darden held his own academically but did not, at least initially, flourish socially.

He went to classes and attended the school dances but because of his insecurities did not date. Yet his hormones raged on. His emotions overwhelmed him at times. To make matters more difficult for him, there was absolutely no encouragement of interaction between the races. And interracial dating was verboten. Back then, at school dances, all the guys would stand on one side of the room and the girls would sit or stand on the other side. Thom knew how to dance, but he didn't dare approach a white girl. He somehow knew that he just wasn't supposed to dance or interact socially with his white female classmates. Neither the white community nor the black community in Sandusky supported that type of integration.

While in junior high, Thom did have a platonic relationship with one of his white classmates. As it turned out, years later she married one of his school friends. Thom said that perhaps the culture in Sandusky prevented him from fully developing or learning how to make lasting friendships. (Of course, since then, as he psychologically matured, he became better equipped as far as developing friendships.) Being an only child, he was selfish with this time. He liked being alone and was good at it. At home, all Thom had to do to be alone was to shut the door of his room. When his door was closed, his parents left him alone.

Thom's social life was primarily based around athletics. He played football, basketball, and baseball during the summer, and fostered friendships on those teams with the white kids. Likewise, he made friends among the school choir.

In fact, while in high school, he became president of the Cappella Choir. (He has his mother to thank for that.) However, in his neighborhood, he didn't have many opportunities to hang out with his black friends. Instead, he attended the practices of his various sports teams and stayed occupied with a lot of school homework. Both parents kept after him to do well in school, so he studied at home.

His football coach encouraged him to go out for the wrestling team. Thom said that back then, when a coach told you to do something, you just did it. He never questioned it at all. It was blind faith. He thought maybe the coach wanted him to become stronger. He somehow got into the finals of a wrestling tournament…and got crushed. "I never went out for wrestling again. I don't even know how to wrestle," he said. But perhaps wrestling did help him to develop his speed, agility, endurance, and quick-thinking skills.

In high school, Thom played basketball—according to him, his best sport. His positions were guard and forward, and the team went to the district finals. There they were upset by a team they had beaten twice during the regular season. It was an early lesson in humility. Thom was picked to play in the North-South All-Star Game. In that game, Thom scored 19 points and had 10 assists. Basketball legend John Havlicek of the famed Boston Celtics (and the Ohio State Buckeyes) called Thom "the best-kept secret in Ohio." If the Boston legend said he could play basketball, he could play basketball.

Thom thought that his school competed in the second-best conference in Ohio. Schools like Massillon, Canton-McKinley, Niles, and Warren Harding were considered to be among the toughest in the state. (Although Sandusky scrimmaged famous football powerhouse Massillon, the schools didn't play during the regular season.) Of the 10 football games Sandusky played, seven were conference and three were nonconference games. The championship was decided by the AP, a poll voted on by sportswriters, and the UPI, which was voted upon by the coaches. In his sophomore year, his football team won the vaunted state championship. And in his junior and senior years, they were ranked second and third. As a senior, at least 10 players on his team acquired football scholarships.

Football has always been a big deal in Ohio, taken seriously by fans and players alike. On game days, the football players wore blue blazers, a dress shirt, and a tie to school. Thom felt a sense of pride wearing the spiffy outfit to classes and pep rallies.

Only a few years after he graduated, the Sandusky school board claimed that Sandusky High School was placing too much emphasis on athletics and too little on academics. The decision baffled Darden, who said, "Remember that most of the black kids went to college on athletic scholarships. Back then there was community support, and people always voted for tax in school-related issues. Why would a successful sports program in a community made up of maybe 40 percent blacks want to cut off or limit players' chances of getting scholarships?" Underneath the question, he suggests the element of racism, pure and simple.

At first, Thom's position on offense was as a wide receiver. His freshman coach, Mike Currence, assisted the varsity coaches during their summer program. He made sure that Thom lifted weights in order to get stronger. And in his sophomore year, Thom was allowed to dress for the games and play during their mop-ups.

In his junior and senior years, he played wide receiver and defensive back. Then, in his senior year, the first-string middle linebacker broke his leg during one of the team's practices. Thom's defensive coach told Tom that he wanted him to move from defensive back to middle linebacker. At the time, Thom was still skinny, six feet tall and maybe 173 pounds. He had a fear of facing bigger linemen—usually the offensive guards were much bigger, about 220 pounds or so. So the lightweight linebacker had to come up with a strategy. He either had to hit or collide with them straight on or avoid them altogether. He was hesitant to take on the big guys since he didn't have the muscle and was afraid of getting hurt. But the compliant Thom did what his coach asked of him and moved to middle linebacker. The appreciative coach made sure to tell college recruiters that Darden was really a defensive back first and foremost. Then a surprising thing happened: the outstanding athlete, a 173-pound middle linebacker, made All-Conference. Once again, Thom would probably attribute that to such things as speed, quickness, football knowledge, competitiveness, and a commitment to overcoming insecurity. And he'd be right.

Thom thought that his high school coach, Milan Vooletich, assisted him with the cerebral part of the game. Darden would visit the coach, and together, during the summer, they watched game film together. Watching game film helped him, and with the assistance of his coach, he learned about the opposing teams' offenses and plays. He would spend this time productively with Coach Milan, who helped him look for strategies to predict what the offense was attempting to accomplish on each play. He also observed how the defense attempted to counter each particular offensive strategy.

With this one-on-one training from his coach, Thom became increasingly fascinated and intrigued by the complex game of football. He began to study offensive strategy and examine how the offense exploited mismatches or defensive weakness. "Remember, every offense and every defense has weaknesses," Thom said. "It's a coach's job to exploit those weaknesses. So you have to attempt and anticipate to make the right call for either the offense or defense, depending upon the down, the yard line, time left in the game, and so forth.

"As you become more knowledgeable, you really begin to understand and can somewhat predict the plays that the offense likes to run. This means you're looking for tendencies, and figuring out their tendencies and their favorite plays. So the job on defense is to anticipate and look for those tendencies." Accordingly, Thom believes that his main strength as a player was his football IQ; he "understood" the technical aspect of the game.

He admitted that a less enjoyable aspect of the game was contact. He did everything he could to avoid getting hit by an opposing player. As a wide receiver on offense, he got hit or tackled, while as a defensive back, he did the hitting. As such, it did not take him long to learn that he'd rather play defense. That made the transition from wide receiver to defensive back much easier.

Thom's initial meeting with Bo Schembechler came during the recruiting process on a 1967 visit to Miami of Ohio. (Coincidentally, while there, he met another football player who happened to be from Barberton, Ohio—a young man named Billy Taylor.) The naïve Darden thought that recruiting trips were generally special occasions. In fact, he thought that he was going to receive a steak dinner, among other things. To his surprise, instead Bo said brusquely, "Change into your workout clothes." He had both of the high school stars participate in 40-yard dashes, agility drills, and more. After completing all of Bo's workout tasks, Thom went back to the locker room and changed into his street clothes, along with Billy. They looked at each other with weird expressions on their faces and said, "We're not coming here. This guy's nuts." "Not only that, I [did] not want a steak dinner. I just wanted to get out of there as quickly as possible," Darden said years later. It was Thom's first meeting with Schembechler, and that first impression of Bo was imprinted on Thom forever.

On another occasion, legendary Woody Hayes came to the Dardens' home, which was in row-project apartments. Woody walked into the Darden household, met Thomas Sr. and Wilma, and quickly turned the discussion to war and the battles, comparing them to football. Woody got so excited that he started cursing, which was his way. After a short while, Thomas Sr. escorted Woody to the door. "After he left, my father said to me, 'You can go anywhere, but not [Ohio State].'" Woody committed a sin in the Darden household. You just don't swear—and that meant anyone and everyone, even the venerable Hayes. Mr. Darden was consistent with his values and his beliefs.

In spite of Woody Hayes' initial impression, the family traveled to Columbus and met with the coach again. There Thom found out that Woody wanted him to play a hybrid position on defense: linebacker on the line and then drop off to defend the pass in the flat when necessary. Thom said he wanted to be a defensive back and that he didn't want to be a linebacker.

Later on during the visit, Thom opened the door of Woody's war room and peeked inside. On the chalkboard, he noticed a ranked listing of recruits and their positions. He noticed that his name was written toward the bottom of the list. Thom thought to himself, *I don't think that's a good sign.* Sometime later in the day, he walked back into the war room with his parents to meet Woody again. This time, Thomas noticed that his name was near the top of the list. Thom said to himself, *That does it. I'm not going to Ohio State to play for him. How can I trust him?*

Darden also visited Minnesota and met Sandy Stephenson, their black quarterback. He also visited Michigan and Northwestern. He was recruited by Purdue but didn't visit the campus. Thom liked Northwestern both academically and because he related well to their coach, Alex Agase. He also liked Northwestern because they had a black team doctor. It was important for Thom to feel supported and to be able to identify with other successful African Americans. He didn't have much of an opportunity for that in Sandusky. But at the time, Northwestern had a lousy football team, and that was not good for the competitive Darden.

Tony Mason, Don James, and Bump Elliott all recruited Thom for Michigan. But it was Coach James who won him over because of his knowledge about defensive backs in the secondary. (Years later, after James became the University of Washington's head coach, he invited Thom to speak to his players. That was quite an honor for him.) Thomas Sr. also liked and was impressed with Don James.

Thom's first impression of Bump Elliott was of a man who carried himself very well. In fact, he thought there weren't many who could make a better impression than Bump. Bump was soft-spoken, a terrific dresser, and a real gentleman. And the coach knew football—its coverages, various offensive and defensive plays, and his players. Darden was amazed that unlike some others, he had a real conversation with Bump. The coach just made you feel like you were one of the guys. And the fact that Michigan was a premier academic school sealed the deal for this recruit.

Of course it didn't hurt that Coach Elliott was very courteous, too, referring to Thom's mother as Mrs. Darden. In fact, Bump made quite the impression with Wilma. She knew he was no phony. Neither parent advised Thom on which college to attend; they simply left it up to him to make this decision. However, they did say that Coach Bump Elliott was very different from the other coaches. Thom knew what that meant, and that message was not lost on him.

Bump brought in more quality players from Michigan and Ohio. Thom believed that Bump had to get more minority players, because he had only four on scholarship. He already had outstanding black players in George

Hoey, Ron Johnson, and Billy Harris. In Darden's class, Bump recruited seven minority players. Two Michigan alumni—Bill Steuk, an attorney, and Marshall Brown, a businessman—had come to the Darden home and took him out to dinner. Before that, going out to dinner had been going to one of the relatives'. This occasion was a big deal, and Thom ordered a steak. Both men took an interest and talked with him. They made Thomas feel that they were impressed with him. Having a sense of belonging and acknowledging him as a person was important for this young man.

Even today, Thom continues to have a good relationship with Coach Elliott. He added that Bump was kind, trustworthy. "You knew he was telling you the truth," Darden said. He added that football was different back then, you looked to your coach to get you fired up. "Coach Elliott made sure that you felt part of the team. I liked him a lot and appreciated that he helped me feel part of the team. Fitting in, and being accepted was very important to me," he said.

Thom was thrilled to play for Coach Elliott. Bump had even been instrumental in helping Darden and his fellow Mellow Men secure their house off campus. "Mike Oldham and Glenn Doughty showed Bump the house listing and he thought it was a great idea. He thought it would be great for us, and great for the sake of the team, as we were seven of the top 15 players on the team." The Mellow Men made sure that they all got to practice on time, and made sure that they took the correct bus in order to get to their classes on time. Being in the house helped Thom, too, since football was the main focus there. Butch Carpenter and Mike Oldham, the smartest according to Thom, kept everybody in line and were good role models as far as the importance of academics were concerned. Glenn Doughty's dad made a sign that read THE DEN OF THE MELLOW MEN, and the friends framed it and placed it in front of the house.

Bo probably didn't like the idea at first, Thom said, but soon the coaches and parents gathered at the Den after games. The parents would fix food for the feast to follow. In fact, position coaches like Hunter and Moe even came. Once *Sports Illustrated* even came—that made it a big deal because it was a very special thing to be black, athletic, and playing exceptional football.

After the parents left, the party began. Of course, the Michigan players all joined in the festivities. Reggie McKenzie was appointed social director, and he was excellent at getting females to the party. It was because of this job, according to Darden, that Reggie honed his organizational skills. He took the job seriously and did it very well. On top of that, he came up with themes for the girls, such as how to dress. For instance, one of Reggie's famous themes was for the girls to wear "hot pants." If the whole thing sounds reminiscent of the movie *Animal House*, Thom said, "Now, we didn't have food fights, we were not out of control, and we never had a fight in the house. We were respectful.... We didn't go to the bars. We just hung out at our house."

It was a tremendous experience for Thom to be aligned with a good group of black men who were smart, competitive, and highly athletic. In Sandusky, only a few black students back then went on to college. In their house, there were six other guys with similar backgrounds. As a result of the Mellow Den, the outstanding group of men dealt with beliefs and prejudices together. They also dealt with the pressures of being in the spotlight as black athletes. They became de facto ambassadors, and they paved the road for others who followed.

Amidst campus unrest, athletes were expected to focus on education and football—but not necessarily in that order. Walking through the beautiful Michigan campus, it was pretty common to see a Black Panthers demonstration, a Nixon protest, an anti–Vietnam War demonstration, and plenty of other campaigns. After class, the group of men had the opportunity to go back to their sanctuary and talk about these issues. They knew they had to represent themselves as Michigan men, not to be foolish. The intellectual discussions helped clarify where each of them stood on the issues and then what to do about it. As a group, the men decided to support the Black Action Movement. As one unit, they decided to consult with their head coach, and talked about the options. Not only was Bo open to the issue, he also changed the spring football practice time so that the players could demonstrate with the rest of the campus activists.

All seven of the Mellow Men blocked the entrance to the economics building so that students could not enter the building to attend class. All of them wore their letterman jackets. The Mellow Men closed the building down and made their point.

Thom attended summer school before the football season and remembered on one occasion seeing a group of hippies come out of the student union. All of a sudden they started performing an improvisational play. Not only that, but they stripped off all their clothes. This was all new and shocking to Darden; he wasn't in Sandusky anymore.

Feeling more comfortable socially, Thom began to date in college. Of course, being a football starter, he was a magnet as far as women were concerned. Other teammates were doing likewise, and it didn't seem like a conflict at the time. He eventually married a gal who became his first wife.

After classes and practice, he would get together with his guy friends. They would talk and hang out. Looking back, he called that time the very best years of his life. He had the opportunity to make a lot of choices for himself, and it was paid for on someone else's dollar. Today he regrets that he didn't study harder and feels his biggest mistake was not achieving a professional degree or going to law school. As it happened, he got married just before participating in the College All-Star Game in 1972. His wife was smart and her father was a well-connected Cleveland doctor. At the time, Thom thought that his father-in-law would assist him in starting a career after he played in the pros. He could introduce him to all the influential movers and shakers. Then Thom would be set.

Wolverines Football

At Michigan, Thom bonded with Reggie McKenzie and the other African Americans from his recruitment class. They all connected and bonded with each other. They also knew that Michigan was the place. Even though Ohio State had more African Americans and was even more progressive than Northwestern, Purdue, or even Miami of Ohio, they liked their decision.

Some other players that Coach Elliott recruited in Darden's class were Mike Keller, Jim Brandstatter, Frank Gusich, Bruce Elliott, and Leon Hart Jr., among others. At the beginning, the athletic and competitive Thom thought, *I'm scared to death. How can I compete with these guys? I'm from a small community, not the big city.* Soon after arriving at that first practice, the players were in T-shirts, shorts, and helmets, and set about doing drills. Once again, Thom played both ways, as a wide receiver and in the defensive backfield. Soon it became crystal clear to him that in the drills he was able to keep up with all his teammates. Not only that, he could be a leader, his hands were good, and he had solid football knowledge. His football fundamentals were good and he began to feel more at ease. Before long, he gained self-confidence.

Sometimes the freshman squad scrimmaged against the second-team varsity—and they held their own. In fact, one time, Thom, as a defensive back, stuffed the running back at the line of scrimmage—and it was on that one play that Thom began to believe, *I belong.*

The talented group of freshmen were all quality players, and no one shied away from competition. That was the hallmark of Thom's class of ballers. They became tough guys on the field. If a player got knocked down, he got up; if a player messed up on an assignment, he would do it right the next time. And of course, those freshmen still made a whole lot of mental mistakes.

The freshman football team gathered together at the Crisler Arena to watch the last game of the season, their varsity Wolverines against Ohio State, which was telecast live. "I couldn't believe that they got beat like they did," Thom remembered. "I certainly didn't feel part of that varsity team at that point." The seven Mellow Men sat together watching that game. It seemed unreal. They made a group vow to each other while watching that blowout: they would not allow any team to beat them that badly. That historic vow was probably led by the social chairman, Reggie McKenzie. And with Ohio State, the vow took on a special meaning in the sense that they all knew how good that Buckeyes team was. They realized that they would have to play their very best in order to beat them. Worse, when Thom returned back home to Sandusky, he had to deal with his friends and neighbors bragging on Ohio State. In his hometown, most everyone wore the Scarlet and Gray proudly.

Then Bump got ousted, which came as a shock to Thom. When he heard that Bo Schembechler was hired, he thought back to his initial meeting with the coach back in 1967. Then in January 1969, he remembered walking into

Bo's office at Michigan for the first time. Bo barked, "Shut the door." Then, sarcastically, "You thought you got rid of me, didn't you?"

During that first Schembechler-led off-season, it seemed to Thom as if Bo was trying to kill the young players—and he almost succeeded. He remembered running and more running and of course that slap-and-stomp drill. Darden said he didn't get hit too much during that slap-and-stomp drill because of his footwork. He was also a fast runner, perhaps the third-fastest guy on the team behind Glenn Doughty and Bruce Elliott. He remembered witnessing a mountain of a man, Cecil Pryor, knocking a kid out of the ring with a fast punch during the drill, though. Then just as quickly, Bo leaped into the ring and said to the gigantic Cecil, "If you want to fight somebody, fight me." Right then and there, Thom knew that Bo could control the team. "I hadn't seen that before," he said.

He added that he thought the players wanted to win for Bump because he was loved; he was like a father, and players didn't want to disappoint him. Or perhaps he was more permissive, like a mother. On the other hand, with Bo it was more like a love-hate relationship because he was so strict. But then, maybe Bump was too easy.

Thom remembered that first spring practice, in one of Bo's early scrimmages, when he made a terrific bone-jarring hit and absolutely nailed the running back behind the line of scrimmage. On that one play, Bo was jumping up and down, as were the other coaches. Remember, back then the coaches never verbally said "good play." In fact, Bo never said *anything* to Thom about his defensive play. You were expected to do your job. But it was likely that because of that one play that he was promoted to the No. 1 position of wolfman.

As a sophomore, he weighed about 173 pounds and was placed in the wolfman (Bo's term) position on defense full-time. Once again, he was scared to death. He had to take on offensive guards, tackles, and fullbacks who weighed much more than him. He realized quickly that he seemed to be getting hurt regularly, too. Even though he had become a starter, he was afraid that position coach Dick Hunter would take him out of the game or demote him if he made a mistake. Sure, Thom got beat up physically but the football-smart Darden didn't make a whole lot of mental mistakes. Since high school, it was drilled into him that if he made a mistake as a safety, it was going to result in a touchdown. (Once again, certain things are imprinted that you don't forget.) And of course, certainly making a mistake or allowing a touchdown is a big one, and one that you can't take lightly. Thom certainly didn't.

Darden will always be known as the first wolfman for the Michigan Wolverines. What exactly is a wolfman, then? In essence, Bo took Woody Hayes' defensive scheme and implemented it at Michigan. At Ohio State, All-American Jack Tatum played a similar roving defensive back position, something Bo earmarked for Darden.

As wolfman, Thom would have to take on the offensive guard; or if it was an option play in the I formation, he might tackle the quarterback while taking on the fullback. In dealing with the fullback, the trick was to hit the fullback in an attempt to turn the play inside. His job was not to allow the blocking back to get to his outside shoulder. In order to do that, he had to keep the left side of his body as well as his left arm free and not tied up by the fullback. If successful, he was able to grab or tackle the running back. He didn't want to be blocked, and Bo wanted him to crush the fullback every time and all the time. It was a physical position, and Thom had numerous separated shoulders, ankle injuries, as well as arm and finger injuries as a result.

As wolfman, It was important for him to read the key signs in order to determine what that offensive guard would do. Thom, being quick, was able to react quite well. The technique was simply learning to keep his left side and arm free so he could grab, if need be, the fullback who was attempting to block him low at the knees and either drive him back or hit him high. Thom quickly learned that if the fullback got to his chest area, he was in trouble. He credits his high school coach for helping him to read the plays so he could anticipate what he had to deal with as a player.

Thom, Doughty, and Keller all became starters in their sophomore year. And in that backfield along with Thom were Tom Curtis, Barry Pierson, and Brian Healy. "We weren't exactly friends, but they were cool and nice to me," he said. He was the only African American in the defensive secondary. Later on Billy Taylor and Mike Taylor started, likely in their junior years. Reggie McKenzie was in Bo's doghouse, so he didn't start until his junior year.

* * *

The 1969 Missouri game was a real eye-opener for the players and the coaches. Thom was still feeling insecure and doesn't remember many details. He thought that maybe he or the team might not be that good if they could get whipped that easily. The brutal defeat really stung. As a result, the players just didn't talk much about that game. Thom remembered Coach George Young talking about creating "a sudden change" after Mizzou's Jon Staggers returned a punt for a touchdown and the Wolverines suffered a blocked punt.

In the aftermath, Michigan worked very hard on the mistakes that following week of practice. In fact, it seemed to Thom that Bo ran his squad nearly to death, running stadium laps in addition to their usual sprinting tortures. Thom thought the coaches seemed more quiet or subdued after that Missouri loss.

Even though the team lost their next matchup, to Michigan State, Thom thought the team defense played much better. He also remembered beating Iowa but didn't remember the final score. On the plane ride back from Iowa, and especially on the bus ride back to the Yost Fieldhouse, the players were singing enthusiastically, "Bring on Ohio State." Everyone was singing together. The mood was electric. Ohio State would be their final opponent of the season.

Just prior to that memorial game with Ohio State, Bo stood up to speak to his players. Thom remembers it going something to the effect of, "This is the biggest game, they are the No. 1 team in the country, and they took three-quarters of our playing field during practice." The coach was pissed off. "They disrespected you. We are going to show them. Let's go get them!" He pounded his fist through the blackboard, exploding it. Then the seniors got up and started throwing chairs around. Thom said, years later, "Holy crap, I was scared to death. This was the raw height of emotion." It was frightening, it was unbelievable, and something that he and many of his teammates had never experienced before.

As a rule, it took Thom quite a while to dress and put on his pads after coming off the pregame warm-ups on the huge playing field. He thought he was probably near the end and in the back going through the tunnel but remembers the unrestrained energy and emotions of his teammates.

As for the game, "we dominated them," he simply said. The Wolverines choked the Buckeyes' running game, and Thom made a good block on a punt return that opened up a lane for teammate Pierson to score a touchdown. Overall, the team had six interceptions, and Darden laid claim to one of them. He also remembered making a number of tackles behind the line of scrimmage in his wolfman position. One thing that always added fuel to his fire was when the Columbus crowd booed against Michigan.

He also added that Woody's sideline antics were a remarkable sight to see, and motivated them. And at game's end, Jim Mandich was picked up by the fans as they surrounded the players on the field after the final whistle. In all the commotion, Thom can't be sure that Woody Hayes even shook Bo's hand after the game. But he did remember that the team partied the entire week afterward.

In his junior year, Thom became a cornerback, and as a senior, a free safety. Thom said he became much more confident, even arrogant, after his sophomore year. He relished team victories with the guys, and that bonding experience they shared has never been duplicated. Simply, there's no comparison to that connection with his college teammates. He didn't bond like that with teammates playing for the Browns, and certainly not in his life after football.

He remembers the 1970 season in broad strokes. There were a number of close contests, in which it took field goals to win games. He made a super interception against Minnesota, placing his feet perfectly before falling out of bounds in a game they took against the Gophers. Thom was a third-team All-American that year. And Bo told him before the start of the next season, "You better have a good season and play like an All-American." Of course, he admitted that he had already spent a lot of time thinking about becoming an All-American, and Bo's directive only further motivated him.

Before that 1971 season, he stayed on campus, working out with his teammates every day. He ran and lifted weights with his Mellow Men. Some days, the players worked out twice a day. During the summer, he worked for the Ford Motor Company in Livonia, locating parts in the very large warehouse and packaging them for delivery.

As a senior in 1971, Thom intercepted a pitch-out on an option play against UCLA and ran it back 92 yards; it was as good a start as there could be in mounting an All-American campaign. Thom played with an injury against Minnesota. But with a torn hamstring, he could not run very well. Still, Bo said he needed the free safety in the game, hobbled or not, so he played. Afterward, Bo said he appreciated what Thom did—a rare instance of verbal reinforcement from his coach. Later that season, Thom scored a touchdown against Indiana. ("Friday before that game, coach Jim Young had us do psycho-cybernetics, and when doing so, I remembered imagining that I intercepted a pass and scored a touchdown, which I did.")

He had come a long way since his doubt-clouded first days in Ann Arbor. By his senior season he was very comfortable on the playing field. Mike Taylor called the defensive signals and Thom would help his brother out with calls. Thom understood the game better and was very good at going to where the ball was going to be.

In his final regular-season college game, against Ohio State, he acknowledged that Michigan was supposed to kill them (the reverse of the 1969 game, in which OSU went in as a huge favorite). The Buckeyes were not a great team, and had maybe two or three losses. But reading the newspapers and listening to the reports is not always a good thing. Thom acknowledged that it might have negatively affected the Michigan team. The players (Thom included) might have bought into their own hype and become overconfident.

In the game, the Wolverines defense controlled the Buckeyes' running attack with superior play by the line and linebackers. They were not throwing the ball very well either. It took a special teams breakdown for them to score their early touchdown.

Thom made a spectacular interception (his second of the game, and one that ESPN chose years later as one of the "100 plays, performances, and moments that define college football") toward the end of that game. The ball was thrown by quarterback Don Lamka to his tight end Dick Wakefield.

Darden was well positioned and coming up fast behind Wakefield when he saw that the ball was thrown low to this receiver. Thom had a couple of options on that particular play. He could either go for the ball or tackle Wakefield. Instinctively—there wasn't time to think—Thom leaped over Wakefield, cupping his hands as he dove for the ball. Now picture Wakefield going to the ground as he's reaching to catch the ball. Darden dived over Wakefield and he made sure that his hands were in front of Wakefield's face in order to steal the interception. Darden caught the ball in the air, rolled over with the ball cupped in his hands, quickly leaped to his feet still holding the ball, and showed it to game official Bill Quimby as he raced off the field. Thom realized that by leaping over Wakefield, his head went down and touched his chest. He knew that Bo wanted him to knock the ball down.

On the sideline, Woody Hayes went ballistic. He ran on the field, kicked and broke one of the yard markers, tearing up everything in his way. Spittle coming from his face, he yelled "pass interference" over and over. He was out of control, to put it simply. In fact, he earned not one but two unsportsmanlike penalties for his behavior. I asked Thom if that catch was pass interference. He smiled and said, "It was the greatest interception in the history of football." (Then he added, "Between you and me, it could've been pass interference.") The play was huge, sealing a 10–7 victory for the Wolverines. Bo never said anything to Thom about the grab, but position coach Dick Connor did say "Great play."

Michigan advanced to the Rose Bowl that year, against Stanford. It was Thom's second Rose Bowl. Unfortunately, he uncharacteristically dropped two punts that afternoon, something very unusual for the usually sure-handed Darden. He said years later that he had a terrible feeling of not being in control during that game. It seemed that Michigan could not do anything right, and that he could not explain it.

Part of the reason may have been that Michigan's best-throwing quarter-back, Kevin Casey, was in Bo's doghouse. Casey could run, throw, and think on his feet, but he was cocky, a free thinker, and had an unusual lifestyle. Because he was out of action for the day, Michigan was left with a running attack and not much else. And when Stanford placed 10 men on the line of scrimmage, Bo *still* wanted to run. Michigan's quarterback Tom Slade just couldn't throw the ball; and when did, it sailed into the stands.

Thom believed that his team was given the opportunity to win that game but that they were preoccupied thinking (as was he) about obtaining the national championship. Bo's focus was on winning the Big Ten championship, first and foremost. But Thom would've liked to have been on a team that won the national championship and felt that his Michigan team was certainly worthy. The loss to Stanford (13–12) was a major disappointment.

As a final act in his college career, after the season Thomas participated in the College All-Star Game in Lubbock, Texas—coached by none other than Bo and Alabama legend Bear Bryant.

A Pro Career

The first-team All–Big Ten and All-American Darden was the 18th player selected in the draft, chosen by the Cleveland Browns. Thom admitted he was gung ho but also naïve when he joined the Browns. There were some veteran players from that 1964 Cleveland championship team whom he thought would show and model leadership qualities. Then, to his surprise in the locker room, he would see the guys smoking after games, not at all shaken up by a loss. Thom was shocked by the dissonance. It didn't fit his thinking. How could a professional, a competitive athlete at the top of his game, be so cavalier about winning and losing? "It messed me up," he said, and in the course of things he lost respect for the game and the guys in the organization.

Thom later realized that professional football is a business, and that players are usually playing for next year's contract, not the glory of a win. After all, they also have families to support. Football, at first, might be for the love of the game for most players. Unfortunately, as a pro, economics become more important for many.

Another stumbling block in Cleveland for Darden was that there was no one of color in the organization's front office from 1972 to 1981. Coming from a supportive and ethnically diverse environment at Michigan, this was tough on him. He also felt that the league put emphasis on "thinking man's positions," such as quarterback, center, middle linebacker, and free safety. Back then, in the pros, there were very few African Americans in those positions. Thom aspired to be a free safety, because essentially the safety was the quarterback of the defensive backs. He was the one who called the plays and signals. He helped defend on the run and patrolled sideline to sideline, defending the passes. As a senior at the University of Michigan, Thom had first played free safety. But with the Browns, they had Thom at strong safety. Then in his second year, he was moved to free safety. "I loved that position," he said.

Thom talked about motivation and the desire to push, push, push. He was never satisfied with his play or understanding of the game, always striving to get better. (It was a lesson learned from Bo as well as his father). Thom knew that he always had to work harder to eradicate any self-doubts. And he believes that he did that throughout his entire career. His belief was that every player can always do more. He acknowledged that he was blessed by having been able to play with special and exceptional athletes at both Michigan and Cleveland.

As a player, Thom's focus was always on the game. It had to be in order to play, execute, and be in the correct defensive position on the field. When playing, Thom never allowed his personal troubles to interfere. He was able to block out extraneous stuff and focus on the task at hand.

Once, when playing against Pittsburgh, Thom intercepted a pass thrown by Terry Bradshaw. He was able to do that because he was able to pick up on the quarterback's idiosyncrasies. He'd look at the offensive formation, then look at the tight end and wide receiver to determine if they were on the strong or weak side. He would then anticipate where the ball was going to be. He could eliminate maybe half the field, which gave him a much better chance at anticipating where the ball would be thrown. And if he was correct, he'd be in a splendid position to catch or bat down the pass.

He acknowledged that in the pros, there was always somebody better. So the task for the player was to improve and master his position. Thom attributes his longevity in the NFL to this commitment.

* * *

A turning point occurred in 1975, when Thom realized for the first time in some time that he was not invincible. In the past, he had overcome separated shoulders, rib injuries, broken hands, ankle sprains, and hamstring pulls and tears. However, this time it was noticeably different. He had a serious knee injury. In a preseason game, on artificial turf, he remembered either hitting or being hit on his knee, and although it didn't seem to hurt during the game, the injury lingered.

In the next game, the Browns were playing the Philadelphia Eagles. Thom was lined up and ready to receive a punt from the Philadelphia kicking team. On the kick, a Philadelphia rookie was bearing down on Thom to make the tackle. One of Thom's teammates, also a rookie, was positioned to block for him. "While catching a punt, I'm supposed to keep one eye on the ball and quickly take a peek at the player ready to tackle me. And while returning punts, I didn't want the ball to hit the ground or allow it to bounce because you never know how the ball is going to bounce. Of course, the other options include either making a fair catch or getting out of the way and allowing the ball to bounce.

"I took my eye off the ball and it hit me in the chest, and as I quickly started to look down for the ball, I saw two Philadelphia Eagles coming toward me. I thought I could get by the first guy and then deal with the second. However, as I was looking down toward the ground, I got hit by that player. His helmet hit my left knee and I was immediately taken to the locker room. The first thing I know is, they are talking about doing surgery the next day in Cleveland," he remembered.

Thom, not totally trusting the Browns organization's doctors, wanted a second opinion. He called Dr. Gerald O'Connor, the University of Michigan team physician, whom he trusted from his playing days. If anyone would give him the straight story, it would be O'Connor.

For a football player, it's important to have legs and an upper body free from injury. As a free safety, Thom had to tackle and run and run and run, in addition to the ability to change directions on the spot. Legs frequently go in one direction and one's body in another. It was only a matter of time before an injury occurred, and it happened frequently to players in his position. But you can't allow an injury to get in the way of your play; you can't play scared— because if you play scared, you won't play very well.

According to O'Connor, the injury was indeed significant. Thom had a medial lateral ligament tear and cartilage damage. The surgeons could reattach the ligament and take out the broken cartilage. The Browns had their own arrangement with this one hospital in Cleveland, but Thom went to the Cleveland Clinic because Dr. O'Connor referred him to his medical school roommate, who ran the clinic. At the time, the Cleveland Clinic boasted the first sports medicine clinic. Browns owner Art Modell wasn't happy; he wanted Thom to have that surgery done elsewhere. Still, the Browns took care of Thom's medical charges. (Unsurprisingly, the Cleveland Clinic, one of the nation's premier hospitals, later became the Browns' team hospital).

During rehabilitation, Thom wore a cast that ran from his hip to his toe. The entire rehabilitation process took about 10 months. He would get up in the morning, exercise, have lunch, take a nap, and then exercise again. He did not play for the entire 1975 season. In spite of his injury, the Browns wanted him to play the last two games of the season, but Thom was smart and declined. Sidelined with injury, Thom's salary was paid for.

During that 1975 season, Thom instead returned to Ann Arbor, attended school, and helped Bo Schembechler install a different defense all while completing his compulsory rehabilitation. Coming back to the Browns in 1976, Thom believed that he was in the best physical condition of his life. He was goal-oriented, focused, and determined to play again at the level he had exhibited, and beyond.

During part of his rehabilitation, when he was still on crutches, he talked with Browns secondary coach Richie McCabe about learning more about the game. Coach McCabe suggested that he should sit in a box at the top of the Municipal Stadium, where he would be away from everybody. From there, he could observe the game uninterrupted. But to do so, he would have to confront a huge ramp in order to get up to that box. The coach suggested that going up the ramp would be worth it because a view from the top would allow him to see the entire field. And then afterward, both of them could talk more intelligently about the game. Thom confronted the ramp, as well as his mental obstacles. He studied the game from a different viewpoint, and it allowed him to get a deeper, more thorough understanding of the brutal game. It was a dismal season for the Browns, who only won three games against flagging opponents. It took at least three different players to fill in as the free safety. When Modell asked why they were having such a problem, McCabe simply said, "You don't have Darden in that position."

Thom became a more complete, valuable, and total player with the help of McCabe. Under his tutelage, Thom learned to read progressions, learned to read the routes of the runners and receivers, and began to anticipate what plays would be run. Prior, although he understood the game, he relied a lot on his physical ability. He became much more cerebral in anticipating how the plays would develop. Of course, being better able to anticipate resulted in better execution, and in fact, he became a much better player.

Thom set the record for most career interceptions (45) and single-season picks (10) for the Cleveland Browns. He was also the NFL interceptions leader in 1978. One of the league's leading tacklers, he made All-Pro in 1978 and 1979 and played in the Pro Bowl after the '78 season.

He thanks Coach McCabe for molding a willing student, and underscores that he didn't take shortcuts. Darden's NFL career spanned a full decade before he retired in 1981.

Thoughts About Bo

Although Bo was a tremendous motivator, he was by no means, according to Darden, the greatest offensive strategist. Bo had certain plays that he thought would work regardless of the defense. But in life you have to adjust and you have to find a way to adapt, said Thom. For example, in the 1972 Rose Bowl, Bo did not make the proper adjustments. He thought that Michigan could run their dependable plays, and that the offense would always get that necessary yard. He would never consider that if the offense was unable to get that yard by running those plays, something might be wrong with the play calling. He expected to get that yard, period. The coach was stubborn and critical. And indeed, the Wolverines didn't throw the ball very much in the Rose Bowl, and paid the price.

In 1975, Bo called Thom on the phone. "Get your ass out here," the coach ordered. Bo wanted Thom to install the double zone defense for Michigan during his spring practices. The Pittsburgh Steelers of the NFL had been the first team to come up with this first successful defense in defending against the pass. In this alignment, the object was to make the quarterback throw the ball between the linebacker and the cornerback. As a result, it would allow the free safety a great opportunity to make a play on the ball and perhaps make an interception. This zone defense was designed to take away parts of the field, making it more difficult for the quarterback to complete his passes. The purpose was also an attempt to neutralize the efficiency of the quick wide receivers.

During this period, the Big Ten was becoming a more pass-oriented division and moving away from the traditional three yards and a cloud of dust. Bo wanted to get on top of it, so he called in his former player. Thom relished the idea of assisting his former coach and didn't expect to be paid, since he was getting his salary from the Cleveland Browns. He was simply happy to help his Wolverines succeed. Jack Harbaugh was then the backfield coach and continued coaching the cornerbacks. Thom coached the safeties, including Dwight Hicks and Mike Jolly, who both went on to fantastic careers in the pros. He also became good friends with Mel Owens, a linebacker (and later first-round pick of the Los Angeles Rams).

Many years later, Thom visited Ann Arbor in order to see Bo. He had been in contact with his coach regularly over the years, but during this particular visit, Thom did not know that Bo's son had recently been killed in an automobile accident. Bo told him about his son, and then broke down in front of Thom. Feeling his coach's raw emotion, Thom broke down also. In a perfect illustration of their complicated relationship, he admitted that he didn't like Bo, but he loved him.

Over the years, Bo and Thom talked about their wives, their divorces. In doing so they became closer, and as a result their relationship evolved. Whenever Bo called or needed Thom, wherever he was—it could've been Cincinnati, Cleveland, Toledo, or Sandusky—he would go, without question, and be there for him. Thom was there whenever Bo needed him in the recruiting process. Thom loved and excelled at being an ambassador for Michigan football.

And they talked careers, too. Thom remembers once while playing with the Browns, Coach Schembechler called him. The Cleveland head coaching job was available, and Bo wondered whether he might be the right fit. Thom told him simply, "Bo, you don't want this job, not with the Browns." He had four different head coaches during his 10-year playing career with the team. Perhaps it was just the advice Schembechler needed; in any event, he didn't pursue the job.

During the NFL off-seasons, as part of staying in shape, Thom would play basketball at the Jewish Community Center in Cleveland conveniently located near his home. At the Jewish Community Center, Thom played against such Cleveland Cavaliers players as Austin Carr, Campy Russell, and Nate Thurmond. He added that he loves that game. He also told me that growing up in Sandusky, his peers in the neighborhood told him that he wasn't good enough to play basketball. Of course, they said that in order to put him down. However, even the older guys in the neighborhood told him that he wasn't big enough, strong enough, or fast enough.

On another note, Thom wasn't happy that his high school basketball coach didn't promote the basketball players for college. He thought that limiting that opportunity might've been because of a racist attitude. There were lots of good ballplayers who played basketball but didn't have the opportunity that Thom did.

While at Michigan, the players played basketball at Yost Fieldhouse on the dirt floor against their coaches Gary Moeller, Dick Hunter, and Jim Young. Those games would take place after football practice and mostly after spring practice. He thought that playing alongside and against these special group of coaches endeared him to them, and put him on an equal level. In other words, the players could hit the coaches and the coaches could hit the players—legally of course. Some of those games were actually rough. Thom liked it that way. Thom, at various times, thought that if he played professional basketball, he would likely have been less injured. It's certainly a possibility. And his father would say, "It is what it is."

On Mental Toughness

Thom learned that one has to have perseverance, one has to be able to take or withstand the blows, fall down, then get up and take the blows again because they will always keep coming. To him, mental toughness is the ability to continue to push yourself even when pushing yourself may not be the best thing for your body to do. Your mind can fool you, especially if you have a high pain threshold. Mental toughness is also the ability to stand up and deal with defeat.

While playing with the Browns, Thom liked the away games because he got to go out on Saturdays, have fun, and associate on a personal level with his teammates. (Still, he was never able to bond with his professional teammates like he had at Michigan.) When the team stayed in a hotel, Browns management would have policemen on the floor to keep away the women and others from the players. "They thought they were protecting us from all these women. Now ask me, what 20-year-old...guy wants to be protected from women?" he laughed.

Thom admitted that he probably played about two years longer with the Cleveland Browns than he should have because of injuries, and was basically injury-free for maybe only one year. But by his eighth year with the Browns, he was pretty well beat up and his head was not totally into the game. He should have retired. He recalled one NFL coach (he does not remember who) saying to him, "If you play this game, expect to have at least two major-injury surgeries." The coach was right: Thom had one major surgery, but after his career ended, he had another. Yet he said that if he had to do it all over, he wouldn't change anything.

Playing professional football, he was at the top of the mountain. Then, when his career ended, it was a complete turnaround; he became just a regular guy. He believed that in some ways being in the pros for 10 years interfered with his maturity process. Making the transition from being a hero and celebrity to becoming an average guy led to a major identity crisis.

After his release the following June, he still wanted to play. But he was not getting ready for the season the way he had before. He was not compulsively working out and focusing on nothing but football. For the first time in his life in many years, he didn't have a focus. He called it the worst time of his life. For one thing, he was no longer on top of the world, the guy people loved and admired. Back then, he didn't need a reservation to go to a good restaurant.

He took the football star's way of life for granted. "I [hadn't] been a regular guy since age seven, when my picture was in the paper and I had all those interviews… What a shock," he said.

During the off-season while with the Cleveland Browns, Thom had taken a couple classes at John Carroll University to complete his degree in education. At one point, he thought he might become a teacher and a coach, but he had a terrible student-teaching experience. Forget about teaching. So he took an off-season job with the Republic Steel Company. There he learned how steel was made, as well as the characteristics of hot and cold metal. In his second off-season stint with the Republic Steel Company, he learned about negotiations, as well as arbitrations with workers and management. In his third year he worked in sales and learned that there weren't any African Americans selling steel in those days. That apparently did it, and he quit. So much for Thom, the man made of steel.

He got some assistance from Art Modell, who provided him with a list of all the CEOs in Cleveland. When asked by the owner what he wanted to do with the rest of his life, he admitted that he wasn't quite sure. So he went back to school and took some business classes at Cleveland State University.

He then interviewed for a sales position for a radio company. This particular radio station was selling airtime to advertisers during Cleveland Browns game broadcasts. Gil Rosenwald, the station manager, liked Thom and hired him full-time. Gil liked Thom a lot and took him under his wing from 1976 to 1981. During those years, the radio station was looking for content, and Thom's creative side blossomed. He actually set up a mock draft on the radio and incorporated jazz music into their programming. (He admits now that there's a likelihood that he got too involved in marketing and TV and lost his focus, football, during that period. Of course, injuries also had something to do with that.)

During that period, he also got involved in cable TV in east Cleveland. He created a station and sold out to his partners after one year. He remembered a conversation with Bo. "What are you doing buying all those radio stations?" he demanded. "You should be coaching." Thom did not want to put all his time into one thing, and didn't think coaching would work out because of its time demands. He knew all too well the rigid schedule and the amount of time that coaches put in during the season and off-season. He didn't think that would be a good fit for him.

Thom talked about being tied to the community while with the Browns. In the 1970s, football was becoming more and more popular. Players started to take advantage of the aggressive marketing opportunities to promote themselves. The better Thom played, the better he was known, which made him a more valuable asset in the economic community. He was able to capitalize on his notoriety. Thom had a number of local endorsement deals, including car dealerships and other retail establishments. He even owned a clothing store. However, he admitted that the amount of money to be made was nowhere near what it is today.

Back then, the players had an NFL Players Association, but the owners didn't share equally in the entire process. Prior to 1973 or 1974, it was not unheard of for a player representative to get cut from his team; in other words, there was no security in being a player rep—in fact, it could very well mean the end of your job. It took a players' strike to change that craziness. Since Thom was a first-stringer, his teammates asked him to be the player representative. Having some experience with arbitrations, he agreed.

Another example of the power the owners held was that the players had to play seven years to become vested in their pension. It was reduced to four years after the strike, and later became three and a half years.

In essence, the players were property of the club; it was called the Rozelle Rule. At one point, the San Francisco 49ers wanted Thom and were going to trade for him. The Browns, however, decided the amount of compensation, and decided they wanted two of the team's top draft picks for Thom. Unsurprisingly, the trade never materialized. The value of the player was always decided by someone else. Over the years, free agency dramatically changed the landscape of pro player salaries. Still, Thom remains grateful for having the opportunity to play in the NFL in spite of being treated as chattel at times.

According to Thom, an NFL player has only so many good years in which to earn a living in the business of pro football. In college, you have the luxury of playing for the team, the university, the tradition, the alumni, the community, and the joy for yourself and others. Playing professional football, the player plays for the ability to negotiate a new contract. So the pro player generally thinks about security and about the next year's contract above all else. And of course, that can get in the way of things—especially the focus on football.

As a defensive back and free safety, Thom was on the low end of the totem pole when it came to salary. Then as now, the quarterback was paid the most. Thom had an interesting way of dealing with the way things were (lower-paid salaries and endorsements), compared to the way things are today (colossal salaries and endorsements). Cognitively, he has incorporated his father's philosophy: "It is what it is." That quote guides him well and takes away the craziness of the cognitive dissonance in today's sports. As his father said, in so many words, you are given your shot at a certain time and place, so make the best of it.

Life After Football

Thom said that he didn't attend much church while in college, and while with the Cleveland Browns, he went only occasionally during the off-season. He said his focus during that time period was achieving, making money, and dealing with all of the temptations. He was faced with a lot of temptations in college and especially in the pros. He had to find out who he was, and has become much more spiritual today some might say, a very different and mature person.

After football, Thom then got involved in mutual funds and became a securities broker. He took class preparation, studied for a week, and then took the test. The first time he was tested, he missed passing by one point; he then nailed it on the second try. Going back to school and studying made him more disciplined again.

He then set up a management company that was called the Cowen Sports Management Group from 1987 to 1992. As an officer of the company, he visited various colleges and universities and talked to athletes making the transition from college to the pros about managing and protecting their capital.

He realized during the course of owning a business that at times, especially in negotiating, he needed a good lawyer. Although he hired a few lawyers, he quickly realized, as his father told him long ago, "No one else has your agenda." A skillful lawyer could indeed be helpful in contract nego-tiations. Back then, Tom did his own negotiations and thought about law school. Reflecting today, he admitted it was an avenue he should well have pursued.

From 1992 to 1996, he was involved in an insurance business with a number of ex-coaches. The company, Aegeon Securities, was originally set up by Forest Evashevski, former coach at Iowa (1952–60), in Cedar Rapids, Iowa. Coach Evashevski had also played football at the University of Michigan from 1938 to 1940. All of the employees at that time were involved in insurance and securities and had backgrounds in sports. Thom took a position selling insurance and securities to others, such as athletes. Again he visited colleges and talked with prospective athletes about investing in their future.

While with Aegeon, he met and married Melissa, a stockbroker. It was his third marriage. Thom's first marriage had ended in a disaster. Being a celebrity, details of the divorce were all over the media. But he has a son, Todd, from that union. His second marriage also ended in divorce, and he has a daughter from that marriage.

Melissa has two children (Leah, 31, and Matthew, 29) from a previous marriage, and together they have Carrie, who today attends the University of Iowa, and adopted Katelyn. Thom described Melissa as a high achiever and good human being who never says a bad word about anybody.

Melissa was raised Catholic and had their daughter attend a parochial high school, in which 98 percent of the kids went on to college. As one of the few minority students at the school, Carrie (who is biracial) had some difficulty in high school. Some of the kids wanted to touch her hair. Thom got involved and told her it was her responsibility to educate her classmates. "Yes, my hair, my skin, my color is different, but my actions, especially expectations and motivation to achieve, are similar to yours." Having been through it before, Thom knew it was important for her to get that respect.

In 1996, he started the Thomas Vincent Darden Group, Incorporated. He helps small and midsize companies and corporations find capital to purchase or reinvest in their own companies. He works primarily by referral. He is his own boss and has no employees. Of the venture, he said, "Banks do not seem to want to give out money, so there's a way for me to creatively find ways in finding capital for these companies."

On Identity

Thom speaks of one major conflict throughout his life. As a young kid, he didn't spend much time with the African Americans in his neighborhood because of his academic placement in high school and time commitments through team sports. Ultimately he developed friendships with white students in his college prep classes and on the athletic field. He said that sports cuts and runs across racial barriers that allow you to have these friendships. He thought Sandusky High School was perhaps 40 percent black, and the high school football team comprised at least that much.

"There were always race issues in Sandusky," he said. "For example, growing up, the blacks could not even swim in the community swimming pool back there. Furthermore, in the '60s, I didn't necessarily see a black in the center position, middle linebacker position, quarterback position, or in the free safety position. These were the 'thinking positions,' and those players had to call the plays. Even in the pros, in 1972, there were not many black free safeties, with the exception of the Oakland Raiders and the Kansas City Chiefs."

Thom believes that there will likely always be racism in our country. He pointed out that his father didn't like mixing of the races, and that things would not change unless people were forced to change. He remembered, with the Browns, a teammate from LSU in 1972. The player had never seen an African American until he went to college; he was simply from the backwoods in Louisiana and had no contact with them. Thom thinks only education will help break down barriers.

Today, Thom's identity in Cedar Rapids, Iowa, is of a businessman who played football. In his past, he generally talked about football a lot with clients. But as he has matured, he finds himself talking about it less and less. His new friendships are from both business and his Methodist church. But he is still close with the guys from high school and especially his Michigan teammates.

By his own estimation, he should've gone to law school or pursued an MBA; both would have aided him in his business life. For instance, there are a lot of liability issues, and he has to be careful in terms of what he says. He also talked about business forms, spreadsheets, and software programs that give him headaches.

He also spends a lot of time working with and giving to his community and his church, and with his family. He still sees himself as young and likes the fact that his daughter in high school tells him that the kids consider him cool. In fact, on a recent religious retreat with a number of black teenagers, he took them out and ran on the track with them. He knew he should have been in better shape but ran faster than he should have. He paid for it afterward.

With his wife, Melissa, Thom seems more at peace with himself. This warrior has indeed moved beyond the gridiron, and has a full life to show for it.

CHAPTER 8

Superman: Frank Gusich

Back in the late 1960s and early 1970s, cocaptain Frank Gusich was known as the toughest Wolverine on the Michigan football playing field. Bo may have called him "a candy ass" (typical for Bo), but the media and his teammates called Frank "Superman."

On October 23, 1956, Frank's young life changed for the very worst. He was not yet six years old when his mother, Wilma, age 33, returned home after taking her husband, Frank Sr., 35, to a neighboring hospital. Frank and his two sisters, Marilyn and Anita, were happy to see her return. Before they could even ask about their father, Wilma blurted out, "Your father died." Frank began sobbing uncontrollably. He simply had no clue that his father had even been ill, and the terrible news completely shocked him. To add to the tragedy, October 23, 1946, was his parents' 10th wedding anniversary. Furthermore, Wilma was pregnant with her fourth child (who would be named Tony).

For the next 13 years or so, Wilma stayed home and reared her four children. Finances were extremely tight for the Gusich family, who received much-needed Social Security benefits to supplement the family income. The children were not indulged and did not enjoy a lot of luxuries. Even though

Frank grew up without extras, he remembered that his mother always had food on the table. It wasn't until the youngest, Tony, entered high school (the other three siblings were out of the house by then) that Wilma entered the workforce. She remained gainfully employed for the next 20 years.

Although she dated occasionally, Wilma never remarried. She had a very close friend named Joe Gorman, who became a father figure and was a positive influence on the Gusich family. Frank remembered one time when Joe and Wilma went out to dinner and then headed to the dance floor together; his mother loved to dance. Frank liked Joe very much. He felt extremely happy that Joe celebrated Christmases with their family. In fact, years later, Joe and Wilma even attended Frank's games together in Ann Arbor. He became, for all practical purposes, a well-loved stepfather.

In grade school, Frank loved all the sports and played, when he could, football, basketball, and even Little League baseball. In the eighth grade, he wanted to attend St. Ignatius High School. This Jesuit school had a superior academic reputation, as well as a superb sports program. Logistics would be a problem since St. Ignatius was located on the other side of town, maybe 15 to 20 miles from the Gusich home. But first things first—Frank had to get admitted to the outstanding parochial school.

He presented his desire to attend St. Ignatius to his mother, and she thought it was a good idea. She wholeheartedly supported his decision to attend. Frank then applied, only to be rejected. He was distraught. Wilma, being a good parent, encouraged Frank to reapply to St. Ignatius. On her own, she made an appointment to meet with one of the "good fathers" at the prestigious Cleveland parochial school. She pleaded, persisted, persevered, and would not take no for an answer. Simply put, she wanted the very best for her son.

And then it just so happened that one of the teachers at St. Ignatius saw Frank playing basketball for his junior high team. The stars were aligned and Frank was finally accepted. Certainly Frank's athletic prowess had something to do with his acceptance. Not only that, but the school awarded him with a tuition grant. The only hurdle left was how to get from his home to school and back.

With the initial problem solved, Wilma, through networking, drove Frank to one of his schoolmates' homes in the morning. From there, his new friend's father drove both of them to school. After school presented another transportation problem. In order to return home after sports practices, the young man—clad in a shirt and tie and loaded down with schoolbooks—could either take a city bus or hitchhike. (Hitchhiking in Cleveland in the early 1960s was considered safe.) With those options, the transportation issue was easily solved by the highly motivated Gusich.

It was in these early years that Gusich learned about goal-setting, removing barriers, and focusing very early in life. Wilma was strong and a terrific role model. Aside from learning how to study more efficiently, obtaining a B average, and putting in three to four hours of homework a night, Frank played the forward position in basketball in his freshman and sophomore years. As a sophomore and junior, he was a member of the track-and-field team and entered the sprints, including the 100- and 200-yard dash. He was also a member of the half-mile relay team.

In football, Frank played tailback on offense and safety on defense. It wasn't until his junior year that he was promoted to first-string for both positions. He liked being with the offense because he was able to carry the ball. He especially liked the notoriety and glamour of being a running back. He admitted that there was a difference in mentality between playing on the offensive side of the ball versus playing on the defense. Still, Frank would have taken any position; he just wanted to be on the field and play. In his senior year, Frank was elected cocaptain along with teammate Fred DeGrandis. And the St. Ignatius High School team won the city championship, which meant that Frank played on a super team that had a national reputation to boot.

While attending St. Ignatius, Frank attained five demerits during one school year. The punishment for the five demerits was attending St. Ignatius on Saturday. This meant, in his peer group, that he was going to "the jug." The punishment task each Saturday was that each student had to recite a verse of a particular poem of someone else's choosing. If you were able to recite, by heart, the particular verse for that Saturday, you were then allowed to leave.

On the other hand, if Frank misbehaved while at home, Wilma had a very different punishment for him to endure. She simply put uncooked rice on the linoleum floor and he would then have to kneel on it for a certain time period. So during his high school years, the school punished his brain and his mother punished him with physical pain.

The two-way football player from a high school championship team was a hot football prospect. He was recruited by such football notables as Woody Hayes, Lou Holtz, Bob Devaney, Marv Levy, and Lee Corso. But when Don James and Bump Elliott recruited him, it was a different story. Bump was a real gentleman in a first-class sort of way. The coach made a strong impression with both Frank and his mother. Frank chose to attend the University of Michigan because of its academic reputation, Big Ten football team, and the belief that he could make the team, and also because of Bump. His family was very supportive of his decision to attend school in Ann Arbor.

Although Frank's other siblings all attended Ohio State, the entire Gusich family rooted for Frank and Michigan when the two teams played against each other. There was no conflict of loyalty whatsoever. Blood was thicker than water in the Gusich family, which speaks to their closeness.

Playing freshman football in 1968, Frank entered at 6'0" and 190 pounds. Frank was a freshman fullback along with Fritz Seyferth and Therlon Harris. (Harris didn't remain in the football program very long and became a wrestler instead. Of course, Seyferth is another story.)

Frank remembered that Bo Schembechler became his head coach in December 1968. He knew very little about Bo at that time, though he had heard from others that Bo was not at all fun to be around as a head football coach. Then early in January 1969, Frank attended that first team meeting with Bo. It was during that meeting that "Bo's law" was unmistakably communicated very clearly. Especially when Coach Schembechler told his players in no uncertain terms, "Do it my way or take the highway."

First came winter conditioning, which was by far the toughest 19-year-old Frank had ever experienced in his life. He remembered different stations (each had a different physical activity) hosted by the various position coaches. That first station was called slap and stomp. In that particular drill, Frank became quickly mentally spent and exhausted because of the unparalleled physical intensity—and that was only the first station! The second was held at the old Yost Fieldhouse: running drills. Players had to run various distances from 40 yards to 100 yards to quarter-mile and then to a mile.

Then came agility training. In this drill, Frank would run in place, knees high, at a fast pace; then quickly turning to his left, he would continue at a fast clip; then he turned to the center, continuing in a fast pace; and then turned to the right doing the same. But that wasn't all. Frank had to drop to the floor on all fours and then quickly get back up to a standing position. Then, in groups of three, one individual at a time would roll over his prone teammates side to side, over and over again. Another drill was like being at a universal weight machine, Frank said. All in all, it was exhausting, brutal physical work.

Frank remembered running from the intramural building to the Yost Fieldhouse in the wintry conditions, sweating in his workout gear. He said that he couldn't understand how being sweaty, smelly, and running in the snow was good for him. However, these experiences are etched in his brain. And perhaps that's what Schembechler intended all along.

The athletes agreed at the time that Bo was a crazy maniac. And thinking the same thing started to bring them together as one. The coach had no trouble being the bad cop. It was okay that all the players hated him at that point. He knew they would eventually get the picture. On one hand, Frank was thinking, *Lock the coach up and throw away the key.* On the other, his thinking became, *How could any other team be in better shape than our Michigan team? Especially in the fourth quarter of a close or difficult game, because of all the superior or extreme conditioning. The better-conditioned team would win the game.*

Of course it took many difficult and exhausting practices and conditioning sessions before Frank could rationalize a positive from the brutal and sadistic treatment meted out by his coach. Not only that, it took lots of whining, complaining and "poor me" from his teammates (gripe sessions)— out of the coaches' hearing distance, of course. But enduring the physical conditioning and sharing in gripe sessions helped to solidify a band of brothers. No one would argue that these players dreaded practices because they were demanding, demeaning, and appeared mean-spirited both mentally and physically. However, how can you argue with the results, as they created a team-first mentality? Even though no one hears football players saying that they love to practice, these Michigan men today cannot and do not argue its value. They are brothers today and will be brothers until they die. Not only that, but they all love that crazy (like a fox) Bo Schembechler.

Bo's rationalization for all this hard work with the myriad of unusual or sadistic exercises was that he was getting his players into playing shape and taking them to new, unparalleled places that they had never been before in time for spring ball. And when spring ball came, they were ready.

During the spring of his sophomore year, Frank was quickly switched from the offensive side of the ball to the defensive side—without an explanation from his position coach. Even so, he adjusted quite well and played, he thought, above average during the tough spring ball session. Frank just wanted to play; it didn't matter to him whether he played on offense or defense. For him, it was about playing the game that he loved. As a defensive back, Frank had decent speed. However, he compared himself to first-stringer Thom Darden. Darden could and did run faster than Frank. Frank's opinion was that he was perhaps a middle-of-the-road athlete himself. He didn't perceive himself as gifted or athletically fluid. But Frank thought that his main strength was the ability to gut it out. He realized some guys were more fluid or more skilled athletically. So Frank had to make up for or compensate for his physical limitations. He thought he did that by playing more physically and mentally tough. And because of Frank's competitiveness and desire to play, he became both physically and mentally tough—eventually meeting Bo's standards.

Because he and his teammates fought together under adverse conditions, they became very special to each other. (Bo would reinforce the bond when he repeated, "The team, the team, and by the way, the team.") Bo was against individualism. In fact, Bo told the players to check their personal feelings at the door. And even though it was difficult to do, they learned how. The players had to play, compete, and execute as a team. It was the team before anything else. And he told them that their game-day play was based upon how hard they had practiced and/or prepared during the week. If a player practiced poorly, his play would likely be poor during in the game. If a player practiced half-assed, game play would likely be half-assed. Make and correct the mistakes in practice, Coach said, so that mistakes do not occur in the game.

At first, young Frank did not fully understand Schembechler's autocratic way or his teachings. But he wanted to play, so he put up with all of it. Back then, Frank thought that Bo was macho. One quote has remained with him all these years: "Those who stay will be champions." (Of course, the Pru Man—John Prusiecki—added, "Those who quit will be lawyers, doctors, and captains of industry.")

Bo's practices were tough, but they prepared Frank and his teammates both mentally and physically. Even when those Ann Arbor weather conditions changed from warm to rain or cold, Bo would blow the whistle and say, "Okay, men, as the late great Admiral King said to his sailors in the North Atlantic, you have to train in the North Atlantic in order to fight in the North Atlantic," Frank remembered. By the time he was a senior, Frank could recite scores of Bo's clever and inspirational sayings.

Game Days

Frank remembered that one and only 1969 Ohio State game. He also remembered the snowfall during the wintry week. He wondered to himself, *Who is going to shovel the snow off our practice field?* He thought it was probably a job for a player or players to do, but he was sorely mistaken. Looking through the window, sitting in his warm clothes, he saw his own coaches hefting the snow off the practice field. "It was so cool that it was the coaches that shoveled the snow for us players," he said. He liked that message sent by Coach Schembechler and his assistants.

Going into the game, Frank thought that his teammates were confident, and that all of them looked forward to playing in the game, which had significance to everyone. He believed Michigan would be victorious and could topple the mighty Ohio State Buckeyes. He really liked the Wolverines' chances. "Remember that this Ohio State team was a 'team of the century,'" he added. "But you never know what's going to happen once the whistle blows, because that's why the game is played."

As a sophomore, Frank played on special teams and also substituted at times for wolfman Thom Darden. Frank also got into games when Michigan had the lead, which was often. That year, Frank practiced with a cast because he had broken a bone near his wrist. But Frank wasn't allowed to play in games with the cast. So when game time came, trainer Lindsy McLean cut off his cast and padded and taped his arm and hand so that he could enter the games. And then after each game that season, Frank had a new cast made (he decorated each in Maize and Blue colors). Unfortunately, he also broke a thumb in one of his practices because that particular thumb wasn't protected. To this day, Frank still has one of those special, treasured Maize and Blue casts.

Frank remembered professional scouts coming by, watching the brutal scrimmages, and saying to each other, "These guys practice hard." Frank acknowledged that he had to hit hard in practice every day—that was Bo's way. And when Saturday's game came, he and the rest of the team were well prepared. Besides, he acknowledged that he was able to release his frustrations and resentments, and focus on those hard hits, punishing the players on the opposing team.

Leading up to Frank's first Rose Bowl game, in January 1971, the Wolverines practiced in East Los Angeles. Frank was on the practice field as a backup to Darden. During that practice, and on one particular play, the first-string fullback Garvey missed a clean block on Frank, who capitalized and made the tackle. Bo didn't compliment Gusich for making the tackle, but he reamed Garvey for missing his assignment. It was a perfect illustration of how Bo operated. He knew what he wanted and he knew how to deal with each member of his team separately. No doubt, Bo knew to push Frank's buttons. As was typical, Bo spent and focused his time with the offense. And if they missed their blocking assignments, he didn't hesitate to get on his players. But it was out of Bo's character to praise the defense for making a good play. Still, it does not mean that he didn't recognize talent when he saw it.

Jim Young was the defensive coordinator, and from him Frank learned how to perform Psycho-Cybernetics during team meetings. Coach Young had the players close their eyes and visualize the upcoming game, employing different scenarios (such as making a tackle, intercepting a pass, recovering a fumble, etc.) in different situations during the entire game. He was a great cerebral psychologist, and his defensive players were introduced to the art of visualization. Back then, Young also coached linebackers. Gary Moeller coached the defensive ends, Frank Maloney coached the defensive tackles and the middle guards, and Dick Hunter was a defensive backs coach and Frank's position coach.

Hunter was Frank's favorite among them. During Frank's junior and senior years, during his lunch hour, he would actually visit Dick and Marie Hunter's home. He worked as "nanny" to their five kids: Dick, Kathleen, Teresa, Billy, and Mimi. He made their lunch and then returned to campus for his remaining classes. Frank really enjoyed being around Dick's family because it reminded him of home. Frank was not at all happy when he heard that the Hunters divorced. He knew full well what it was like not to have a father. He learned later that they were able to remain good friends.

Frank didn't get to know Bo very well until his junior and senior years. As a sophomore, Frank played second string behind Darden. And during Frank's junior and senior years, he was promoted to first-string wolfman, while Darden was switched to the safety position.

Frank thought that Michigan's defense scheme was similar to the one that Bo used while coaching at Miami of Ohio. With his Miami of Ohio team (they were the politically incorrect Redskins) Schembechler coined the term "the Apache" for what became wolfman at Michigan. Essentially, the wolfman played to the strong side of the offensive formation and/or the wide side of the field, but his defensive assignments were varied depending on the offense's actions. Maybe he covered the tight end, maybe the running back, maybe he covered the middle of the field, or maybe he was in man-to-man formation or he covered the wideout. Also in this position, Frank blitzed the quarterback. He thought the wolfman position was fun and varied, and he really understood that it was important to know the assignments. It was far from simple. At root, he was required to do a lot of reacting to what the offensive players did. Each of the defensive backfield players often attacked on a slight angle, and it was crucial for him to know his own guys' assignments too. (He called it "basically a 5-2-4 defensive slanting scheme.") Frank had a lot of responsibility and had to do his job well.

After his last game at Michigan, he remembered Bo coming by and visiting the players in the locker room. That was something Bo did after every game. Gusich had not been recruited by Bo, who was coaching at Miami of Ohio at the time. After that last game, Frank said, "Bo, I'm from Cleveland, you are from Ohio. Why didn't you recruit me?" Bo replied, "Francis, they needed to fill their quota from Cleveland." Bo laughed and Frank laughed as well. Generally the only time Bo called him Francis was behind closed doors. His teammates called him "Guzer."

* * *

Frank had vivid memories of teammate Cecil Pryor. Frank heard the infamous story of Cecil visiting the coach in the hospital years later, at Mille Schembechler's funeral while standing between Bo and Cecil. According to Cecil, he did not travel back with the team after the Rose Bowl game in 1970. Instead, he stayed in L.A. and went to visit Bo at the hospital. Cecil found scrubs, a mask, a stethoscope, and a clipboard, and snuck into Bo's hospital room. He looked down at Bo, and then the coach opened his eyes. Reflecting on the incident, Bo replied, "I remember that when I first opened my eyes I thought I had died when I saw your face." The three of them smiled and laughed during the otherwise solemn occasion.

Frank remembered hearing rumors about Cecil, who was the team's starting defensive end, executing a prank during their pregame TV introductions before the start of the 1970 Rose Bowl. Frank wanted to find a tape of that Rose Bowl game to present to Bo at the 20-year reunion of the '69 team. He called the Rose Bowl committee, as well as NBC, in an attempt to find the tape of the game. He also called Ken Fouts, a member of his church, who had directed one of the Super Bowls for NBC. He was putting the wheels in motion. Once Ken realized the errand was for Bo, he expended more energy. Frank soon received a call from NBC in New York. Yes, they found a two-inch reel in their archives of that particular game. Although the film was broken in parts, NBC spliced it together and made a videotape for the occasion.

During that reunion, the tape was played—including the pregame player introductions. The players introduced themselves one by one; Jim Mandich... Tom Curtis...Dan Dierdorf... Then it was Pryor's turn. He said, totally straight-faced, "My name is Cecil Pryor, I'm from Corpus Christi, Texas, and my major is nuclear physics." The last part, of course, was totally untrue, but he had everyone in stitches. Cecil then told them that there was more to the story. After the game, Cecil got three letters of job offers: from McDonnell Douglas, Boeing, and NASA. In fact, he showed the letters as proof. He said he also received a round-trip plane ticket, so they could fly him to one of the jobs. However, he cashed in the ticket at the airport instead.

Frank believed that the Michigan success story has a lot to do with his legendary coach. He also believed that "the team" still has great relationships and connections, and that winning likely had something to do with it. The players on the 1969 and 1971 teams have get-togethers every five years in Ann Arbor. The turnout is always terrific, and Frank never had to go long without seeing his friends. One of their more recent reunions before he passed away was for the Michigan–Notre Dame game. He didn't know for sure but wondered if other teams had the same camaraderie that his Wolverines teammates had, whether the other teams bonded and had the same cohesiveness of those Michigan boys who endured the conditioning and tough love of Coach Schembechler.

Frank remembered attending one reunion and watching Bo circulate around the room, talking to former players. Frank said that it didn't seem to matter if the player was a starter, an All-American, or a reserve player; Bo made contact with them all. He *cared*. At the very beginning, Frank thought the guy was crazy and commiserated with some of his teammates. It was only after a while that he realized that Bo was setting the tone. At some point, he understood that Bo was consistent with what he preached, that he followed through with the things that he said. He knew that Bo could be trusted. "He was very tough and hard, but we developed as a team," he said. His Michigan teammates got closer, and they hit their crescendo against Ohio State in 1969.

Frank acknowledged that his fondest memories of Bo were years later, long after playing for him. "I love him," Gusich said. "He made us winners, we came together as a team and we won. All this winning might have had something to do with the closeness we experienced. Bo was hard and he was intimidating. Just ask Dan Dierdorf." Looking back, Frank was always extremely happy to be part of the great Michigan Wolverines tradition.

Family

Frank married his wife, Linda, in November 1972. Linda was born in Detroit, attended the all-girls Dominican High School on the east side of Detroit, and then attended the University of Michigan. Coincidentally, this author grew up on the east side, and their high schools were very close to each other, though he and Frank never met.

After graduation, Coach Schembechler referred Frank to one of his personal friends from Miami of Ohio, Joe Hayden. Joe's father started the Midland Company and then became its president and CEO. This company, by barge, moved things like coal, sand, and limestone on the Mississippi River, all the way to New Orleans. They also moved petroleum, coke, and dense rock from China and sugar to their refineries in New Orleans. The company then broadened their base and then went into consumer loans, including the insurance industry business. Frank lived in Cincinnati and worked for this company from 1972 to 2002, eventually ascending to executive vice president.

Frank and Linda currently reside in New Orleans. They have two children. Mike was born in 1976 and currently resides in Scottsdale, Arizona. Mike attended St. Savior High School in Cincinnati. Although he was recruited by seven of the 11 Big Ten schools, including Ohio State, Penn State, and Michigan State, he was not recruited by Michigan. Instead, Mike enrolled at the University of Illinois and became starting safety on the Illini football team. He went on to earn a master's degree from the Wharton School of Business at Penn.

Brad, the youngest, was born in 1979 and lives in Hermosa Beach, California. Brad attended Penn and played lightweight football (cornerback) there. (Today, this is called "sprint football.") The game is played on the condition (major rule) that no player can weigh more than 165 pounds. Famous sprint footballers include Patriots owner Bob Kraft, Washington Redskins titan George Allen (who coached the sport at Michigan for a time), and even

President Jimmy Carter. Brad went on to the University of Michigan and earned a master's in engineering there.

About 10 years ago, Frank had an appointment with his primary doctor. Frank wondered why he was kept in the waiting room for such a long time before consulting with his physician. Once in the office, the doctor told Frank that he had bad news for him. He had treatable, but not curable, cancer. They would know more information once they consulted with an oncologist the following day.

After leaving Dr. Barry's office, Frank called home; he wanted to tell Linda about his visit. She wasn't there, so he didn't leave a message for her and instead returned to his office. Clearly shaken by the news, he was unable to focus on any task.

On that slow drive home, he thought about different ways to tell his wife his bad news. There just didn't seem to be a good way. He wanted to be as honest with her as he could. Arriving home, Linda was there. They sat and they talked. Even though it was a solemn occasion, Linda had a lot of questions for Frank. She was supportive.

Initially, naïve Frank thought that he would have chemotherapy and then continue working. In fact, after 15 days or so of chemotherapy, Frank returned to the office. That night he awoke with a sore throat and shortness of breath. Frank and Linda immediately went to the hospital. The doctors first started treating Frank for pneumonia but were concerned about his shortness of breath. It turned out to be more serious than pneumonia, and at the age of 53, in 2003, Frank had a quadruple bypass.

Frank also had a bone marrow cancer with a multiple melanoma condition. His cancer finally went into remission in March 2012. During his treatment, he lost about 60 to 65 pounds. After further evaluation of his pneumonia-like symptoms, he was diagnosed with aortic valve difficulty and an aneurysm condition considered north of his heart. Unfortunately, the doctors could not operate on his heart because of his weakened physical condition.

Frank's most recent heart surgery was in May 2013. In order to build himself up for that procedure, Frank calculated that he had walked about 337 miles from January 2013 through the end of April. Frank started out walking slowly at first and then built himself up to be able to walk at a pace of 16 minutes, two seconds per mile. He said that was a great improvement for him; in the summer of 2012 he was only able to walk slowly for about 13 minutes and might've covered maybe a couple tenths of a mile within that time period.

Frank, treated at the Cleveland Clinic, was pleased with his medical care. It helped that his old teammate and cocaptain from St. Ignatius, Fred DeGrandis, was the president and CEO of all the clinic's suburban hospitals. In fact, Fred accompanied Frank to all his doctor appointments there.

Frank realized that he was not in control and had never been more scared in his life. He reconnected with God and believed that God was in control of his being. He told himself that he had to trust God, and that his creator could do whatever he wanted to with him. He said, "If He wants me to be there, I'll be there. If He has other plans for me, then that's okay too." Frank said that he was blessed to be in His hands and the pressure was off because that was just the way it was. Thinking about not having to be in control, just being in God's hands, brought him more peace. He said, "It's like I'm handing off my medical condition, off to my creator, and [must] see what He has in store for me. I know it will work out depending upon His plan."

Reflecting on mental toughness, Frank thought that it had a lot to do with discipline. He said, "It's like developing a game plan and sticking to it. You stick to something, and you don't relinquish your goals." He learned this at a very young age, and then it was ingrained in him by Bo. Bo instructed, if you want to achieve something, you set your sights on it and you don't give up. Frank used the example of his mom who would not take no for an answer in getting him into St. Ignatius. He then quoted a Bible story. In the story, if your neighbor comes to you in the middle of the night looking for food and you see he's persistent, you'd better give it to him, because only then will he go.

Frank said that people have to be clear about the goal-setting. Some people might have to write the goals down. No matter the method, goal definition is important. He said that he didn't necessarily have to write them down on paper, but clarity is important.

He said, "You don't allow the negative circumstances to interfere with meeting your goals, which is mental toughness. Some 40 years later, things are different for me. It wasn't always that way. Now when times get tough, I put myself into God's hands. A lot of this has to do with my incurable cancer. It certainly changed my thinking within the last two years. Because of learning about my incurable cancer, I'm thankful that I have a new relationship with my creator. He gave me a real opportunity and I'm thankful for that. People might think I'm nuts, but that's what happened."

Sadly, the proud warrior for the Maize and Blue passed away in 2014. He will be missed by the entire Michigan family. He was tough to the end.

CHAPTER 9

The Best Athlete: Jim Betts

Jim Betts just might have been the best athlete on the 1969 Michigan Wolverines football team. This is his story.

Jim was born in Memphis, Tennessee, and then his family moved to Flint, Michigan, for about three years. Jim's father, Nathaniel, a carpenter, then moved the family to Cleveland. He also wanted to be near his own father, who was a carpenter in the building industry. Another relative was a foreman in the same industry.

Nathaniel was also an athlete. He played high school football in his home state of Tennessee. Unfortunately, Nathaniel had a drinking problem and was also an alcoholic. Young Jim remembered playing touch football in the street with his friends and his father. His father would yell, scream, and demonstrate how to kick that football a great distance. During one of his famous demonstrations, Nathaniel kicked the ball and made a terrific punt. It was too bad that long punt somehow landed across the street and went right through a neighbor's living room plate-glass window. But his dad was a cool customer. "No problem," the carpenter yelled. He went over and talked to the neighbor, purchased new glass, and immediately fixed that huge broken window.

Playing football and other sports with his father are happy memories for Jim. However, a great many weekends were not as happy, as Nathaniel often took to the bottle. Jim admitted that he grew up in a very unhappy household. He lost his father in 1993. At the age of 63, his father had too much to drink and totaled his car, ramming into a nearby neighbor's house. He died on impact.

Jim was eight when his family moved to Cleveland, and his mother, Anna, was soon diagnosed with MS. By the time Jim was 11 years old, she was bedridden with her illness. She died at the youthful age of 57, in 1985. Jim didn't have what many call the traditional family unit, and he experienced a large void in his life when his mother died. That void was difficult to fill. What made it worse for Jim was that he didn't have a good relationship with his father. On a few occasions, when Anna was able, both she and Nathaniel attended a few of Jim's high school football games. He was happy that she delighted in her son's athletic success.

Jim was born May 18, 1949. In addition to older brother, Gregory, Jim has two younger sisters, Pam and Tanya.

As a second-grader in Flint, Michigan, at St. Matthew's Grade School, Jim had a crush on classmate Wendy Ryan. This precocious boy asked Wendy to marry him. Wendy replied, "I'm too young." To which he responded, "I'll wait." It wouldn't be the last Jim would see of Ms. Ryan.

Jim attended St. Aloysius elementary school in Cleveland, and at about the age of 11 he experienced a rapid growth spurt. While still in elementary school, he was recruited to attend Benedictine High School. At Benedictine, Jim was a member of the student council and earned the all-around athlete, academics, and school achievement award, known as the Mr. Benedictine Trophy. A strong student, Jim also played football, basketball, and baseball. In football, he was a starting quarterback on offense and played safety on defense.

Ohio is well-known as a competitive state for football, and Cleveland, in particular, had a hotly contested football environment. Jim's high school football team was a perennial champion and played the West Senate team for the championship. As a senior, Betts was All-Senate, All-American, All-State, and All-American as a quarterback; he also won awards on defense as safety.

His high school coach was Augie Bossu, who had attended college at and played for the University of Notre Dame. Augie had a good reputation and was recognized as one of the better coaches because he stressed football fundamentals. He coached up to the youthful age of 89. Quite simply, he loved coaching and was able to do it until the end. He died at 91.

Jim thought that Coach Augie was fair and had great character. Prior to Betts, Benedictine had never had a starting black quarterback. Being a devout Catholic, Augie was spiritual; he didn't discriminate on the basis of race, or anything else for that matter. Out of the total student body, there were perhaps 25 to 30 African Americans in the 1,000-student population. In Jim's junior year, maybe five of them were on his football team; as a senior, maybe three.

Jim played baseball and was catcher in his sophomore year, outfielder as a junior, and first baseman as a senior. He could also hit, and served as cleanup hitter. In basketball, he played numerous positions as well. He was a point guard in his sophomore year and played forward as a junior and senior.

The popular, precocious Jim started dating at age 15. All his friends outside of school were black as his family lived in East Senate, a primarily black neighborhood. Despite going to a different school, he still played pickup games—in basketball, baseball, and football—with his black neighborhood buddies.

However, when Benedictine played East Technical High School in football, Jim remembers being called "Uncle Tom." It was the middle guard on defense for East Technical, during their ferociously fought game. On one particular play, quarterback Jim dropped back five steps, released the ball in a screen pass, and then dropped back three more steps to be out of the way of the play. Even though he had gotten rid of the ball, that East Technical guard brutally knocked the hell out of him. Jim got up, looked him straight in the eye, and seethed, "You son of a bitch." Immediately, the ref threw a penalty flag for the unsportsmanlike hit. The team huddled up for the next play, and quarterback Jim called the same screen pass play. Jim then told the center to lightly brush the middle guard with his shoulder and then let him come through cleanly.

Jim took the ball from center and dropped back five steps. He got in a good throwing position and then threw the ball with as much velocity as he could muster, directly at the fiercely charging middle guard. It was released with such great force that it somehow got lodged in the defender's face mask. *Smack*, the middle guard went down to the ground. Jim quickly went over and asked, "How is that for Uncle Tom?" He then looked toward the referee, who smiled; no penalty was called. Jim knew how to get even.

Mental toughness, according to Jim, is comprised of all the things that happen to you in life, within your family and community. These factors help to cultivate and mold an attitude. Jim saw a lot of things from both sides (white and black), so he can appreciate perspective. He would often walk away from a confrontation, but not always. At Benedictine there was a kid who picked on him. Jim finally told him, while in the shower, "You say one more word and I'll knock you out." The bully said something, and Jim stayed true to his word, decking the kid. After that incident, he wasn't bothered by any of the Benedictine kids.

* * *

Lee Corso, the Naval Academy's coach, was a friend of Coach Augie. In fact, he was the only coach that Augie allowed to visit Benedictine during the football season. Augie was smart and didn't allow his high school players to be distracted during the football season, so he did not allow other recruiters to bother his players. Corso visited Benedictine and was interested in Betts and one other player, Larry Salina. (Salina later enrolled at Ohio State.) Jim had considered attending the Naval Academy.

Then, after the football season, Augie presented him with three or four shoe boxes filled with letters from prospective coaches. Jim was overwhelmed—he had no idea how to deal with all of the inquiries. He then began to receive many phone calls and visits from various coaches. He found it all very flattering. Thank goodness Augie was there for him, because he helped Jim sort out the confusion. The coach did that by first asking Jim to consider the following criteria: academics, athletics, distance from home, the quality of the football team, and, finally, the quality of the school. Augie then asked him to rank the variables. That process helped Jim realize that he should attend a Big Ten school.

Even though Augie had played for Notre Dame, he didn't cram it down Jim's throat. But Benedictine's Father Lawrence and another priest thought that Jim would do well and put pressure on Jim to attend Lee Corso's Naval Academy.

Jim learned that Notre Dame sent out letters to the top 13 players in his football community, and he attended a dinner at Notre Dame. There, he had a conversation with line coach John Ray, who told him, "We think you are a great athlete, but we're not going to offer you a scholarship. We perceive you playing as a defensive back. We have a good quarterback coming in, Joe Theismann." Jim didn't get a chance to talk to head coach Ara Parseghian.

Returning home, Jim told his high school coach about his experience at that Notre Dame dinner. Augie replied, "You're not going there, are you?" When Jim told him no, he was certain that it did not upset his coach. In the same conversation, Jim told Augie that he could play quarterback at Miami of Ohio with Bo Schembechler. Jerry Hanlon had been to recruit him. Jim told him he was not impressed with Jerry Hanlon, so Miami was out; furthermore, he had also heard from other players that Bo was crazy. That didn't sound appealing to him.

Gregory is Jim's oldest sibling (by one year) and was a very good football player as well. He played fullback on offense and linebacker on defense. He attended a junior college in Kansas and then transferred to Xavier. Jim was offered a football scholarship (as a defensive back) to attend Purdue, and Gregory would've received one too on the condition that Jim also enrolled there. But Gregory asked Jim if he wanted to enroll at Purdue, and Jim admitted he didn't. "Choose the school you want to attend, and don't worry about me," the older brother said.

Bump Elliott, Jim Mandich, and Don James visited Jim's home in Cleveland. Bump spent more than three hours talking with his mom while Jim spent that time talking with Mandich and Coach James. Jim knew that Mandich was a tight end and thought that he was going to be his receiver at Michigan. Coach James was up-front and told Jim about his competition (Dick Vidmer and Dennis Brown), but assured him that he would have an opportunity to play quarterback.

Growing up in Ohio, Jim didn't follow Michigan until he saw them emerge victorious in the 1965 Rose Bowl. He was only a high school sophomore at the time, but he liked their winged helmets and felt they certainly distinguished them from all the other college teams. The fact that the Wolverines won that prestigious game was important too. There were two other Big Ten teams that were very dominant in the 1960s, and both of them had a number of black athletes: Michigan State and Ohio State. Jim didn't want to go to Ohio State because he did not like their helmets. Instead, he accepted the scholarship and enrolled at the University of Michigan.

At Michigan

Jim's freshman football team played two games. Don Moorhead, Bill Berutti, and high school All-American Jerry Perkins were the other freshman quarterbacks recruited. Jim started the first half against Toledo as quarterback, and in the second game, against Bowling Green, he played the whole game as a defensive back.

During that freshman year in 1967, his teammate Paul Staroba, a wide receiver and punter, came up to Jim and said, "I understand you asked my girlfriend to marry you." Then a very cute Wendy—all grown up—came up and said, "Sorry I didn't wait, but I'm glad to see you." *Boy, is she cute,* Jim thought. *Paul's lucky.* As it turned out, Paul and Wendy got married and had five daughters.

After the football season, in January 1968 Jim tore his meniscus. The injury affected his play in spring ball, and he was the fifth-string quarterback on the depth chart. Very quickly, about a week and a half into spring practice, Jim moved up to third-string quarterback. Then running back Ron Johnson got injured and the athletic, versatile Jim was switched to tailback. Although Jim had average speed for a running back, he had great agility.

Jim started the first game of that 1968 season at halfback against the University of California, a game Michigan lost 21–7. Johnson came back from his injury after the loss, and Jim was demoted to second string. The second game of that season was a road game against Duke University. The running backs coach, position coach Tony Mason, told Jim that he wasn't going to travel with the team for the Duke game. He was dumbfounded. Instead, Coach Mason explained that he was going to take Lanny Scheffler, who had rehabilitated from an earlier injury. Not known for mincing words, Jim replied, "I can run better than Lanny, I do more tricks than Lanny, and if I got to the 5-yard line and fell over, I would get the five yards." Tony Mason was not impressed with the player's reaction and said, "Take it like a man." *Take what like a man?* Jim thought.

Jim knew that Mason had recruited Lanny, but he was still angry. He immediately called his mother and told her that he was quitting the team. She replied in no uncertain terms, "You keep your butt there." Then David Farabee, a wide receiver, broke his arm. George Mans, the receivers coach, came up to Jim and asked, "You want to play offense?" Jim replied, "Hell yes!" He then played as a wide receiver and in that position brought in the offensive plays for quarterback Dennis Brown.

In 1969 Jim's junior year, Bo Schembechler had become his head coach. Jim certainly knew about the coach's reputation. Indeed, the other players called him "a son of a bitch." In those days, there were pockets of favoritism because of the alumni influence on their recruits. They wanted their recruits to play, simple as that—and their influence, at times, determined who played. But Coach Schembechler erased all that from the outset when he said at that first meeting, "I am going to treat you all the same: I'm going to treat you like dogs." The new coach was aware that he had depth at every position, but he didn't know how good the individual players were. As Jim could attest, Bo pushed his players hard. Back then, the offensive quarterback, running back, wide receiver, defensive back Jim was about 6'5" and 200 pounds.

During spring ball, Jim was well aware that he had to work on his quarterbacking fundamentals, especially the option play, which was one of Bo's favorites. Don Moorhead was clearly the first-string quarterback. Bo told him, "You are Michigan's best quarterback behind Moorhead and Rex Kern." (Rex Kern was Ohio State's quarterback.) Jim knew his place on the depth chart.

In 1969, Jim's on-again, off-again girlfriend got pregnant, and they married just before the start of the football season. In July, Jim and his new bride returned to Cleveland to live with her family. As a result, he didn't receive correspondence regarding workouts, reporting back to school, or team meetings. Jim left Cleveland on a Sunday and returned to the Ann Arbor campus. Before doing so, he stopped in Toledo on the way to visit an alumnus who recruited him. Jim mentioned that he wasn't sure just when he had to report back to school for his football commitment.

Arriving in Ann Arbor, he bumped into Coach Jerry Hanlon at about 8:00 that evening. Hanlon told Jim that Bo was mad as hell, that he didn't know whether or not Jim was even returning to school. He said, "You should've been at that meeting at 4:00!" So Jim immediately called Bo, but his wife, Millie, answered and told him the coach wasn't there. Hanlon instructed him to be at the track early the next morning around 6:00 AM to run the infamous mile. The players were all expected to be able to run a mile in about five and a half minutes. Before Jim left school for the summer, Jim had run a 5:25 mile. He purposely didn't run his best since he was well aware that he had to run faster than his spring mark when he returned to school after the summer. Bo, not pleased with Jim, greeted him with a sarcastic remark. "I know you're out of shape. You ran off and got married," he said. (Notice Bo didn't say congratulations or good for you.)

Jim ran the mile with Jerry Dutcher and Mike Hankwitz, among some others. He stayed in the middle of the pack for the first two laps, and both times when he passed Bo standing on the sideline, the coach yelled out to him, "I knew you were out of shape!" Then, during the third lap, Jim took off, with blazing speed, and quickly distanced himself from the rest of the pack. Jim came in third behind Jerry and Mike. They ran a 4:35 mile. While closing the gap, Jim almost caught them and ran a 4:42 mile. Jim ran toward Bo and asked him, "Does it look like I'm out of shape?" Bo replied, "You come every morning and run a mile." How's that for positive reinforcement?

Jim had worked on his conditioning in Cleveland that summer. He knew how to condition himself and in doing so ran on the sand on the shores of Lake Erie with his other athletic friends. The group would run the miles on hard sand, and then do sprints on the soft sand. They would run 40 x 40 yards, 10 x 100 yards, and 5 x 200 yards in the morning. For their second workout of the day, in the afternoon, the well-conditioned athletes would do their passing drills in the sand. Little wonder he got in such good shape.

During that memorable 1969 season, Jim remembered seeing 50–14, the previous year's score against OSU. He said it seemed to be everywhere. "We didn't know at the time, but the coaches both on offense and defense were putting in at least one play every week in preparation for that Ohio State game," he said. Just prior to that game, Jim, who was rooming with Don Moorhead, received a visit from Coach Schembechler. He was talking to Don about the upcoming game being his greatest game. He then turned to Jim and said, "You better have your ass ready in case something happens."

Jim remembered that going into the University of Michigan tunnel to play Ohio State, a fight broke out between the two squads—the tunnel was not nearly wide enough to accommodate both of the fierce rivals. He thought maybe Cecil Pryor started it, but Jim got in a few swings before it ended. He added that, "If Cecil started that fight, that meant he was ready."

At the end of that 1969 season, Jim had talked to position coach Dick Hunter about switching positions (from quarterback to the defensive back-field). Jim wanted to play and knew that first-stringers Tom Curtis and Barry Pierson were graduating. And that left only sophomore Thom Darden in that backfield. Coach Hunter said that the switch would be fine with him. Jim immediately looked for Coach Schembechler to tell him of his plans. Jim, in no uncertain terms, directly told Bo, "I want to play safety. I do not want to sit on the bench behind Moorhead because he's your quarterback." Bo replied to Jim, "You son of a bitch, *I'm* going to tell *you* what you're going to do. You're going to play both positions. You're going to play first-string on defense and second-string quarterback." Bo had to get in the last word regardless of the situation, whether he was right or wrong. Looking back, some of it seemed very funny—but, of course, at the time it was not.

Jim's final football game as a Wolverine was held in his home state of Ohio. Coach Schembechler said to Jim, "Are you ready for this game?" "I have been ready for this game for two years," Jim replied.

Was he ever. In front of his hometown fans and friends, Jim made 14 tackles and intercepted a pass to set up a Michigan score. Jim also received the

Meyer Morton Trophy (for showing the greatest development as a result of the annual spring practice). After the season, he was selected to play on defense in the annual Blue-Gray All-Star Game in Birmingham, Alabama.

Jim and Bo

Jim knew from Bo's players at Miami of Ohio that he was crazy; they were glad he was leaving. Of course, at the time, Jim didn't know that Bo was preparing his players for life after football. But once Schembechler took the reins at Michigan, it became clear that he wanted his tough boys to be strong-minded in the face of all of the difficult situations that life presented. And if they could make it through his extremely difficult practices, they'd be ready to become leaders in their families and in the community.

Jim believed that not only did he have a good relationship with his coach, but that his coach liked him as well. Jim visited him in his office, and they would have conversations about many things, including religion and alcoholism. Since Bo's first wife was an alcoholic and Jim's father was an alcoholic, Jim felt that Bo not only related to him, but also understood the difficulties in living with an alcoholic.

Jim wasn't afraid to talk directly to or bullshit with his coach. During the team's first winter conditioning program with Bo, the coach said, "Men, if you expect to play like a team, you have to look like a team. I want everyone to look the same. I don't want to see a mustache, long sideburns, Afros, or facial hair." The very next day, the athletic Jim visited Bo in his office and said, "I cannot shave my mustache as a black man. I can't shave because it's akin to our culture. Being black, this is part of me." Bo responded, "Is this a joke?" Jim told him, "I'll go through walls for you, but you can't deny who we are as people." The coach then threw Jim out of his office, saying, "This is happy horse shit."

Every five years or so, Bo Schembechler asked Jim about this facial hair "heritage" thing. He wanted to know whether or not Jim had been telling the truth. After about 30 years, Jim finally came clean and admitted he was bullshitting his coach. As if a dam had burst, Bo said, "I knew it!" and mumbled a number of unintelligible words. The coach finally knew he'd been had.

During one spring practice, it was a brutally cold day in Michigan. Quarterback Jim, behind center, fumbled the snap. Bo leaped to the occasion, came up, and kicked Jim, yelling, "Son of a bitch, don't drop the damn ball again!" He was still fuming when he said, "Run the damn play." But Jim refused. Then teammate Reggie McKenzie yelled out "Rope Man" (Jim's nickname). Jim was still mad and embarrassed, but he ran the play—albeit only going through the motions.

The very next day, a proud Jim went into Bo's office, looked him in the eye, and said, "Bo, no one's going to be harder on me than myself. And if God wanted a foot up my ass, I would've been born with a foot up my ass. I don't want you ever to do that to me again." Jim quickly turned around and left his coach's office.

In the very next practice, but not on purpose, Jim fumbled the ball under center. This time Bo asked Jim in a softer voice, "Would you run the play again?" Jim believed that his hard-ass coach respected him. "Of course I had talent," Jim admitted, "and I really wasn't ever in Bo's doghouse like others. That didn't mean that he didn't get mad at me."

When Jim was a senior, his teammate John Pighee asked if he could borrow his car so he could take his girlfriend to the airport. Jim replied, "No, because you'll never make it on time for our Sunday team meeting." Jim figured out a new plan. He would drive them both to the airport and then bring John back to the meeting. So the three of them headed for the Detroit Metropolitan Airport, dropped off the girlfriend, and returned to Ann Arbor. As it turned out, Jim was right the first time—they were five minutes late to the team meeting. Coach Schembechler was very angry; no one came late to meetings. Jim said right off the bat, "Bo, this is my fault. I picked up John a few minutes late. We drove his friend to the airport." Perhaps Jim's willingness to take responsibility ingratiated him to his coach.

After every game, the players were graded on their play. After the game with the University of Minnesota, Bo met with the players. Players were graded on how they lined up, tackled, got themselves in the right place at the right time, and understood the defensive formations. Jim had an interception in that game too. He earned a 100 percent and the defensive game award. The coach turned his back once he realized that it was for Jim and muttered, "Son of a bitch." Jim replied, "Thank you."

Jim said that because of his personal relationship with Coach Schembechler, he wanted to do the best for himself and for the team. Some guys would cuss out the verbally aggressive coach behind his back. Yet Jim knew that Bo wanted senior leadership and he wanted to cultivate his relationship with the older team players. Generally, it was the younger guys who thought that Bo was a tyrant. "So as team leaders, we explained to them why he was doing all the crazy stuff," he said.

Betts remembered that Jim Brandstatter was blamed for missing a block on a punt in practice, and it turned out it was Dick Caldarazzo's miscue instead. Jim's teammates certainly remembered that boondoggle made by the coach. It seemed to them that Jerry Hanlon was the only one who could control the "crazy like a fox" Bo. Jerry had been with Bo for an inordinate amount of time, and Jerry loved him. It seemed that Jerry got fired maybe 30 times over the years. But he understood Bo's rants and ravings. And in the coaches' meetings, Jerry would tell Bo to back off and Bo would reply "You're fired."

Jerry is good people, and Jim has a great relationship with this position coach to this day. It solidified when they went on a recruiting trip to Cleveland. Coach Hanlon and Jim were recruiting Eric Penick, a running back from a private school. Jim and his old coach had dinner with the boy and his mother. Jerry asked Jim, "Would you like coffee?" Jim replied back, "I don't drink coffee. It makes you black." After their dinner, Jerry, confused, said, "Why did you do that in front of Eric and his mom?" "I told Jerry, 'He's not coming to Michigan.'" As it turned out, Eric attended Notre Dame.

Racism

Early in Jim's life, he received advice from his mother about racism. His mother said, "Don't judge everyone by one individual, and don't judge the entire race by one individual." Jim took her advice and learned as a youngster to "defuse the racism stuff," he said. He mentioned that when he first went out for football at Benedictine, he took a low profile in order to put people at ease. He didn't want to be viewed as a threat. He said if stuff was taboo then he would talk about it in a fun way. But if someone said something wrong, he called him on it (though he admitted that he probably didn't do that enough).

Jim's grandmother had Cherokee blood in her background and his great grandfather had French blood in his. Jim's grandmother advised him to treat racism like the weather: "It's how you dress for it." Attitudes, as well as the language, have changed over the years. And personally, Jim has viewed and experienced the changes as he assimilated through society. Perhaps that meant acting more like a white person at times. Looking back, Jim said he had a few biological advantages, including lighter skin color, the absence of kinky hair, smaller lips, and a smaller nose more than likely from his Native American heritage. Other advantages for him included attending a Catholic school, where he learned how to integrate into the white community while still keeping a foot in the black community. Going to a parochial school, he saw the focus on education, while in the black community, it was more about partying.

Jim admitted he wanted to play baseball in addition to football at the University of Michigan. Teammates Thom Darden and Bo Rather were All-State in baseball in high school, while Jim was All-League. The three of them talked about going out for the team and went to their head football coach to talk to him about it. Schembechler said, "Go talk to Moby Benedict." Benedict was the baseball coach. He questioned the three football players: "Did you guys play in a summer league?" No. "You guys are all starters in football. I don't think you want to ride the bench in baseball. Playing here, you would be riding the bench." The players replied, "We could start on your team. We would make your team better," but he did not let them play. After Jim graduated, he came back to Michigan as an academic advisor and found out that Coach Benedict didn't want more than one African American on the team at one time.

Years later, when Jim was an academic advisor at the University of Michigan, he knew that there was an NCAA rule that every sport had to schedule an open tryout. He admitted that most students probably weren't aware of the rule because such things were not necessarily publicized. But Jim knew. So he found Benedict and told him that he had to have open baseball tryouts because of the NCAA rule, and to put out a flyer to announce the open tryouts. For his revenge, Jim went around recruiting every black kid on the campus that he could for the tryout. He said he rounded up about 30 black kids (one had a mitt that looked older than Methuselah's). The rascal's purpose was to get back at Moby and screw up his day, but there was one kid who had talent.

About 15 years ago, Jim and his wife, Marti (who is white), were in Chicago. They were walking together when a car drove by and someone yelled out the window, "Nigger lover!" It seems racism will always be a specter in Jim's life. The Bettses currently live in Milan, Michigan, and have two children, Evan and Eric. Early on, they went to the school and talked with the teachers and the principal regarding potential racism toward their biracial children. The teachers and the principal both assured the Betts' that they didn't think there would be a problem for the kids, and happily, they were right. Perhaps times are changing after all.

I asked Jim about how he dealt with this anger, and he cleverly said, "I play golf and I hit that white golf ball." Additionally, being an academic advisor helped him work out a lot of his frustration by helping black athletes with their issues.

Jim believes that sport was a great conduit for fitting in. It even elevated your status. Having a career outside of athletics was more difficult. Jim kicked himself for not going to graduate school and obtaining a master's degree in counseling.

Jim and Marti

Marti and Jim first met in Naperville, Illinois, a suburb of Chicago. At the time, Jim was playing golf at this country club with one of his former Michigan teammates; Marti was employed at the bar. Jim purchased a hot dog and a Coke and attempted to get a date with her, even though they were both in a relationship at the time. This went on for a while, and Jim continued to strike out. Then a few years later, they finally got a drink together.

Marti is one of nine children who come from an athletic family. An All-American basketball player for Notre Dame, her father, Leo, was also on Notre Dame's All-Century team. He also played professional basketball for the Fort Wayne Pistons. Her mother, Nancy, played golf. Additionally, a few of her brothers played basketball, and another was an expert in martial arts.

After dating for a while, Jim had met a few of her siblings, but not yet her parents. Her brother Kevin told Jim that he might have a hard time being accepted in the family. Kevin thought that his father, Leo, would likely have a hard time with him because he was black. Leo was indeed upset when he found out Jim's race, and Jim sent him a letter regarding his intentions. He first figured that Leo's wife, Nancy, wouldn't go against her husband. As it turned out, Leo carried that letter with him quite a while before he told his wife about it. Leo suggested that Nancy invite Jim to a Christmas Eve family celebration. At that family gathering, Jim and Leo talked for two and a half to three hours while the family members periodically checked in to see what was happening. At that Christmas Eve celebration, the family even had a Christmas present for Jim. Jim told Leo of his plans to marry Marti in Las Vegas and asked Leo for his permission. Leo began crying and told Jim that he was the only one ever to ask for his permission to marry one of his daughters. Jim also told Leo that he did not want Marti to have a hard time with her family.

After Michigan

Jim was drafted by the New York Jets in the 10th round of the 1971 NFL Draft and signed a contract to play backup quarterback and safety. Before reporting to camp, Jim was rehabilitating from ankle surgery (an injury suffered in the Blue and Gray game) and was student teaching at Scarlett Junior High in Ann Arbor. There was a tradition at the junior high that the student teacher would be thrown into the swimming pool by the students at the end of the school year. So a great number of students started to drag Jim toward the pool. Unfortunately, Jim had a whistle around his neck, and one of the students' hands got stuck on the lanyard. While Jim was going into the water, that metal whistle got pulled out, striking him in his left eye.

Jim was taken to the emergency room and the doctor thought he might lose his eye completely, but he was unable to perform any exploratory surgery because of all the swelling. They decided to wait until the swelling subsided.

On a return visit to the ophthalmologist, Jim had a scar on his retina, resulting in a loss of central vision. He has a black spot when using his left eye, and lost 70 percent of vision in the eye. Although he was compensated—a half a day of a regular teacher's pay—his case set a precedent for rights of student teachers. That was a good thing to come out of a bad situation. Jim is sanguine about it today, saying, "No matter how good you are, you can lose it in the blink of an eye—no pun intended."

Jim notified the Jets about his freak accident. With one good eye, and out of shape because of his ankle injury, Jim reported to camp 30 pounds overweight. Even though the ophthalmologist told him not to exercise because it would likely impact his injury, Jim replied, "I can't see anyway." The Jets had one drill in which he would have his back to the coach. The coach would yell as the ball was thrown in Jim's direction. He was supposed to turn and catch the ball, but he could not see it and the ball hit him in the head. If Jim had initially turned around on his right foot, he might've been able to compensate by relying on his right eye to catch the ball. But by turning to his left, he was unable to see the ball because of the blind spot.

Jim thought the Jets training camp left a lot to be desired. In order to get in the running shape and lose weight, he ran after practices. The Jets cut him and he was called to the Minnesota Vikings training camp. The Vikings picked him up, he thought, as a stand-in until another player got healthy. Jim believed that if the Vikings had let him go earlier, he would have been the starting safety for the Hamilton Tiger-Cats of the Canadian Football League (they needed one American player to fill their roster spot). Jim had spent time with the Tiger-Cats, as well. After that football season, he returned to Ann Arbor to complete his degree. He had an opportunity to go back to the Tiger-Cats for the next season, but his heart was not in it. With that, his football career ended. Instead, he stayed in Ann Arbor and took a position as an academic advisor.

As an academic advisor, he performed counseling and tutoring at the University of Michigan until 1979, when he moved to Boston to work for the General Discount Corporation. This company financed big (and expensive) equipment like oil rigs. Jim moved to their field office in Chicago in

1981. (However, when there was a problem with the oil glut on the market, their business took a hit and they closed the office.) In 1988 he took a job with the Washington International Insurance Company as an agent in Chicago, then moved to Milan, Michigan. He later returned to Ann Arbor and was employed by ex–Michigan football player Don Coleman in his multiethnic advertising agency. A few years later, he was approached by Tom Monaghan from Domino's Pizza about targeting his product to a special group. In order to pinpoint the culture and to close the account and get the job, Jim told the true story about when his grandfather purchased insurance from Washington National Insurance in 1929. His grandfather paid weekly premiums until his wife died in 1976. Jim's grandfather told him that at the time, there were only two insurance companies that insured African Americans. Tom told his grandfather that he could get a better deal, but he refused, saying, "No, I'm sticking with this company." His loyalty made a big impression on Jim over the years.

Jim also worked with nonprofit communities in schools, bringing in outside businesses in order for the students to receive work experience as well. He worked with youth, teachers, and businesspeople during the summer. Through his efforts, he was able to change the content of what the school taught. He calls this "project-based learning." While he was involved with the public schools, six new high schools opened and featured co-teaching in courses such as geometry and art, along with computer training.

Jim applied for an academic counseling position at the University of Michigan, but the head of the search team told him they were looking for a PhD to run the program. Jim found out that he needed at least a master's degree in order to interview for an academic counseling position; the same was true for similar positions at Wayne State University and Eastern Michigan University.

While Jim was involved in student tutoring and academic counseling at the University of Michigan, the student-athlete graduation rate improved from 50 percent to 85 percent across the student body. He accomplished all this with a handful of tutors, teachers, and a study table. He cultivated relationships with the dean of students to facilitate his program. In the past, when he played football, it was the coach who asked the professor to give the kids a break. Jim changed all that.

Currently, Jim is involved in a mentoring program with Clay Miller and is considering starting up a program to help athletes with their career transitions after football.

Health-wise, the 6'5", 225-pound Jim underwent a posterior spinal decompression procedure on December 3, 2013, and began professional rehabilitation in March 2014. By all accounts, the ironman is recovering just fine.

CHAPTER 10

Keller 90: Mike Keller

I n 1968, Mike Keller a 6'4", 200-pound Catholic Central High School senior from Grand Rapids, Michigan, with both football and basketball honors, questioned why the University of Michigan's Bump Elliott offered him a football scholarship.

Keller knew that football competition in Grand Rapids was at best on a fourth-tier level. Ahead of him were the Lansing-area high schools and the Bay City–Midland schools. And the cream of the crop, in his day, were the high school football players from the Detroit area. What's more, he also knew that Tom Hoskins, Michigan's High School Player of the Year, was planning on attending U of M. He figured that he could expect a whole lot of big-time competition with the Wolverines. Was he good enough to perform on the big stage? Perhaps he could at least make the traveling squad before graduating.

Michigan head coach Bump Elliott was a football All-American, and his Wolverines had been victorious in the Rose Bowl. Both Michigan and Bump Elliott had superb reputations. In any event, he would be close to home.

Yet even though the insecure young man, one of eight siblings, from little Grand Rapids started out sixth-string on Bill Dowd's University of Michigan freshman football team, Keller became a three-year starter (1969–71), achieved All–Big Ten and third-team All-American honors in 1971, was selected to play in the annual College All-Star Game in Chicago against the world-champion Dallas Cowboys, and was the 64th pick in the 1972 NFL Draft by the Cowboys. He was also voted as a member of the All-Time Michigan football team (modern era). How did he get there?

This is the Michael Francis Keller story. Mike was born on December 13, 1949, in Chicago, Illinois, to Dorothy and Lee Keller. Dorothy was born in 1919 and initially married Jack, a pilot, during World War II. Tragically, the very year they were married, his B-17 bomber was shot down over Germany, and he and his crew were killed. Jack never got a chance to see his son, Jack Jr. Dorothy married Lee Keller in 1947. Lee, also a veteran of World War II, was a marine who fought in Guadalcanal and on other islands in the Pacific. Incidentally, prior to the war, Jack Sr., Lee, and Dorothy were all friends in their home state of Illinois.

Dorothy then gave birth to Lee Jr., and Mike followed shortly thereafter. He was followed by Jim, Patty, Mary, Tom, and, last but not least, Billy. With all those mouths to feed, Lee, a former college football lineman, was away from home a lot, earning a living to support his family. And Dorothy, very religious, spiritual, and educated, ran the Keller household like the marines at Camp Pendleton.

Michael's father, Francis Lee Keller, is an even-keel guy. It seems that nothing bothers him. He worked hard and had a materials-handling company (forklifts, hand trucks, etc.), which had him out of the home maybe two or three days a week making calls. Lee is still alive, and Mike remains very close to him.

One of Mike's earliest memories is at age four, when he challenged his mother to a foot race. Although the distance was not long, at least by adult standards, Dorothy didn't allow Mike to win. She told him, "Race me again when you are faster. I will give you another chance." With that, the earliest seeds of competitiveness were planted.

While attending St. Stephen Elementary, seven-year-old Mike was selected to take part in a basketball exhibition during the halftime of a middle school basketball game played by junior high–aged kids. The kids would perform both dribbling and shooting drills. In addition to the exhibition, Mike scored the winning basket in a brief 4–2 game. The importance of this event was not lost on Dorothy as she sewed the No. 8 on Mike's playing jersey.

On another occasion, one Sunday morning after attending morning Mass, he accompanied his Pee Wee football team to play a "game" at Tiger Stadium during the halftime of a Detroit Lions football game. Having a fan base, parental support, hearing the cheers of an enthusiastic crowd came early to him—and he relished it.

Mike competed with his older brothers, and for him it was always a competition. In fact, at times, Mike got so mad at himself that he would tear up. Even though brother Jack, at 14, was seven years older than him, Mike would still compete with him, even at games like golf. He certainly liked playing cards with his older brother and went at it with him furiously. They played gin rummy, and also war, using at least three decks of playing cards. For Mike it was a battle to dominate and to win at all times.

As an adolescent, Mike was extremely large for his age, having undergone a series of growth spurts. He learned about competitiveness, being active, and developed an early love for all sports. Additional parental support and positive reinforcement for his achievements became apparent, and the Keller home became the gathering place for all the different-aged kids in their well-to-do neighborhood. Mike's father even built and installed a basketball net on the garage so that Mike and the kids could shoot hoops on the Kellers' lighted court. And even after his father turned off the outdoor lights for the night, Mike would still be out there, shooting that ball. After all, it was perfect practice, he rationalized—"like being blindfolded. Just think what I could accomplish when I could actually see the basket."

Mike learned responsibility when his parents allowed him, at the age of eight, to deliver the *Detroit Free Press* each morning. In order to pick up the papers, even when there were snowy conditions, Mike would have to get up around 4:00 to 4:30 AM, ride his Schwinn bicycle to the warehouse, and deliver all of the newspapers along his route. By the time he returned at about 6:30 AM, he had pedaled four miles. And then he had to attend church, since he was an altar boy for Mass. He kept his paper route until age 15. And then he resigned from being an altar boy. His mother said something to the effect of, "Of all the things you did, you are giving up on the Lord." The quick-witted Mike replied, "I'm just resigning. I am not giving up on the Lord."

Mike generally bought all of his sports equipment from the earnings he made on his route, or at other jobs. However, if he was short moneywise, his father would become the banker and lend him the money on the one impor-tant condition: that he be paid back in full. Mike didn't have to pay interest on the money borrowed, but he could not welch on the business arrangement. He learned very early on that if he wanted something bad enough, he would have to pay for it.

It might've been in the seventh or eighth grade that Mike wanted his parents to buy him a powder blue sports coat—probably to impress a girl. His parents said no, so he bought it himself. Mike even purchased his own set of golf clubs.

Mike learned to be active and productive at an early age. He thanked his mother for that. She would say such things to him as, "You're not making the best use of your time; you're capable of so much more." His mother was relentless in keeping the kids working all the time. "She'd give us a job like using a toothbrush to clean the woodwork or sweeping the streets or cutting the grass even if was done yesterday, and she would even have us sweep our neighbor's porch," he said.

By the time Mike reached junior high, he had really grown. He was disal-lowed from playing competitive football because of his size and weight. (As an eighth-grader, he was about six feet tall and weighed about 160 pounds.) The football coach allowed him to practice with the team, and placed him on defense against the first-team offense. Mike indicated that even though he was bigger than everybody else, he did not attempt to hurt them. He did admit that he made most if not all of the tackles.

The importance of academics was stressed to him as well. Dorothy expected him to do well in school. She kept on him, and he indeed performed well. One of the reasons why Mike attended parochial school was because of the importance and value of education stressed by his mother. Although Mike was a good student, he laughed when recounting these stories. His second-grade teacher, Sister Rosalie, was perhaps 5'4", and young Mike was 5'6". He had just seen the movie *Juvenile Delinquents* with Jerry Lewis. In the film, a number of juvenile punks are questioned by the police, and sit chewing gum, shuffling their feet, and shoving their hands deep in their pockets. A disobedient Michael Francis did something wrong in class, and the Sister asked him to stand up out of his seat. Sister Rosalie approached him and started to discipline him verbally. Michael Francis responded by doing his best movie invitation of the punks. All of a sudden, little Sister Rosalie smacked him with her famous roundhouse right hand across his punk face. He was stunned, stood up at attention, and never messed with her again. With that, he quickly learned one important lesson: don't mess with the nuns.

While in high school, Mike was in a class with another nun who shall go unnamed. The high-strung nun walked around the classroom closing all the wooden classroom windows, but as she closed each one, one of the students quickly and quietly opened it again behind her back an attempt to drive her nuts. Although well-known as a prankster, Michael Francis would not take credit for being the window opener. In the same class, on another occasion, a classmate threw BBs onto the floor, making all kinds of noise. That episode did it—the delicate nun ran out of the room in horror.

Mike's mother was a smart and talented academic. She received her PhD and was a professor of English literature at Aquinas College near Grand Rapids. She was relentless on dictation, usage, and even had him diagramming sentences. She would have him read Dickens' *A Tale of Two Cities*, Melville's *Moby-Dick*, the Hardy Boys mysteries, and other classics. Mike even joked about reading *Beowulf* as a kid. Yet education and mastery of the classics were no laughing matters in the Keller household. Dorothy challenged everyone in the family to do and be at their best and said, "Whatever you do, do it well." She was a great role model.

Whenever Dorothy was angry or when Mike was in trouble with her, she called him Michael Francis. To get even with her, Mike called his mom Bucky up until the end. One of Mike's—or Michael Francis'—favorite stories involves driving his mother bonkers. The Kellers had a gigantic dining table for their family of 10. His mom would start cooking early in the afternoon, and then all of them would come to the table. However, "the drill sergeant" (his mother) had a rule: no one—and that meant no one—could touch a utensil or hand to any morsel of food until she, the drill sergeant, took the first bite. Mike and his siblings were a band of carnivores, waiting to pounce on their food—but this hungry pack had to wait. After she took that first bite, it was pandemonium as the kids started devouring the food with glee. And following that explosion, it wasn't too long before she would have to leave the table because she began hyperventilating. At some point after she got her breath back, she returned to the table and completed her dinner. Wanting to solve this problem, she visited her family physician, who suggested that she breathe into a paper bag when needed. That was all the wild bunch needed, as they would call out, "She's in the bag again." This bunch was sadistic.

Dorothy attended the 6:30 Mass each morning because, according to her, "All you kids would go to hell otherwise." She said things like, "An idle mind is the devil's playground." The Keller home was spotless, since the drill sergeant kept her kids occupied with chores seemingly nonstop. Mike figured out very early on that if he got involved in enough sports, he would be spared from some of the chores.

Once her kids were reared, Dorothy went back to school to get a PhD in English literature. Mike thought his mother was out of her mind to read old stuff like that, but she became an expert in archaic English. She also played tennis, golf, and bridge at the country club. It seemed there was never enough time in the day for her.

The precocious Mike learned to play the trumpet. Another of the Keller family rules was that each member of the family had to play a musical instrument for at least three years. But after three years, when they had their foundation, they could continue to play or give it up. Mike acknowledged that he couldn't impersonate Louis Armstrong, so he discontinued his trumpet play.

At the time Mike began secondary school, Catholic Central High school was the only Catholic parochial school in Grand Rapids. Back then, Grand Rapids was a melting pot. Mike lived in the wealthier part of town, with primarily Irish and German descendants. The other part of town was considered poorer and was made up of primarily of Polish and Romanian immigrants.

As a sophomore, Mike was a varsity starter in football, playing tight end and wide receiver on offense and middle linebacker on defense. Unfortunately, the team was not very good (1–9–1). After that season, the coach was fired and a new football head coach from Central Michigan by the name of Jerry Sieracki was hired. Coach Jerry was selected to change the mind-set of this losing team (losing was indeed uncharacteristic of the Catholic Central football tradition). He did so that very next year. In Mike's junior year, he made second-team All-City on offense and the team went 6–4.

Mike made it a point in his senior year to become All-City and All-State. (He did make All-City and earned honorable mention in All-State selections). During that season, he essentially played the entire game. He started on offense, defense, and served as the punter on special teams. Mike relished all the playing time. His team compiled a 7–2–1 record, and tied for the city championship with two other public schools.

It hadn't been until Michael's senior year, when he started to receive letters of interest from colleges, that he began to consider playing college football. Mike wasn't too knowledgeable about the recruiting process. Did they contact his coach, or did his coach contact them? In fact, he didn't even have a discussion with his coach about playing college ball. He received letters of interest from colleges in the Big East and from Colorado as well as from Catholic colleges and some Ivy League schools. He also received interest from Bill Doolittle, Western Michigan's football coach. As the letters rolled in, his thinking began to change. *Maybe I can play.* Of course, a high grade-point average, good ACT scores, and positive input from the academic-minded nuns at Catholic Central all helped too.

In the end, maybe 30 or so universities recruited him. Likely because two of his former high school teammates, Mike Kadish and Clarence Ellis, were playing for the Irish, the nuns also wanted him to attend Notre Dame. Mike's father was even willing to pay for his school expenses there. Coach Ara Parseghian told Mike that he didn't have a scholarship for him at the moment, but that he was sure that he would have one for him If he attended. Mike was also recruited to play basketball at William and Mary, Davidson College, and a handful of others.

Even though Mike was a "rock star" in little Grand Rapids, he still had his doubts about how he'd rate on a national stage. Little Grand Rapids was better known for its basketball competition. Mike made All-City in basketball, and thought it was his better sport. He considered himself as a bruiser, fast on defense, a skilled rebounder, excellent at steals, a hard worker who could score 14 or 15 points a game. Indeed, Mike's basketball coach would often say, "Give the ball to Mike and he'll make the play." And of course, his team won the city championship in basketball. They even had their own version of the March Madness, and his Catholic Central team averaged 43 points per game. However, he thought that his height was a limiting factor, and he was not a terrific ball handler. As far as college competition, he saw himself becoming a role player or the sixth or seventh man on the team.

The popular teenager committed to the University of Michigan in large part because he perceived himself as a student first and a football player second. He also didn't want his father to pay for his college education. (However, he did accept a car from his generous and proud father while at Michigan.) At the time, Michigan's football program was floundering. But it had a superb reputation as far as academics were concerned. He thought he'd get solid education and earn a degree that would place him in a good position for the rest of his life—and he would be close to home to boot. He thought that he might even attend law school and become an attorney.

As far as football was concerned, he also liked the idea of the possibility of going to the Rose Bowl. The nuns at Catholic Central clearly felt it was Notre Dame and told him, "The highest call on your way to heaven would be God's favorable opinion, if you went to Notre Dame." Mike didn't have a response then, but today he would say to them, "If Jesus was on earth today, he would have been smart and gone to Michigan."

Bo

Some of the first words that came out of Bo's mouth during that first team meeting in early January were: "Your reputation is that you are good athletes, but you are a bunch of pussies." That remark, one of many, made a lasting impression on Mike Keller.

It was during spring practice that Mike, Jim Brandstatter, Fred Grambeau, Tom Hoskins, and other sophomores were sitting, in full uniform, on the grass just before drills. They were complaining about how hard it was playing for Bo. It just wasn't worth it. They were all going to quit the team and give up their scholarships. Just think about what they could do with all of the free time they would then have. Of course, they had to figure out exactly how they would explain their decision to their parents.

Then out of the blue there was a loud, screeching whistle. Each player quickly scrambled for his helmet, stood up, and got into a running stance. They ran quickly across the grass, sprinted swiftly across the railroad tracks, past the locker room, past Crisler Fieldhouse, and in a flash arrived at the stadium practice field. It might have been all talk, but those grief sessions helped solidify and bond the men for life.

The first game of that 1969 season was against Vanderbilt. Schembechler had weeded out a lot of those Michigan football players during the course of his demanding spring practices. In fact, out of 130 players, only 70 or so were left by that first game. Against the Commodores, Keller played well. Depending upon the defensive alignment, Mike played either as an end or as a linebacker. His terrific speed, quickness, and control had a lot to do with his success. Also, playing on the short side of the field with Thom Darden helped too. Additionally, All-American Mike Taylor also played behind Keller.

During that first season, there was a tremendous level of commitment, going full speed, and physical contact in practice. Mike had to do his job and he had to know what his teammates were doing as well. The coaches expected a lot from him. Defense position coach Gary Moeller would joke, "Well hell, Keller, you can't get out of your own way."

Keller had long hair in 1969, as was the style of the day, but Bo didn't like it. He often said, "Keller you'd be a hell of a player if you could only cut your hair." The quick-witted Mike replied, "Baldness runs in my family. My father has it, my grandfather has it, and all my brothers are bald. I'm going to be bald in a few years, so I'm keeping it as long as I can." The coach looked at him, dumbfounded, and just walked away scratching his head. Mike's humor disarmed the tough Schembechler.

In that first year, the Wolverines lost to the Missouri Tigers. Bo was mad as hell and said that the players didn't pass the test. "You should be embarrassed. Goddamn son of a bitch, bunch of pussies. You didn't work hard enough," the coach fumed. Then he continued his tantrum by breaking chairs, blackboards, or anything else in his way. He also referred to this team as being "a bunch of country clubbers." To him, football was war, and it wasn't for weaklings. "You don't quit, and you don't take a day off," he'd say. Another favorite expression was, "Don't let the door hit your ass on your way out."

According to Mike, the team's day off was on Saturdays during game time, when they would play against some of the weaker kids and kick the crap out of them. One of Bo's strategies was to tell his players that they were going against the greatest athletes, "they were better than us, and don't worry about their poor record since they were better than their record shows. So we quickly learned not to take any game for granted," Keller remembered.

Coach Schembechler loved to insult his players. And of course, the bigger the insult, the more respect the target received from his teammates. But Bo was not without a humorous side. During one practice, the coach was all over the field. He put his best players on defense, and during those years the defense would always beat up on the offense. Bo said, "If the other team can't score, they can't win." On one particular play, a pass play, both the wide receiver and cornerback went for the ball that was thrown to the sideline. Unfortunately, the coach ended up in the middle of the collision as the ball arrived. Bo went down to the ground with a thud. Some wondered, *Did we kill the coach?* Then Bo leaped to his feet and said, "That would've killed an ordinary man."

Bo knew how to deal with people. He paid close attention to details and one could learn a lot by just watching him. And Bo Schembechler made Mike tougher. He expected a lot, and Mike had faith in him. Mike learned that he could not let his teammates down by blowing or not knowing an assignment, not going all-out during practice or in a game, or arriving late to a team meeting. He also learned how to deal with his many aches and pains. He had to work hard since there was always somebody in the wings ready to take his place.

Sure, Bo used salty language. He was a unique dude, and he was certainly uncompromising. For him it was all about hard work, and it certainly paid off. Players may have disliked it as it was happening, but every last one of them appreciated it in retrospect. It took longer for some than others, but in the end they all got it.

Bo's philosophy on defense was simple. In Bo's words, "How do you know that the running back is not going to break a tackle? I want all 11 of you going to the ball at a proper angle for a gang tackle." The idea was to eliminate a quick score by the offense because psychologically that might turn the tide and change the score for the game. The coaches assessed those players who never quit and who never took a day or a play off.

Some questioned why the Schembechler teams didn't do well in the Rose Bowl. Mike thought it was because of the lack of intensity, lack of focus and the weak motivation. The Ohio State game was circled on the calendar as one of the more significant goals. The winner of that game likely won the Big Ten championship as well. For the team to go to the Rose Bowl, that was simply a reward. Not only that, but going out to sunny Southern California, the team had unusual distractions like Disneyland and all the good-looking girls. These distractions made it more difficult to focus on that game, and as a result, Michigan never played their best. In fact, both times they lost close games, by close scores, in upsets.

* * *

Mike talked about his position on defense, covering the offense's tight end. He said that he would either chuck the player at the shoulder pad or head to disrupt or control the line of scrimmage. Then he would look to tackle the quarterback or running back. Whenever Michael felt physical pressure or resistance by the tight end, he knew instinctively that the offense was running the ball. Conversely, if he didn't feel the physical pressure from that tight end, then he knew it was a pass play and adjusted accordingly.

On running plays, after dealing with the tight end, he then looked for a confrontation with the fullback coming to block him. If the fullback didn't come after him, then he would look down the line of scrimmage for that offensive guard (who invariably weighed at least 50 pounds more than him) advancing to knock Mike on his butt. Being in a stationary position was to Mike's disadvantage, because he had to make sure, if possible, only to give that guard one of his shoulders to hit as opposed to both of them. If the large offensive guard made contact with both of Keller's shoulders, he would not only succeed in knocking Mike flat on his ass, but would open a hole for the running back. Keller could not let that happen—that was his job, and his job alone.

While playing for Schembechler, each player was graded from 1 to 100 on their performance in each particular game. Attaining a score of 80 was considered about average, and a low score of 70 was below average and not acceptable at all. In fact, if the player scored 70 or lower, he was more than likely demoted.

If a player was graded at a high level, he then earned the right to be in the Victors Club. On top of that, the player was permitted to wear a special jersey during that week of practice. Keller said he received a lot of ratings of 90+ for his game performance. In terms of the grading system, Mike didn't have to make a tackle or intercept a pass, but he had to do his job within the scope of the defense called. He acknowledged that playing on the weak side might have made it easier to receive a higher score, since he had less territory to cover. Michael received Victors Club honors in 38 out of 40 games, at that point a Wolverines record. Additionally, the player who received the most Victor Club jerseys received a trophy at the end of the year—Michael had three of them.

The defense may have had soft-spoken coaches, but the players actually were, at least on the field, a bunch of crazies. He thought that playing defense gave him a different mentality. Off the field, he considers himself a cream puff.

As a sophomore, Mike weighed about 192 pounds and was the fastest sprinter among all the other tight ends and linebackers. Gary Moeller was Mike's position coach—Mike thought of him more as an older brother since Gary was only 28 at the time. He said Gary had passion, enthusiasm, and a love for his players. He coached the defensive ends and linebackers and became a good mentor to the entire squad; all of them loved him. Though a stickler on details, Moeller was also very animated, and his players had fun during their practices. Many times Coach Moeller turned practices into fun games. At times, Mike would be laughing and having fun while his other teammates were miserable. Mike acknowledged that his rapport with Moeller made him play even more enthusiastically.

There were a total of seven or eight defensive ends on the team. Phil Seymour, Paul's cousin, was a starter and was All–Big Ten. When they moved Phil to the other side of the line, Mike was fortunate enough to take his position. One of the other defensive ends, backup Don Easton, wound up marrying Don Canham's daughter. Clint Spearman was a backup to Phil Seymour.

Mike lined up on the short side of the field. The wolfman and the other defensive end lined up on the wide side. But according to Mike, Michigan's strength was really on the short side of the field, even though they had one less player. (Don't forget that the sideline or the out-of-bounds marker was like having an extra player.)

During their grueling practices, the first-team defense often played against the second- or third-team offense. Sometimes Mike had one-on-ones with offensive guard Reggie McKenzie. And he knew from very personal experience that Reggie was tougher than nails. The two tight ends that Mike faced were Paul Seymour and Jim Mandich. Mandich was also a fraternity brother. McKenzie and Mandich were by far the toughest guys Mike faced during Michigan's practices—and maybe the toughest he ever faced on the field of play.

Sometimes in practice, the reserves practiced like they were All-Americans themselves. Mike talked them out of going full speed because if they continued, he promised them that he would have to knock them out. (Of course, he didn't say any of this within earshot of the coaches.) After all, he didn't want to beat himself up with the second- or third-stringers before Saturday's game. But because of Bo's regimen, Mike thought of game day as his day off—it was a break from the exhausting practices under Bo.

Mike came to the conclusion that because the players worked so hard in practice, they might as well win the game. They were the best-prepared. They slaughtered teams like Iowa and Illinois in part because the Michigan players were so much more talented. Mike gave credit to all of his teammates for their success, but especially those who didn't get to play in the game. Those players were tough, because they got beat up like punching bags every day in practice. (Mike's younger brother Tom was a walk-on at the University of Michigan. One of those aforementioned "punching bags," he received an award for sticking it out during all the practices.) Those guys, according to Mike, were mentally tough without a doubt. They didn't complain and accepted their roles.

Mike assumed leadership positions, but not on the football field. The team captains were Frank Gusich, Jim Mandich, and Guy Murdoch—and they were more serious, buttoned-down types. Mike remembered making jokes, chasing girls, and going to the bars. His group didn't hang out with the captains all that much. But he was still a positive role model for them on the field. And hell, Mike believed that Bo liked him even with his long hair.

During Mike's junior year, he was approached by his former coach Bump Elliott, who was then assistant athletic director under Don Canham. Bump asked Mike to run for the Board of Control of Intercollegiate Athletics. To this day, Mike remains in the dark as to why Bump approached him. The board consisted of Don Canham, the athletic director; regents at the University of Michigan; and influential financial backers, maybe 10 in all. Mike got elected and served the two-year term. While on the board, Mike went around the state of Michigan promoting Michigan football to the various booster groups. He talked about the status of the football team and learned to overcome his fear of public speaking when he realized he was good at it. In fact, he knew more about the subject than anyone else. He called his two-year stint "the rubber chicken circuit" (named, of course, for all those quasi-edible banquet dinners).

It was at that time that Mike became cognizant of the enormous business of big-time athletics. He learned about all the policies, who was hired, and who was fired within all the sports. He found out that the Michigan athletic complex was huge, as well as powerful. It was an eye-opening experience, the politics and the wheeling and dealing, and it served him quite well throughout his career. He found out that people, their agendas, and their personalities do not always work for the common cause. Navigating through the maze of the big business of sports is no small task.

Mike had first met Bump as a high school recruit. Like the others, both of his parents loved Bump because he was soft-spoken, a real gentleman, good-looking, and extremely humble. On top of that, Bump was very articulate in telling the Michigan story. He spoke from personal experience because he could—he went through it all, from being a student to an athlete to a head coach. The Kellers also knew that he was a fierce competitor. And Mike's mother was really impressed with Bump's communication skills.

While at Michigan, Mike learned just how great Bump was in terms of Michigan's history. He also met his brother, Pete Elliott. Pete's son Bruce, a quarterback, was also recruited to play for the Wolverines. Mike felt close to Bump and remembered his lifelong interactions with him. Bump would often check in on him: "How is your class going? How are you doing?" And even at reunions many years later Bump would ask about his kids, Michigan football, Mike's teammates, and even about the NFL. Mike thought of Bump as a favorite uncle and considered himself part of the Elliott family.

Mike also got to know Don Canham, the athletic director who had been an All-American in track at the University of Michigan. According to Mike, Don was a marketing genius who also supplied sportswear for Michigan athletics. He was a successful businessman and was great at generating revenue. He simply revolutionized the business of college athletics and maximized the business side of sports. In fact, many other colleges followed his lead. He also transformed the alumni association, cultivating big donors. Under Don, Michigan Stadium sold out. He marketed jerseys, and had price differentials in the Stadium, charging more money to the alumni groups. He became and was the pioneer. And for it, he was loved and hated. Michigan athletics had long been a giant operation; Don made it big business.

Canham also mentored Keller in the business aspect of collegiate athletics. Mike said he became a sponge and took it all in. And this early experience in the business of big-time football became his model and set the stage for things to come. He could begin to think big.

Still an excellent student while at Michigan, Mike was in the honor societies in both his junior and senior years, with the Sphinx and the Druids. One snowy, wintry night about 30 men from the society came to his dorm. Their mission was to drag him out of bed, pull him into the driveway, and then hose him down with cold water while sprinkling brick dust all over him. This procedure was called being tapped, and it was the society's initiation rite. But when the gang arrived, the clever, wide-awake Mike got out of bed quickly, speedily got dressed, and snuck out, heading for his trusty Plymouth Valiant. As he was quietly and slowly backing out of the driveway, one of the members of the society grabbed the car's passenger door. The door swung open and the hanging man was going to collide with the nearby tree. Fortunately, he jumped out of the way as the door caught the tree with a loud crunch. "Too bad," the fraternity members shouted as Mike sped away. Incidentally, Mike became president of both honor societies later on.

Academics came easy for the fun-loving party boy Keller, and he graduated (a bachelor's degree in general studies, college of literature, science, and the arts). In particular, he loved history, political science, psychology, and sociology. He studied somewhat but didn't hit the books very hard. One can argue that he actually majored in networking.

Mike took a few history classes from Dr. Rickenback. The doctor had a grading key that might've looked like this: A for athletes, B for boys, and C for coeds. It was a history of Europe class, and Mike remembers liking it because it actually was about drinking good wine at spectacular restaurants throughout Europe. He enjoyed a speech class with teammate Jim Brandstatter, in which Mike delivered a speech on the Bantam Rooster of Alabama politics: George Wallace.

Socially, Mike identified with that movie classic *Animal House* ("I could've been either Otter or Boone"). In his fraternity, all the class papers went into their archives. That allowed any fraternity brother to use them if necessary. Of course, the jocks, according to Mike, took the path of least resistance at times. After all, playing sports was a full-time job—about eight hours a day during the school year. So in order to remain academically eligible, the players got creative in writing papers, taking tests, etc. Nowadays, the universities keep statistics on graduation rates, thereby keeping an eye on their coaches as one component of the evaluation process.

Make no mistake about it, Mike took advantage of having a good time. This music lover has varied tastes, but his favorite song is "The Victors." The Michigan fight song defines his life and his thoughts. It's even the ring tone on his cell phone.

During Mike's summer and winter vacations, as a freshman, he worked in the furniture factories in Grand Rapids. Then he worked for an interstate trucking company. He put in a full workday and toiled in the heat, loading and unloading trucks. (One time there was this six-to-eight-ton piece of metal that was leaning against the wall. The forklift operator somehow lost control of this piece of heavy metal and it proceeded through the floor of the truck while Mike was in it. Luckily, he jumped and managed to land on top of it. If he had missed he would have been seriously injured or killed.) After putting in a full day's work at the trucking company, Mike then worked out for a couple of hours, doing a lot of running. Indeed, his quickness and endurance were two of his major football strengths.

After his sophomore year, Mike stayed and worked in Ann Arbor. He had a great job as a security guard at the Willow Run Nova plant. The workers at the Chevy plant adopted Mike and the other teammates who worked at the plant. The full-time workers at the plant advised him not to get involved in the various employee fights. Because he was well-liked, they wanted to protect him from possibly getting accidentally knifed, hurt, or killed. They were also protecting the Michigan team and its success. Though a precarious work environment, the job was simple: he had a specified circuit route and his one job was to put a key in a lockbox, which resulted in meeting insurance requirements. He was a salaried union worker and made approximately $5,000 per month—big-time money for a young kid.

Mike Keller loved his University of Michigan playing days. He treasured his time there, and it still resonates today. He currently attends more college football than pro games. He loves this game. It permeates his life because of his unique experiences in football and his current involvement in putting together the FLA (Football League of America). Mike continues going back to Ann Arbor for family reunions, and attending games every year. However, Keller is not ready to hang up his cleats because he realized that he doesn't do well in the retirement mode.

The Game

"My Wolverines started slow during [1969] and then we began beating teams like Iowa [and] Illinois…by huge margins. We were methodically destroying these teams as we became a juggernaut of a team toward the end of the season," Mike remembered. Michigan was coming on strong. He added that his brother Jack in Manhattan Beach, California, was listening to the game outside on the street, and was quickly joined by his friends and neighbors. According to Jack, the street was abuzz and cheering for the underdog, the Maize and Blue.

Then, on November 22, 1969, "the 10-Year War" between Bo and Woody began. On that day, the mighty (undefeated in 22 straight games, favored by 17 points, ranked No. 1 in the country) Scarlet and Gray traveled to Ann Arbor to play the Wolverines in front of a stadium-record 103,588 screaming football zealots. It was the first meeting between the two coaches, and it would be a doozy.

The game was televised on ABC and announced by alumnus Bill Flemming, with Lee Grosscup providing the color commentary. During that historic season, the Buckeyes scored at least 34 points a game and only had one team (Michigan State) score 21 points against them. (The Spartans still fell 54–21.) Many in the media had anointed OSU the greatest college football team of all time. The Buckeyes were unbeatable, they said.

Some of OSU's stars included quarterback Rex Kern; running backs Larry Zelina, Jim Otis, and John Brockington; wide receivers Jan White and Bruce Jankowski; middle guard Jim Stillwagon; and defensive phenom Jack Tatum. Mike remembered seeing a cartoon in the *Detroit Free Press* (that same paper he delivered as a kid) of Woody Hayes driving a steamroller, accompanied by Kern, Otis, Tatum, and others, rolling over a flattened U of M football team.

Michael discussed his goals for that game. "I wanted to be a team player, and in order to win, it was my job to follow the game plan," he said, betraying none of the significance he and his Wolverines put on the matchup. The defensive game plan was designed to stop OSU's off-tackle running game, eliminate mistakes, contain big plays with pressure, so they couldn't get to run to the outside. Mike's job in a passing situation was either to rush the quarterback or drop back in the passing lane to look for a possible swing pass. The players he expected to battle most often were Jim Otis, Rex Kern, and Jan White—all leading lights on the team. But Mike had confidence. If he did his job, and played according to the game plan, his team would likely be in a good position to win the game. It's easy to forget, too, that in all the breathlessness about that OSU team, that Michigan was itself a solid team that year. Indeed, Mike was surrounded by good players. And his Maize and Blue team was ranked maybe second in the nation, with a particularly stifling defense that didn't give up many points to opponents themselves.

Michael said that he was spent both physically and emotionally in the big game. He only became aware of the degree of his exhaustion on the last play of the game, when his legs buckled. He was fearful that the crowd of joyous students were going to trample him as they rushed on to the field in celebration; instead, they lifted him and carried him halfway up the tunnel and out of harm's way as a security guard let them all pass. He was thankful that his elixir, adrenaline, helped him focus long enough to make it through the game.

Becoming a Pro

In 1972, there was no NFL combine like there is today. Mike knew he came from a good college team but hadn't had any face-to-face contact with pro scouts or coaches. He thought his stock had risen, but he wasn't totally sure; only the results of the draft would tell. Far from the media circus it is today, there was a two-day, untelevised draft for the 26 professional teams. Most of the players, including Mike, stayed at home while it transpired. At that time, he was rooming with Paul Seymour, Fred Grambau, and Dick Lindenfeld, and he could have passed the hours with his fraternity brothers, but he admitted that he was nervous and likely not very good company. There was nothing he could do but wait for that phone call.

Leading up to the draft, he had received letters and/or questionnaires from the Los Angeles Rams, New England Patriots, Miami Dolphins, and Dallas Cowboys, and from limited information he had the sense that the Cowboys seemed most interested. In fact, Gil Brandt (vice president of player personnel for Dallas) met Mike at the Metropolitan Airport in Detroit—though Mike did not remember much of that meeting. Still, Keller had a real affinity for the Cowboys because George Andrie, a former Catholic Central High School player, was playing with the Cowboys.

Keller thought he was going to be drafted, but it was not a foregone conclusion. Yes, his teammates and coaches had high expectations for him. In fact, some of his teammates were drafted in the first and second rounds. (All in all, 18 Wolverines teammates were drafted.) Yet it's hard not to let doubt creep in as the hours pass. After all, some skills from college didn't necessarily translate to the NFL.

Keller was drafted by the world-champion Cowboys as the 64th player taken overall. He was ecstatic that the pressure was off, and called friends and family to share the good news. In May, he traveled for a rookie weekend meeting with the Cowboys. There he met with the position coach and trainers, who gave him some idea of what to expect. Meanwhile, he had been selected to play in the Chicago Tribune College All-Star Game against his future teammates, the Cowboys, in July 1972. He had learned that none of the pro teams could have more than three rookies on the squad, and he was one of three rookies from the Cowboys selected to play in the game; he took that as a good sign, as well as a source of motivation.

It was a busy time. A week prior to the game, Mike and his wife, Kathie, married. The fact that he had All-American honors, was the 64th pick overall in the draft, and was selected to play in the All-Star Game somewhat helped his fragile confidence. For one thing, the Cowboys had three All-Star linebackers in Chuck Howley, Dave Edwards, and Lee Roy Jordan. The experienced veterans knew how to play in what was called Dallas' Doomsday Defense. And since the pro teams had a 40-man roster limit in those days, the Cowboys carried only five linebackers. That left little room for Keller, rookie standout or not.

To make matters worse, Mike sat next to the All-Pro and original Doomsday Defense member George Andrie one day at breakfast. Mike said to him, "I'm glad you guys didn't thrash us in that All-Star Game." George replied, matter-of-factly, "We hadn't prepared much for that All-Star Game and we won easily." It was yet another cognitive dissonance, and it completely took the wind out of Mike's sails.

Afterward, Keller thought that perhaps if he had been drafted by a lesser team, or if he had not been selected to play in the college All-Star Game, he would have had more practice and playing time with his NFL teammates. Being selected to play in that All-Star Game was prestigious, but it stalled his development of the skills he needed for that special Cowboys defense.

As a rookie, feelings of insecurity again surfaced. *These guys are good,* Mike told himself. *How can I make first string? Is this really what I want to do? How long am I going to be here? I do not like being a backup. It's not much fun.* Indeed, Mike hadn't played backup for quite a long time and had gotten used to center stage.

In high school and in college, Mike dominated. He was one of the best, if not the best, player at his position. But suddenly that wasn't the case. Chuck Howley, Lee Roy Jordan, and Dave Edwards were better linebackers, and the Cowboys defense was the best in the league. Maybe he could make the team, but it was unlikely that he could supplant the veterans to make first string. He thought he was physically better, stronger, faster, had good coaching fundamentals, and was smart, but because of the complicated professional defense, he was not able to pick up all the specialized nuances with the Dallas Cowboys. He realized that he had to be on the field, playing, in order to learn the defense. He also quickly learned that in order to supplant or replace a starter, he had to be significantly better. Coaches, he found out, were generally reluctant to make changes. He became well aware that you don't graduate from the pros; instead, a player reaches the ceiling and then goes home for good.

Although he recently married, his honeymoon consisted of five days in Montréal before reporting straight to the All-Star training camp, then the Cowboys camp and the 1972 football season. Adjusting to the world of professional football was very difficult for Kathie, too. Mike knew she was terribly unhappy with their situation. She would've preferred him returning to Michigan and working for her father.

Mike started over again in Dallas—but this time he had to play opposite Mike Ditka, the Cowboys tight end, in practices. He knew that the teams rarely cut a third-round pick, and he worked pretty hard thinking he'd make the team but was unsure.

As a new rookie, he once sang "Dixie" with a Southern drawl in front of this veteran team. To his surprise, "Bullet" Bob Hayes rushed over to him and said, "You son of a bitch—you're either stupid or you're purposely insulting the black guys." Of course, Mike pleaded ignorance—he wasn't thinking about the deeper implications at all—and apologized to the veteran, but he was worried about his place in the team culture.

Aside from being on the bomb squad and not making first string, his first year with the Cowboys was relatively uneventful. For Mike, being a professional lacked all of the structure of college. He was out of his comfort zone; the Cowboys expected him to be responsible for himself. During the off-season, he was scouting and he did what was necessary, including running and weightlifting. He later realized that he should've done more and wanted it more. Mike did not make the necessary adjustments to become a professional football player. There were too many distractions for him, and they got in his way.

That first year, players seemed friendly at training camp and appeared to welcome him. Kathie got pregnant and told him, "Your job is to make me happy." It was a rocky start to a professional football career. Looking back, he realized that getting married at that time and taking her away from her family was a large mistake. He had trouble focusing totally on the team because of these demands. It was very difficult to replace starters, and it was a tremendous adjustment for him, something his wife couldn't understand or fully support. Mike believes he did the best job he could under those circumstances. He made the best team in the league, got more money, was part of the playoff team, but was only a backup on a good team.

During that season, he got to know Walt Garrison, the former Oklahoma State fullback. He held his own against the runner in practices in addition to dealing with offensive guard Blaine Nye. Mike said, "If you are able to hold your own at least 50/50 or more, when playing, then more than likely you earned their respect." It's important to win these confrontations and to win incrementally. A mistake might be mere inches. The goal was to get that edge over your opponent. As a rookie, Mike felt good while scrimmaging if he won about half of those battles. On a good practice day, when Mike did better than 50/50, that was a huge positive statement. As a pro, it takes time to win those battles because the veterans have experience on their side.

In that shaky first season, Mike started saving—beginning with $20,000 from his first signing. He was thinking of the future because he had a wife to support, and he had learned valuable lessons about financial responsibility from his parents. Added to which, he didn't know at that time if the NFL was going to be a long-term deal for him. He learned quickly about the realities of the NFL. On average, a player's career spanned just three and a half years. He had conversations with his agent, Chicago attorney John Denison, who also represented his friend Tom Stusic. The attorney's philosophy was that there were no guarantees with the contract; the only way you'd make it each year was by being on the team. That essentially meant that there was a week-to-week money guarantee. Mike trusted him and started preparing, knowing that his NFL career might not last long. Meanwhile, he started looking else-where. He saw working in the front office as a great opportunity, a stepping stone to a different future.

To Keller's surprise, he had an opportunity to work in the 10–4 Cowboys' front office during his first off-season, in 1972. It was great summer employ-ment income, but it also got him thinking about life after a playing career. However, it might not have helped his standing as a young player with the Cowboys. In fact, the front-office work resulted in him becoming a scout sooner rather than later.

In his second season, 1973, Mike positioned himself to take over Dave Edwards' outside linebacker slot because of his superb play. Then in maybe the third or fourth game of the preseason, Mike suffered a shoulder injury that required surgery. Actually, it was nothing new; Mike's shoulder issues started at the University of Michigan and just got worse in the pros. He had a rehabilitation period of six to eight weeks. While in rehab, Mike spent lots of time in the training room, working out with weights. Mike had a detailed rehabilitation program designed by the strength-and-conditioning coach. It started with him squeezing a ball and then progressing to lifting weights. The program was designed to strengthen muscle and tendons of the surgically repaired shoulder as well as build the muscles situated around the injury.

It was the first time that he really committed himself to bodybuilding, and he was lifting more weight than he ever had before. It's possible that being overzealous with weights might have contributed to further injury, unfortunately. Still, he was bigger, stronger, and still had his speed. He ran about a 4.65 40-yard dash and he considered himself explosive.

During that injured reserve time, he was part-time with the team and part-time in the front office. He heard comments from the players like, "Here comes Gil's spy." He believed that he had been well-liked by the players, but fair or not, his reputation suffered.

Being out of game action helped him as a scout. He was learning the operation in this outstanding, state-of-the-art front office, from the ground level. He felt a part of the team only during home games; when the team traveled, he was left out. Likewise, players on the injured reserve were not part of the preparation and planning for the game. "It sucked," Mike said.

Being on injured reserve left Mike with a lot of time to think. Was he injury prone? Could he rely on his physicality? He thought the Cowboys downplayed his injury, and he consulted the University of Michigan team orthopedic doctor for a second opinion. In the past, he had relied on his body (his speed, quickness, strength, and toughness) to deal with players who were larger than him. Suddenly there was a chink in his armor, so to speak; his invincibility was no longer infinite. Insecurity began to set in on the young player, and that helped to set the stage and subconsciously seal his fate on the football field.

It was clear that being on the injured reserve was psychologically the kiss of death for Mike. He knew that the Cowboys valued him. And he rationalized at the time, he said, "I'm young, I was just going where the current would take me. It's an opportunity."

Mike talked to the Cowboys trainers about his pain because he knew that something was terribly wrong. He frequently got twinges, and the pain "was like having a needle or knife stuck in you," he said. The pain was far from constant, though; at times, he even had relief between snaps and into the next play. But the pain quickly returned. The injury required major surgery, period. Perhaps Cowboys management thought to themselves, *No one can come back from this injury*, but Mike was never told that by anyone on his team. Mike had suffered a gradual tearing of the tendon in his shoulder that likely started while playing for Michigan. The most recent X-ray revealed that his tendon was gone.

Mike believed he had a decent (not great) training camp in his third season with the Cowboys. He thought he was finally getting it, and believed he was "ready" to take over and become first string. He better understood the Cowboys defense, and the game started to slow down for him. His reaction times began to quicken, too. He didn't think he was far off from supplanting that first-stringer, but he knew he had to keep out of the training room and could not afford to miss practice time.

How does a player differentiate between pain and injury? The player certainly has to know his own body and has to rely on the information given to him by trainers. It certainly is possible to play with pain, especially when a body is taped and the person receives shots like cortisone or other painkillers. Professional football players undergo many extraordinary treatments (in part) because of the belief that they are needed. It's considered important to be on the field regardless of how you're feeling. And of course it was difficult to think clearly when adrenaline is coursing through your veins.

Mike generally kept his comrades in his thoughts while undergoing treatment. It was important for him to differentiate between the various types of injury. One can break a finger and can still play—because that's what a player was supposed to do. Players play to fulfill that macho image. It was better to be dragged or carried out of the game than to walk off of your own accord. The coaches as well as teammates expected this toughness. And players always had to look over their shoulder since there was always somebody in line to take their place.

He seemed to get better, but he was cut in his third year with the Cowboys three or four weeks into the 1974 regular season. Mike remembered being cut by Coach Tom Landry. The Turk (NFL parlance for the reaper of bad news) came to Mike and told him to grab his playbook and report to the coach. He was making about $28,000 as a player, and his salary as a scout was $20,000 plus expenses. Coach Landry told him, "I'm going to have to let you go. But report to Gil Brandt and Tex Schramm for your next assignment."

As quickly as his playing career ended, his front-office scouting career began. Maybe that injury worked to his advantage; maybe it gave him a new lease on life. It certainly was another opportunity—one by which he could stay in football, a game he loved. Still, being cut was a major disappointment. He knew, in his mind, that he was bigger, stronger, and faster than the current first-string Dallas linebackers. It's true that they were experienced, more knowledgeable, and unhampered by injuries. But all that was cold comfort.

He began to rationalize that his new opportunity was a really good position. He didn't have to go home with his tail between his legs. After all, he wasn't backed into a corner without a job. In fact, he would bring in even more money than he had as a player. His wife and daughter were financially secure. Alternately, he had applied to the University of Michigan law school and was accepted. In the end, he chose to be a scout. And for the first time in his years in the pros, he felt secure.

Mental Toughness

Based upon 38 years of experience as a player, scout, front-office staffer, and CEO, Keller had a lot to say about the importance of evaluating players' mental toughness. According to him, the most important qualities for success in the pros are physical, which might account for 50 percent; psychological, 25 percent; and emotional, 25 percent. He believed that many front-office evaluators place much too much emphasis on physical size, speed, agility, and strength, and not enough on the intangibles. Mental toughness, he thought, was extremely important to a player's success. After all, he added, mental toughness is the key component in overcoming adversity, from injuries, internal struggles, and family circumstances, among other problems.

The term "intangibles" is regularly used in the National Football League by the front office and media as a catch-all for anything that can't be measured or quantified. These intangibles might refer to instinct, focus, and the ability to learn from mistakes made on the field. It also might refer to a player's ability to overcome insecurities. In essence, it's a broad definition, but the intangibles can make or break a player at the professional level.

For the past 40 years or so, the NFL has employed the Wonderlic Cognitive Ability Test to assess its players' intelligence, problem-solving skills, and reasoning. Each individual has 12 minutes to complete the 50-question test. According to the Wonderlic website, an average score on this test was 21. To give an idea of the breadth of results, the scores of a few current and past players include: Sebastian Janikowski, 9; Hakeem Nicks, 11; Donovan McNabb, 14; and Dan Marino, 16; John Elway, 30; Steve Young, 33; Drew Bledsoe, 37; and Ryan Fitzpatrick, 50. Potential NFL draftees' answers are compared to successful players in the past, in an attempt to get more insight about the players and predict their potential NFL success.

Roughly ⅓ of current NFL players are undrafted free agents. This suggests that the NFL Draft is hardly a science, as so many of the drafted players fail to make the cut in this highly competitive league. An April 25, 2013, story in the *Wall Street Journal* reported that in the 2009 NFL Draft, a total of 12 players were drafted by the Dallas Cowboys; three years later, in 2012, only two of those players remained on the Cowboys roster. The Oakland Raiders drafted seven players in that same draft, and none of them remained with the Raiders team by 2012. Obviously player evaluation is far from an exact science.

Perhaps a better assessment tool can be established to evaluate the components of mental toughness, Keller said. But if so, what are the predictive variables? Keller stated that there are players in the NFL who are physically bigger, stronger, faster, and more talented than others. College players report to the NFL Combine at the beginning of each year and go through a series of drills that measure just how fast they are in the 40-yard dash, how high they can jump, how far they can jump, the number of repetitions they can bench-press 225 pounds, and so on. Yet Mike believes there is far too much attention paid to such physical traits. It's easy to understand why these tests are used in part because they're easily quantified. Remember, the NFL game is about simple arithmetic. Ten yards = a first down; a punt travels X number of yards; the ball is placed on the X-yard line. And statistics are embedded in football culture, from the coaches who evaluate their team's progress to the players striving for individual superlatives to the talking heads who dissect their on-field performances to the fans at home refreshing their fantasy team scores.

Mike acknowledged that measuring intangibles, even though much more difficult to quantify, would more than likely add a different and valuable set of information and would likely be a better predictor of future performance than the current Wonderlic and Combine results.

* * *

As a defensive lineman and linebacker, Keller engaged in many physical battles. He had to work his way up the roster. Although Keller was never told by his Michigan coaches why he was promoted to first string, he figured that he had the following attributes: he was tall and fast, he worked hard, he played with enthusiasm, he had a good attitude, he was always on time for meetings and practices, and he displayed a team-first attitude. Furthermore, he didn't allow injuries to interfere with his playing, he was competitive, he gave full effort in practices, he was intelligent, and he had the desire to win. These were some of the characteristics expected from him by position coach Gary Moeller and head coach Bo Schembechler. And he looked for those "between the ears" qualities in the players he evaluated in his scouting career.

Other illustrations of Michael's mental toughness included his self-talk and a studious viewing of game film. He frequently thought: *How do I match up against this player? If I throw a forearm into his face sooner or later he'll duck. This guy is getting weaker, he's not as tough as I am. I'm wearing him down, and he's going to give up. I'm looking for him to quit. I see it in his eyes: he does not want to get hit. Now I've got him, he's mine, and I've beaten him down.* Although these conversations were never voiced aloud, they provide insight into Mike's thinking, competitiveness, and self-motivation.

For Keller, building self-confidence was imperative. One of his successes was blocking a punt in his first collegiate game against Vanderbilt. Bolstered,

Mike had more success on the field. Eventually Mike began to believe that maybe, just maybe, he was good enough to play at the Big House in front of all of those screaming admirers.

Mike admitted that the tough and brutal game of football is not played perfectly; players make mistakes. The issue becomes, *How does a player overcome his mistakes?* He gave the example of quarterback Tom Brady and how he might operate. When Brady throws an interception, he doesn't allow that mistake to get him down. He doesn't press or get uptight; instead, he quickly forgets about the mistake. Brady never allows negative or irrational thinking to take over. Mike called this "greatness," and it's what separates Tom Brady from other players.

Other quarterbacks are often referred to as having "happy feet." When they begin to fear the pass rushers, they likely allow the negatives to take over and begin to fear the pressure, which interferes with their performance. How a player handles a mistake is significant. It's important for a player—especially a quarterback—to keep focus. And indeed, the successful quarterbacks are the ones who expect to have success in their game performance.

I asked Mike to construct a "robot" with the qualities necessary to reach the highest heights in the professional game. These are his thoughts:

1. **Competitiveness.** is about a player that hates to lose. He never quits. He plays as if every play is the most important in the game. He never takes a breather and he's always going and running at top speed.

2. **Being a team player.** This means the individual is willing to sacrifice his own personal glory for the sake of the team. His job, so to speak, is to take care of his own position, to defeat the guy in front of him and then to pursue the play. You have to beat your opposition and have containment. The thinking is, *I'm one of 11 or one of 40.* The player doesn't subvert all of his personality, however; he knows that if the team is going to be successful, the individual players are also going to be successful.

   There can be a problem, of course, if you're great but play for a bad or inferior team. Since football is a team game, it's imperative that you rely on the player or teammate next to you. You have to pay attention to your assignment, be part of the team, and never, ever freelance. If you freelance, that could likely cause a breakdown. Second, it is important to be on time for meetings and practices and to obey the training rules. This translates to respect for the team. It also extends to learning the playbook and not getting into trouble, and then playing all-out on the field.

3. **Intelligence**. The Cowboys had a flex defense, which meant that the players had to make quick decisions on the field. The NFL uses the Wonderlic test as a cognitive measure of intelligence. However, some players scored very low on this test (despite having success on the field), so management had to figure out the reasons for the low score. Some of those reasons include a reading disability, poor math skills, or other impairments.

Football intelligence can also be called instinct—making good decisions, avoiding mistakes, and knowing how to react in battle when the 250- or 300-pound opponent is coming at you as in combat. Players know something bad can happen in a game, but they are trained to do their part and make good decisions under pressure. Take, for example, the quarterback, standing back in the pocket when attempting to pass. The quarterback knows he's going to get hit. Getting hit likely means getting clobbered and being in pain after the collision. No one likes to get hit, but the quarterback still has to wait for that receiver to get open and deliver the ball. If the quarterback has happy feet, or gets nervous, it likely means he gets rid of the ball before taking the hit but doesn't complete the pass. Other examples of intelligence include engaging the enemy in trash talk and motivating one's teammates at the line.

4. **Mental Toughness.** According to Mike, players had to differentiate between pain and injury. Players expect to play with pain, and most also have a high pain tolerance since daily pain is a major component or part of this game. Sometimes it's hard to think of professional football as just a game—indeed, it is a job. One can be in pain and have torn ligaments, but if he can still play, he should play. Many take an aspirin

or some other pain reliever to play. That's the kind of pressure these athletes put on themselves. The game is about current performance, not what the player did yesterday. In the pros, one common joke was that being a rookie, the player's pain is likely gone by Monday. The second-year player had to wait until Tuesday before his pain was gone. And for the veteran, the pain was likely gone by the next game or a week later.

Over the NFL's history, some mentally tough players come to mind—like Jack Youngblood, who played with a fractured tibia. Walt Garrison played with a broken clavicle. Conrad Dobler, who had had numerous leg issues, took injections and played with significant physical injuries during the game. Today Dobler walks with a significant limp as a result of all his football surgeries and injuries. Were these players foolish to press on with significant injury?

During his playing career, Keller had tendon and muscle damage resulting in problems with the supraspinatus muscle-tendon, resulting in eventual surgery and thus ending his professional career in Dallas. And he didn't take drugs or pills to cope with it; he just has high pain tolerance. Today, he is unable to hold a 20-pound dumbbell in his outstretched right arm. He laughed, saying that he can still play golf.

As a player scout, Mike would talk with coaches, position coaches, trainers, and the athlete himself while attempting to assess the player's toughness, endurance, and ability to play in pain. He also looked at game film. He was interested in the player who didn't want to miss practice as opposed to the one who hung back in the locker room. As he visited certain schools over and over again during his professional career, he got to know the coaches and trainers and therefore cultivated much more reliable information on prospective pro players.

Another mental toughness aspect is focus. Can a player focus and put out of his mind outside factors such as personal issues and still play the game at 100 percent? Mike believes that there were different degrees or levels of competitiveness. To illustrate that, he gave an example of his son Sam's determination. At the age of 12 or 13, Sam weighed about

160 pounds. Around that same time, his parents were divorcing. Sam wanted to play football, but he weighed too much. Michael told him that he had to lose about 30 pounds to be in fighting shape, and that if he put his mind to it he could do it. Sam lost about 35 pounds and joined the football team—and it changed his life. Mike told Sam that when you set your mind to it, you can accomplish many things. He also told him that he had to dedicate himself to work hard, focus, and not take the easy path. Sam took his dad's words to heart, and made a commitment to succeed.

We realize that the average playing career of an NFL player is about three and half years. Players drafted in rounds one through three are more than likely to make the team, but that's no hard-and-fast predictor. One reason why the average playing time in the league is limited is because by playing three games into their third year, professional players' pensions become vested. So teams generally cut players after the second year to avoid paying into the pension fund (regardless of their football talent). From a personnel perspective, there are plenty of other players available and qualified to play the game.

At the young age of 28, Dallas Cowboys scout Keller joined Dick Mansperger who was hired by the new NFL expansion team, the Seattle Seahawks. In Seattle, Mike eventually was promoted to assistant general manager. Gil Brandt was not too thrilled when Mike left Dallas, although Keller thought that Tom Landry and Tex Schramm were fine with it. Either way, his life's chapter in Dallas was over.

As a professional football scout, Mike assessed teamwork, reliability, and the ability to sacrifice—again, all those intangibles. Other scouts may have been hung up on the measurables, but he believed that the true measure of a man was more subjective. He assessed them through observation, talking with coaches, and even talking with the player's parents and family members. He also studied the characteristics of great players and attempted to pinpoint the source of their greatness. He said he "might not figure out the 'why,' but you can generally can determine the 'if.'"

For Mike personally, he didn't leave his own competitiveness on the field. The young, aggressive, and bright man wanted to be the best scout, period. He set out to find new ways to improve the scouting process. He also thought of opportunities beyond scouting, either as a personnel director or general manager. He admitted that his fear of failure was behind his drive as a player and working in the front office. According to Mike, his fear of failure helped sharpen his instincts and heighten his senses. Indeed, he felt his fear of failure gave him an edge. It pushed him to work harder than anyone else.

He also remembered what his mother said: "You either get better or you get worse." He had to overcome his weaknesses. He learned that he didn't have to be the most talented, just the most committed. And when you overcome your deficiencies, that's how you separate the good from the great. He did this time and again in his life, on the football field and in his career.

Mike's least favorite part of working in the front office was cutting players and giving them their walking papers. He looked into their eyes and saw the devastation they were experiencing and feeling about never playing football again—something he could well relate to from his own playing days. With some, he was able to rationally talk about it with them. And indeed, most of the cut players knew that it happened to him once; he had been in their shoes. Some others wanted to fight him. Or they'd say, "You're making a big mistake. I'm a good player and I'm going to come back and kick your ass." Some of the players saw it coming and were resigned to it. Other players were relieved, saying things like, "I'm ready to get on with my life." And still others would cry. Mike explained to them there was more to their life. Yet some had nowhere to go or nothing to do afterward and some were embarrassed.

When a player had to bring in his playbook, he knew he was being executed; Mike was the executioner. Seahawks management felt he was the right person for the job for many reasons, but that never made it easy on him. Management also had him cut coaches, which was just as bad if not worse.

Mike said he never felt guilty; after all, he was just the messenger. There was nothing he could do about it. No one wanted his job, and he could see why. Football, especially at the professional level, is full of harsh realities. His advice for any player is, "Evaluate your strengths and think about the next chapter for you. Remember, every player will either retire or get cut, and most are cut. Just think how special you are to have made it at this level. You played out your dream of playing professional football."

* * *

While in Seattle, Mike went fishing with four or five buddies. They traveled to the Deschutes River, which at the time was flowing violently. They arrived at the Warm Springs Indian reservation, where they would fish for rainbow trout. While casting, Michael's fly landed in a tree branch. It being his favorite fly, he started climbing up the tree to retrieve it. Then he got to the limb and slowly moved his body, stretching toward his caught fly, when he heard it strain. Then suddenly the limb broke, plunging him into the river. The river was flowing strongly and his waders started filling up, adding maybe 30 or so pounds of water to his fame. Luckily he was a strong swimmer and was able to swim to the shore. But it was a scary moment.

Another time, Mike took his father to the Icicle River in central Washington, where he taught his father how to fly-fish. It was a very special weekend for Mike. He was living his life and his father was living it vicariously through him. Though no one came into peril, it was a powerful moment for both of them.

While with the Seahawks, Mike received a call from Bo Schembechler. The coach offered him a job as assistant athletic director of recruiting. Suddenly Mike was faced with another career decision. Should he go back to his beloved Maize and Blue or should he stay with the pros? If he returned to Michigan, he might become athletic director one day. On the other hand, if he stayed with the pros, he could become a general manager. He started listing the pros and cons of each scenario. He liked his quality of life in Seattle and saw himself as a pro guy. Then his thoughts turned to his family. If he went back to Michigan, he'd be near them.

Before making a decision, he went in to talk with the assistant personnel director of the Seahawks, his boss, Dick Mansperger. Mansperger was fuming, and carved him up, saying things like, "You ungrateful son of a bitch! You're crazy if you're going to leave for Michigan. If you leave, you are never going to work in the NFL again. I expect you to be loyal to me for the rest of your life." Mike was crushed by Dick's response. He walked down the hall and talked to the general manager, John Thompson. The GM reassured him and told him to settle down. He said, "Dick is overreacting. Make sure you talk to me Monday morning before getting back to Coach Schembechler."

That Monday morning, the GM offered Mike the position of assistant general manager. That did it; Mike would stay with the Seahawks.

While working as assistant general manager for the Seahawks, Mike received a call regarding the formation of a new spring football league. The year was 1982, and the league was called the United States Football League (USFL). Keller had just completed the season with the Seahawks, and the new USFL Michigan Panthers training camp would start in the winter. One of the principal owners of the Michigan Panthers was Alfred Taubman, who made his money as the first shopping-mall guru.

The other owner wanted to hire Jim Spavital as the GM; he had prior experience with the Saskatchewan Roughriders—possibly the worst team in the Canadian Football League—as coach and general manager. He had also coached the Chicago Fire in the World Football League in 1974. Mike was 31 at the time, and though Taubman wanted him as GM, he was ultimately told that he wasn't old enough—but he could be the assistant general manager or the director of operations. He left the Seahawks in 1982 and took the job as assistant GM. Meanwhile, Chet Simmons was the USFL commissioner who delivered ESPN and ABC television rights.

General Manager Spavital was uncomfortable with Mike from the beginning, and often excluded him from meetings or gave him stupid jobs. That didn't bother Mike. He had to figure out how he could build this team and set them apart from the other teams in the league—teams that had established NFL coaching greats such as Marv Levy and Chuck Fairbanks, to name a few. Mike was up to the new challenge. He had figured out how to recruit NFL and college players during the course of his career. And in the process, his Michigan Panthers became the best team in the league.

The league had a huge ripple effect on the professional game, and the USFL saw many players decamp from the NFL as a result. In those days, the average NFL salary was only $80,000. The NFL was able to limit that amount because they essentially had a monopoly on professional football. Once the USFL was established, the average NFL salary quickly jumped to $240,000.

In their first season, the Panthers started the season with one win and four losses. Mike went to the owners and told them that he needed $50,000 for bonuses and $200,000 in salaries in order to get three quality veteran players on the roster. At the time, the team had a number of rookies and needed to add veterans to stabilize the offensive line. They agreed to give him the extra money. Mike first hired Ray Pinney formerly of the Pittsburgh Steelers as left tackle. He also signed Wayne Radloff for the center position. The moves immediately solidified the line, and the running game improved dramatically. Likewise, the line was then able to protect quarterback Bobby Hebert. The team quickly jelled and won its next six games in a row.

The Panthers advanced to the playoffs and ousted George Allen's Chicago team. "I earned my bones," Keller said. At first, the GM thought Mike was some young punk. In fact, Spavital called Bo Schembechler to ask about the young Keller. Bo replied succinctly: "Mike Keller is the best young guy in the NFL." And indeed, through his professional actions, Mike got credit from the players, coaches, and the front office. Then after that first year, the Panthers tore up his contract; he was then making twice as much as he had with the Seattle Seahawks.

The first USFL championship was played in front of 60,000 Denver fans in July 1983. The Panthers were victorious and beat the top team from the East, the Philadelphia Stars. The Philadelphia Stars had big talent in Jim Mora as head coach and Carl Peterson as general manager. Winning the championship in the first year was a serious statement, and Keller was proud of the team's achievement. The Panthers were the toast of Michigan and averaged about 30,000 fans at the Silverdome in Pontiac, Michigan.

The Panthers did well in 1985, and hosted a playoff game against the Oakland Invaders, coached by John Ralston. That game was played in front of 65,000 fans at the Silverdome. On the personal side, Mike was living in Rochester Hills, Michigan, renting a 25-acre ranch. He started his second marriage, and the following year, his son Sam was born. Meanwhile, 32-year-old Pete Rozelle was appointed commissioner of the NFL.

In that first year of the USFL, the league was strong and attendance was good. There were initially 12 teams. In the second year, six more teams were added—with questionable owners. But the initial 12 owners got their money back by adding the additional teams. Donald Trump came in the second year as owner of the New Jersey Generals. Trump started a campaign for the USFL to compete with the NFL in the fall. He convinced the owners to move the season to the fall after the third season, 1985. Because of problems with stadium leases, the Michigan Panthers moved and merged with the Oakland Invaders. Suddenly the Invaders became the strongest team in the league along with the Philadelphia Stars, who moved from Philadelphia to Baltimore. They played in another championship game in the Meadowlands in New York. The Invaders were stopped deep into Stars territory in the final seconds of the championship, and fell to the Stars 28–24.

At the Oakland Coliseum, the Invaders team averaged about 30,000 fans a game. Enthusiasm remained high, but many USFL teams had trouble getting stadium leases because the spaces were already used by the professional baseball and football teams. Meanwhile, the NFL had a monopoly on TV rights. The USFL started a lawsuit against the NFL for antitrust statutes. The USFL won the lawsuit, but the jury awarded the USFL just three dollars. It was Trump's attorney who handled the lawsuit for the USFL. Trump had been snubbed by the NFL trying to force his way into the league. Ultimately, he won the battle but lost the war. The USFL folded after just three years, and the NFL went back to football as usual.

Moving on

In 1996 Keller moved to Scotland to run the Scottish Claymore Football Team in NFL Europe. While in Scotland, Mike bought his first Harley-Davidson and was soon riding his new motorcycle throughout the Scottish countryside. That bike was a perfect fit for the larger-than-life, black-leather-clad Keller. He even joined the local Harley club. To this day, Mike loves the sound of "rolling thunder."

There was additional synergy. Before Scottish Claymore football games, 40 Harleys—complete with cheerleaders on the back of the bikes—roared on to the playing field and did a victory lap before going out the tunnel. And the papers, full of articles about the team, turned Scotland on its ear. Just the year before, Claymore's Gavin Hastings had been a rugby player, and his team won the Rugby World Cup. Suddenly everything was turning up American football.

One of the NFL Europe conditions was that the Claymores had to have a minimum of two Scottish players on the roster. Mike hired long-range kicker Gordon Beckham for long field goals. For extra points and short field goals, Mike hired rugby star and national heartthrob Gavin Hastings. Hastings was a fullback in rugby, and once claimed that he would never play the violent, aggressive game of American football. But Mike was able to turn him around, and hired him to kick extra points. The Scottish football team benefitted since Hastings had a positive attitude. He absorbed himself within the team, and helped assimilate players into the Scottish culture. Wouldn't you know it, Mike's team won the NFL Europe championship (or World Bowl). Another feather in Keller's cap.

Jim Criner was a head coach for that 1996 championship team. At that same time, Scotland was a Hollywood hotbed; the epic *Braveheart* was filmed on location at the Edinburgh Castle and around Scotland. Mike was a special guest at the movie's premiere and even wore a kilt to the event. From 1995 to 1998, Mike was having the time of his life in Scotland. He was offered additional jobs helping set up soccer teams (which is king there) as well as rugby clubs.

But American football took the country by storm, and in the first year the Claymores averaged 18,000 to 20,000 people in attendance. Outside of the national rugby team, his team had the highest attendance among sports teams. NFL Europe really promoted American football and the attendance soon climbed to 27,000. They became the top spectator sport in the country.

While in Europe, Mike got engaged to Anna. He called her the "Viking Princes." A model from Newcastle, England, she had a wonderful personality. You'd be likely to find her dancing on tables at the bar. She was outgoing to say the least. She was also adventurous, and even went bird hunting with Mike.

Mike—this motorcycle-riding hunter and outsized American—thought he must have amused the Scots. He was a large part of their entertainment. Although some Scots had claim to royalty, Mike had Anna. A weekly TV celebrity, Keller had notoriety as a glittering fish in a small pond.

In 1993–94, the NFL and Roger Goodell hired Mike as a consultant. Mike became an intermediary, working with NFL owners and the new expansion franchises in Jacksonville and Carolina. The NFL was interested in expanding everywhere; they had global aspirations. Mike also consulted for the Canadian Football League. He had become an expert on startups, as well as turning around flagging franchises in arena football as well.

After leaving the World Football League (NFL Europe's successor), Mike went back to Grand Rapids and started up a sports commission. In that position, he helped Grand Rapids bring in baseball and basketball tournaments. One day he received a call from David Dixon, asking him to talk to Vince McMahon. The idea was for Mike to set up a new league under McMahon. Keller declined, and kept on saying no until he finally decided to meet with the impresario. The charismatic and deep-pocketed McMahon convinced Mike to join him in his new venture, called the XFL (the *X*, of course, standing for *extreme*). Mike was the first employee of the fledgling league, and developed all aspects of football operations.

The league was intended to be considered alongside with other major professional sports. However, there were significant off-season, internal hurdles with television partners. Vince McMahon's original plan had been to purchase the Canadian Football League. But when that didn't happen, the media attacked the new league with a vengeance. The league was perceived as having poor-quality production and was considered pure entertainment. This league lasted just one season, 2001.

Mental Toughness Revisited

Mike looked at the concept of mental toughness through the wide lens of his football career.

First and foremost, there is goal-setting. In setting a goal, the individual alone has to have complete control over goal attainment. The goal has to be concrete and easily measured. Goals could be learning the Dallas Cowboys playbook, getting to practice on time, or putting in 100 percent effort on the practice or playing field. Regardless, the individual has to have control over the outcome. So being cut by the Cowboys was not totally under Mike's control, nor was the failure of the USFL or XFL.

Mike admitted that when he was a player with the Cowboys, he actually put a lot of energy into scouting—more, even, than into his playing. He also admitted that he fell behind because of his injury. On the other hand, he was moving ahead as a scout. So he had this approach—approach conflict. He liked both, but it seemed that he had more success with the Cowboys as a scout than as a player because of a number of variables.

Mike thought that out of 1,000 NFL players, maybe 75 to 90 percent of them will say they had a more positive experience playing football in college than with the pros. In the pros, there is always uncertainty—someone is always right behind you, waiting to take your place. There's a lot of failure in the NFL, and only the greatest survive. A few get lifetime security after their first pro contract, but they are a very precious few.

Having success is another aspect of mental toughness. By having on-field success, Mike's expectation level continually became greater. Conversely, when he experienced failure, that lowered his level of aspiration. Having more successful experiences results in attaining more success.

Mike had a plethora of successful experiences during his three years while playing for the Wolverines. Unfortunately, during his three-year playing experience at Dallas, he did not have the same experiences in the pros. Those failure experiences led to negative thinking and loss of confidence for him, which was detrimental to him as a professional athlete. However, as a scout for Dallas, he received positives, excelled, and forged a new career path for himself. One laden with success.

Mental toughness also includes the concept of reframing. Mike remembered that when he was playing football, he'd tell himself, *I'm going to beat the heat at the hottest point in the day, so that I'm going to do better in the cooler weather.* He didn't complain about the heat; it was an obstacle to overcome.

Even today, Mike Keller walks during the hottest part of the day. Sometimes he thinks he might melt the bottom of his shoes, but he convinces himself to do his best.

While scouting, Mike observed that some of the other scouts said they could not or would not be able to cover all those different schools. Mike realized that if he could cover more schools, more ground, he would have more reports and therefore be more valuable to his team. *I can sleep on the plane, or even take the red eye. And look at what I can accomplish by sleeping on the plane.* Indeed, when he traveled to Europe, he would fly all night so that he could accomplish more during the day.

Mike added that our society has changed in that we are unlike our ancestors. In his opinion, we are becoming soft as a country because not everybody is willing to pay the price. He thinks that people do not always force themselves to get things done and that things are too easy in our society. Mike said he always found a way to do more. He attempts to use positive thinking at all times. It is clear these lessons were imparted from both his mom and Bo Schembechler.

Reframing, in other words, is when you analyze the situation and put a positive spin on it and use it in your self-talk and thinking. It's not about whining or having a "poor me" attitude; it's about making the best of each and every situation.

Another mental toughness concept is the need to achieve. This is tenacity and perseverance. When he got beaten by Rex Kern, OSU's quarterback, Mike would tell himself, *I'm going to figure him out. I am not going to make that mistake again, and I'll get him in the next play.* Mike never quit on the field. Instead, he learned from his mistakes. There are lessons to be learned from failure, Mike acknowledged. But succumbing to failure was never an option.

Mike always wanted to break down the opposing player. He realized that if he hit him as hard as he could on that first play, that would be a good thing. He might even injure or hurt himself in so doing. Yet Mike wanted the opposing player to know that it was going to be a tough afternoon for him. He wanted him to realize that the hard hitting would go on for the entire day. Yes,

Michael said, it was intimidation. But he wanted to win the day. There was no path of least resistance when it came to beating your opponent, no shortcut.

Mike admitted that success was a driving factor in his entire life. In Michigan, at the beginning, he thought that Bo Schembechler put the team through a lot. But if his test was passed, it proved that player wasn't a quitter. Furthermore, he prepared his players for the game, which was a second test. Bo's Wolverines didn't think of quitting—ever.

"Look at all these startups" he said. "You see my persistence. I'm not going to quit. I paid the price. As a kid, I wanted to race everyone. I played every sport and I loved the competition. When I swam, I trained hard. In basketball, I would shoot until it got dark. Competition was very important. You have to have the physical and mental makeup, and then your chances of success are great."

Mike is not sure why he became so competitive, but that quality has always been there. Perhaps it was being in a large family, or the fact that his mother always challenged him. Or maybe it was the reward that came with success. He wanted to be special in his parents' eyes and strove to achieve in every way that he could.

Mental toughness is also associated with affiliative needs. Reflecting on this, Mike said, "Look at all those connections from my Michigan team…. We all suffered together and we were winners together," but in the process they became bonded—a true band of brothers. The cohesiveness that developed contributed to the concept of team, team, team. Their individual egos in essence were merged, and they became part of something greater than themselves.

On the playing field, each did his own job, and they didn't want to disappoint their teammates by being out of position or making a mistake. At all costs, it was important for them not to let the team down and to play through pain. And when Coach Schembechler got on Preston Henry or Jim Brandstatter or anyone else, the players appreciated and rallied around their teammate. "It was like we had a boot camp," Mike said. "The warfare, it made us closer—especially when a guy got hurt or injured."

Today, the teammates remain connected. They know what is going on in each other's lives, they email each other, and they attend scheduled and unscheduled reunions with one another.

Mindfulness is also a component of mental toughness. This means self-awareness. Mike said, "I became very aware of how my body works. I got to know my body very well, especially while in training. I had twinges and learned that I could not afford to overlook them, and it was very important to have a sound mind and a sound body."

Mike gave an example of being in touch with his body, while playing with the Cowboys. He said that at times, his pain was like being stuck with a needle. The pain was not continuous, but on and off. And the only time (not every time) he felt relief was between snaps. He became accustomed to experiencing the pain. Still, with the Cowboys, his discomfort became much more frequent and much less tolerable. After talking with the Cowboys trainer about his discomfort, he knew something was terribly wrong. And indeed, the injury effectively ended his professional career.

There is no doubt that Mike Keller exhibited and utilized the virtues of mental toughness during his illustrious playing career at the University of Michigan. He was one of the players who made Bo Schembechler look good and assisted the coach in becoming one of the football gods.

During Mike's professional playing career with the Dallas Cowboys, he did not have the same mind-set as he had at Michigan and as a result didn't have nor could he duplicate that field success. Other variables such as a recent marriage, playing at the highest level, severe injury, and other employment possibilities affected what took place between his ears while with the Cowboys.

It seems to this author that mental toughness has to do with conscious mental processes, including perceiving, remembering, imagining, conceiving, judging, and reasoning. Being able to utilize rational cognition to the fullest equates to, broadly speaking, Plato's "know thyself" maxim; transforming that into performance equals mental toughness and success.

Today

Recently Mike was contacted, along with CEO Scott McKibben, to form a spring football league called the Football League of America. The league will feature eight teams in the following cities under consideration: New York/ New Jersey, Baltimore/Washington, Miami/Tampa Bay, Louisville, Detroit, Chicago, Dallas/Fort Worth, Denver, Phoenix, Houston, Philadelphia, and Seattle. The league will schedule a season consisting of 14 regular-season games in major league stadiums, then have a series of nationally televised playoff games with a championship game hosted on July 4. Dallas will host the league office.

President Keller believes that the league will succeed because the game of football has become the most popular both in terms of TV and game attendance. In part, it's a psychology of violence for the American public. Football fans desolate after the conclusion of the NFL season will have an outlet to enjoy their favorite team sport in the new league.

The FLA expects to black out the upper deck in stadiums, making it about 40,000 seats per stadium. They also plan to control the cost and make it more affordable for families, something market research has shown that NFL fans have criticized. There are lots of opportunities for players coming out of college, and the quality of play is excellent.

There are also plenty of available coaches out there, some of whom have been blackballed by the NFL. So Keller does not expect any difficulty in stocking his rosters and management with talent. He added that the league might even consider Tim Tebow, a onetime NFL standout who's been cut by three different NFL teams. Tebow may well fit in with this new league, but even the Heisman Trophy winner might not have the necessary skills for success.

The FLA will have the highest quality of football played anywhere in the world, outside of the fall league.

Mike believes that sport in general is important to America. He said we are sportscentric, perhaps the most sports-centric country in the world. "Just look at the focus and the support for sport in elementary, high school, and college for both boys and girls," he said. It is a major part of the fiber of our country. "It's certainly a major part of my makeup," he added.

Mike also has a dream to take youth sports development to another level. His idea is a startup that he calls the San Diego Sports Academy. This program will be extensive and plans to cover youth through professional athletics. It will incorporate education, moral concepts, proper nutrition, and community wellness into a training process. He envisions associations with professional and semiprofessional athletic organizations, the fitness community, trainers, physical therapists, dietary specialists, and other related groups.

The San Diego Sports Academy will likely include elite athletic training, summer sport camps, leagues, dormitories, cafeteria/food services, classrooms, and other facilities. The indoor and outdoor fields will host football, soccer, rugby, baseball, basketball, volleyball, and cheerleading. The indoor facilities will boast Olympic-quality swimming and diving pools, classrooms, meeting rooms, a dormitory, physical therapy rooms, and a cafeteria within a 40-acre compound.

Judging by Keller's tenacity, the new ventures will receive his full enthusiasm and go on to great success.

Family

The fly-fisherman, hunter, golfer, and dreamer Keller has two children, Jessica and Sam, from two marriages. Sam, a quarterback, started his football career at Arizona State. When asked why Sam didn't play for the University of Michigan, Mike replied, "His girlfriend wanted him to go to Arizona State, but he would've been a perfect fit for the Wolverines." At ASU Sam was a starter until he got injured, then his backup remained the starting quarterback. Sam was unhappy, and Mike helped facilitate a transfer to Nebraska. Sam was redshirted in his first year but became the Practice Player of the Year for the Cornhuskers. He was leading the nation in passing, averaging more than 300 passing yards per game until he was injured again. A Sun Bowl MVP, he threw the winning touchdown in the closing seconds of that game. Although Sam wasn't drafted, he did have professional tryouts with the Raiders and the Buccaneers.

Sadly, Mike is currently estranged from his daughter, Jessica.

Mike met Kimberly in Seattle, and the couple married in Jackson Hole, Wyoming. These days, you'll find them flying back and forth between Florida and Texas with Lulu, Kimberly's lapdog, and Mike's new Visla puppy, Maggie.

AFTERWORD

The Secrets

Eight outstanding University of Michigan men were chosen to represent Bo's Warriors. These men exemplified the great Michigan tradition both on and off the field. Not only did coach Gary Moeller accompany Bo to Ann Arbor, but he served with him in a number of coaching capacities over the years, including defensive coordinator. Gary went on to become the head coach of Michigan from 1990 to 1994. During his five seasons as head coach, his teams were 44–13–3, for a winning percentage of .758. Gary was a leader, a communicator, and the players related very well to his style and creative coaching drills. The young, athletic Moeller also played basketball during the off-season with the young footballers. His exuberant physical style on the basketball court sent a clear message and modeled physical play. Playing sports was not for sissies.

The seven players were chosen because they signify the Michigan tradition of excellence, and they are good examples of the mentally and physically tough caliber needed to play the brutal game of football. Additionally, they have gone on to become well-known spokesmen for the university and leaders within their communities. And of course, the seven were outstanding athletes who contributed greatly to the team—especially in the 1969 Ohio State game. The "magnificent seven" played important and critical positions, manning the backfield and the line of scrimmage, and playing on the line and in the defensive secondary on the defensive side of the ball. Woody Hayes had his Jack

Tatum, but Bo Schembechler had his Thom Darden and Frank Gusich as wolfman.

These men are no random sample; they were identified and significantly chosen as a representative sample of the 1969 Michigan team. Were there other stars on that particular team? Of course. But these eight were chosen to best represent the dynamism of Michigan football.

After interviewing these individuals and hearing their stories, I learned a lot about Coach Bo Schembechler and the magic he created both on and off the field. Did he make them champions (they won 27 out of 30 college games from 1969 through 1971), or did they make him the legend? That's for the historians to decide. But the following are the top secrets of the success for Bo Schembechler's 1969 warriors.

Don Canham, the newly appointed athletic director was a visionary. He knew that he had to change the direction of Michigan football. Previously, Michigan legends like Fritz Crisler, Benny Oosterbaan, Tom Harmon, and Coach Bump Elliott were conservative and personable men. As Michigan's track coach, Canham recruited talented black athletes from places like Jamaica. Canham knew that he had to recruit outstanding athletes from different backgrounds in order for Michigan athletics to be successful as a whole.

By bringing in Bo Schembechler, he delivered a very different Michigan head coaching message. With him, it changed from the country club set to more of a workingman, get-your-hands-dirty mentality. While controversial at the time, the passage of time has validated Canham's vision. And since that 1969 game with Ohio State, Michigan has always had a Big House sellout. In 21 years, Bo Schembechler's coaching record included 234 victories, 65 losses, and 8 ties. His teams either won or shared 13 Big Ten conference titles.

Bo brought fellow Ohioans to Ann Arbor. About 80 percent of the coaches were from Ohio, and many of the recruits were from Ohio as well. All these Ohioans absorbed Wolverines DNA. Their blood flowed Maize and Blue—they were Wolverines!

Bo inherited players recruited by previous Michigan head coach Bump Elliott, and those recruits excelled at more than football. They were good athletes, quick, had good hands, were agile, and above all they were coachable and intelligent.

During that first spring practice in 1969, players may not have liked Bo. And not many were ready for what the coach brought to the table (his seemingly unorthodox training, conditioning, and coaching methods). But Bo beat them down and then built them up, and in doing so fundamentally changed their thinking. He wanted to take them to higher levels that they had never experienced.

There were about 120 players who showed up for that first practice—too many, according to the coach. By the end of that practice, there were 80 players. Those who did stay learned about work ethic, loyalty, commitment, and discipline. They developed a passion to get better, established a common bond, and internalized the superior belief both mentally and physically that they were better than the opposition. After all, they never heard of any other teams going through on the practice field what they did.

The 1969 team had great senior leadership, starting with captain Jim Mandich, Tom Curtis, Brian Healy, Barry Pierson, and others. The seniors had been humiliated (especially the ones from Ohio) in 1968 when they were thrashed 50–14 by Ohio State. They wanted another opportunity to play the Buckeyes, and revenge played a significant part in 1969. The seniors did not have to verbalize their desire to beat Ohio State. Nor did anyone have to tell them about the importance of winning that game. All this was in motion before Bo was hired.

The Mellow Men—Reggie McKenzie, Thom Darden, Glenn Doughty, Mike Taylor, Billy Taylor, Butch Carpenter, and Mike Oldham—made a vow that November that such a defeat would not happen again. And indeed, the talented athletes played an important part in the 1969 season.

The transition from easygoing Bump to Bo was difficult for the players, to say the least. The Wolverines were 3–2 after five games in 1969. In the sixth game, against the University of Minnesota Gophers, the Wolverines trailed at halftime. The boisterous, loud, and crude Schembechler entered the locker room. The players expected him to be ranting and raving, but Bo, in a calm voice, told them, "We are better than them. Don't waste this opportunity." With a little guilt trip, Bo's statement made clear to his young men that he had confidence in them. The players left the locker room reenergized, and the final score was Michigan 35, Minnesota 9.

If it can indeed be pinpointed to one moment, the team came together as one on that Saturday, October 25, 1969, in Minneapolis. Both the offense and the defense began to jell—the defense by controlling the Gophers offense, essentially putting the Michigan offense in a great position to score points, and the offense by Michigan sustaining drives and allowing the defense to rest on the sideline. Together, they were playing as a team. This was the turning point. Bo had made his imprint on the team and they had become "we."

The following Saturday, November 1, Michigan played Wisconsin and prevailed 35–7. The next week, Michigan played Illinois. 57–0. On the 15th of November, Michigan played Iowa and won the game 51– 6.

The week of the OSU game, with snow and ice on the practice playing field, Bo sent another message as his coaches went out in the cold and shoveled away the ice and snow so players could practice on a small portion of the field.

During that OSU week, the players practiced with an intensity that was never duplicated. They were high in spirits and motivation—so much so that the coaches thought the players might burn themselves out prior to the game. But Bo, in his wisdom, let them go. He had faith in his players. As a result, the players' intensity and energy rubbed off on the coaches, and they also began to believe in their team in turn.

No one entertained losing that game. The coaches knew the players were well prepared. They knew they wanted to beat Ohio State and that everyone had a will to win. It was a once-in-a-lifetime experience. The magnitude of the game was immense. The Buckeyes were abundantly hyped by the press. The other story was that Bo was set to play his former mentor for the very first time.

The classic photograph taken after the game of the players on the bench erupting in joy tells the story: Michigan 24, Ohio State 12. These players demonstrated their mental toughness and left it all on the playing field that day.

After their victory against Ohio State, Michigan was selected to play in the Rose Bowl on January 1, 1970, in Pasadena, California. The intensity during practices for the game against the University of Southern California was nowhere near the level it was at for Ohio State. This, coupled with Bo's heart attack the night before, most certainly affected the final score, and Michigan fell 10–3. Additionally, there was a controversial call when USC tailback Charles White reached the end zone—although he didn't have the ball. The Wolverines believed that the ball was down on the 3-yard line, but the play was still called a touchdown—and, as it turned out, that was the difference in the game.

Yet the Wolverines knew how to throw a good party. As the team, the men—from very different socioeconomic and racial backgrounds—all partied together. Bo didn't allow cliques; it was *the team, the team, the team*. As a result, this group of men remains close today—and their attendance at frequent reunions is exceptional, even by Michigan standards. Certainly winning had a lot to do with it. At any rate, they are a true band of brothers.

The amazing experience at Michigan was never duplicated again, especially that resounding 1969 victory over Ohio State. Even the players who went on to outstanding pro careers agreed and said that nothing came close to their Michigan years.

Will there ever be another Bo Schembechler? Will there ever be anything like the infamous 10-Year War between Bo and Woody? Maybe, maybe not. But Schembechler's legacy is secure. And college football remains extremely popular, especially at the University of Michigan.

It's been said that Bo Schembechler was a true "psychologist." Whether or not he studied the field of psychology and its tenets, he intrinsically understood human nature. When he arrived in Michigan, he inherited a group of young men who loved the game of football. In order to work with the ones who loved the game the most, he weeded out the others by extremely physical means through his brutal practices and scrimmages. Schembechler believed that man has many needs and goals, and that the human motivational system works as a result of tension that can either be generated or reduced.

The psychologist Schembechler knew that his players had needs of **abasement** (the accepting of blame or criticism during practices and games); **achievement** (the need to overcome obstacles, to excel, and to surpass others, whether in competition with a fellow teammate or an opposing player); **affiliation** (loyalty with teammates; Mike Keller referred to it as "a band of brothers"); **aggression** (overcoming opposition and forcefully beating opponents); **counteraction** (overcoming weakness and maintaining self-respect through practice, practice, practice); **deference** (to admire a superior); **dominance** (controlling one's environment to achieve a desired outcome); **exhibition** (making an impression); **order** (achieving precision, such as by running a play over and over in practice); and **succorance** (the need to be loved).

Schembechler also knew that he could, through his practices, place physical and emotional barriers in the way of his players, thereby thwarting their needs and, as a result, either increasing or decreasing their tension systems. In doing so, once their needs were met, their satisfaction and drive would be like no other. Just ask Brandstatter, Keller, Curtis, Darden, Betts, McKenzie, and Seyferth about their experience, their self-esteem, and their identity with Coach Schembechler. Coach Moeller would agree, too.

The Michigan story goes on. One has to be there to experience it. Just go to the Big House and you'll know what I mean. Go Blue Go!

—Frank Lieberman, PhD
Cool, California, May 2014

About the Author

Dr. Frank Lieberman was born in Detroit, Michigan, on November 26, 1939. A college football player at the University of Detroit, he attained a master's degree from the University of Michigan in 1965 and a PhD in 1973 from Wayne State University.

Lieberman is a psychologist, author, TV producer, and talk show host. He is also the author of *It Has Nothing to Do With Age*.

Lieberman is married, with five children and seven grandchildren. He and his wife reside in the Sierra Nevada foothills of Northern California, where the city of Auburn has rightfully claimed the title of "endurance capital of the world." He is one of four individuals in the world to have completed the Swanton Pacific 100-Mile Ride and Tie, in 2008; the 100-mile Tevis Cup horse race, in 2000; and the 100-Mile Western States Endurance Run, in 2002. Additionally, he is the only participant to have completed all three mountain ultra-events in his sixties. He continues to compete in ultra-running marathon events today.